The Signs of a Savant

Language Against the Odds

Every once in a while nature gives us insight into the human condition by providing us with a unique case whose special properties illuminate the species as a whole. Christopher is such an example. Despite disabilities which mean that everyday tasks are burdensome chores, Christopher is a linguistic wonder who can read, write, speak, understand and translate more than twenty languages. On some tests he shows a severely low IQ, hinting at ineducability, yet his English language ability indicates an IQ in excess of 120 (a level more than sufficient to enter university). Christopher is a savant, someone with an island of startling talent in a sea of inability. This book documents his learning of British Sign Language, casting light on the modularity of cognition, the modality neutrality of the language faculty, the structure of memory, the grammar of signed language and the nature of the human mind.

NEIL SMITH is Professor Emeritus of Linguistics at University College London.

IANTHI TSIMPLI is Professor of Psycholinguistics at Aristotle University of Thessaloniki.

GARY MORGAN is Professor of Psychology at City University London.

BENCIE WOLL is Director of the Deafness, Cognition and Language Research Centre at University College London.

The Signs of a Savant

Language Against the Odds

Neil Smith, Ianthi Tsimpli, Gary Morgan and
Bencie Woll

CAMBRIDGE
UNIVERSITY PRESS

CAMBRIDGE UNIVERSITY PRESS
Cambridge, New York, Melbourne, Madrid, Cape Town, Singapore,
São Paulo, Delhi, Dubai, Tokyo, Mexico City

Cambridge University Press
The Edinburgh Building, Cambridge CB2 8RU, UK

Published in the United States of America by Cambridge University Press, New York

www.cambridge.org
Information on this title: www.cambridge.org/9780521617697

First published 2011

Printed in the United Kingdom at the University Press, Cambridge

A catalogue record for this publication is available from the British Library

Library of Congress Cataloguing in Publication data
The signs of a savant : language against the odds / Neil Smith . . . [et al.].
    p.   cm.
Includes bibliographical references and index.
ISBN 978-0-521-85227-2 – ISBN 978-0-521-61769-7 (pbk.)
1. Savants (Savant syndrome)   2. Language acquisition.   I. Smith, N. V.
(Neilson Voyne)   II. Title.
BF426.S54   2011
153 – dc22   2010035474

ISBN 978-0-521-85227-2 Hardback
ISBN 978-0-521-61769-7 Paperback

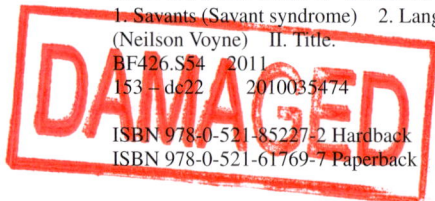

For Christopher and his Family

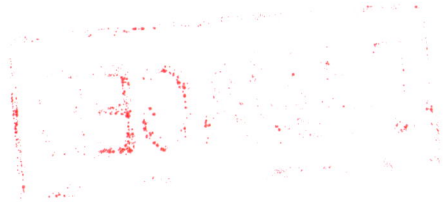

Contents

Appendices

Figures

Appendix 1

Tables

Preface

We have been studying Christopher for nearly twenty years, documenting – and marvelling at – his remarkable linguistic ability. The fruits of our earlier research resulted in a dozen articles and a book, *The Mind of a Savant* (Smith & Tsimpli, 1995),[1] in which we spelt out our interpretation of his skewed abilities. This work raised more questions than it answered, and one in particular has preoccupied us ever since: how would Christopher with his flair for languages but with severe apraxia, some of the characteristics of autism, and limited intellectual ability, cope with a signed language? The tension is obvious: he has a huge talent for language but signed languages require precisely those social, visuo-spatial and kinaesthetic abilities in which he is most lacking. Hence we decided to teach him British Sign Language (BSL) and observe the results.

Some of the findings reported here have been published in articles (Morgan *et al.*, 2002a, 2002b, 2007; Smith, 2003) but most of it is new. We have also presented parts of this material at conferences and seminars at UCL (University College London), Korea National University Seoul, the Aristotle University of Thessaloniki, the University of Oxford, the University of Cambridge, the University of Reading, the University of the West of England in Bristol and Gallaudet University in Washington DC. We are grateful to the various audiences for their input.

In addition to this we have received a vast amount of help from others in the preparation of this book. Our major debt is to Christopher, whose patience and enthusiasm have been a source of inspiration, and to his family, especially his sister, Ann Fairclough. We are likewise indebted to the Camphill Village Trust, especially John Carlile and his family, for help and advice and for providing an environment in which Christopher and others can thrive. In addition we are grateful for comments, conversation, criticism and help both practical and theoretical to Noam Chomsky, Annabel Cormack, Frances Elton, Uta Frith, Annette Karmiloff-Smith, Jill Lake, Ann Law, Peter Lovatt, Peter Möbius, Laura-Ann Petitto, Deirdre Wilson and Cambridge University Press's anonymous referees. None of these should be held responsible for what we have done with their contributions.

We would also like to thank Helen Barton and her colleagues at Cambridge University Press for their help and long-suffering patience as we spent more time writing and re-writing than we had ever planned. We are grateful to Elsevier for permission to reproduce fig. 3 from Baddeley (2000a), and to Wiley-Blackwell to reproduce figs. 2 and 5 from Smith & Tsimpli (1995). Finally, and perhaps most importantly, we are grateful to the Leverhulme Trust who, under grant F.134AS, have supported our research for many years. Our investigations of Christopher, and hence this book, would not have been possible without their contribution.

1   Introducing Christopher

Every once in a while Nature gives us insight into the human condition by providing us with a unique case whose special properties illumine the species as a whole. Christopher is such an example. On first inspection his fate may not seem fortunate. Because he is unable to look after himself, he lives in sheltered accommodation; on a variety of standard tests of intelligence he scores poorly, with particular difficulty on non-verbal tests; his horizons seem to be limited to the performing of routine tasks of a non-demanding nature. His life looks sadly circumscribed. Until one turns to language.

Despite his disabilities, which mean that everyday tasks are burdensome chores, Christopher is a linguistic wonder: with varying degrees of fluency, he can read, write, speak, understand and translate more than twenty languages. Playing noughts and crosses is beyond him, but interpreting between German and Spanish is easy; he doesn't understand the kind of make-believe play that 3- or 4-year-old children indulge in – pretending that a banana is a telephone for instance – but he learns new languages, from Berber to Welsh, with enviable ease. His drawing ability indicates a severely low IQ of between 40 and 60 (a level hinting at ineducability), yet his English language ability indicates a superior IQ in excess of 120 (a level more than sufficient to enter University). Christopher is a savant, someone with an island of startling talent in a sea of inability.

1.1   Personal background

Christopher was born in England on 6 January 1962, the youngest – by about ten years – of five children: he has two brothers and two sisters. His mother was 45 years old at the time of his birth, and the pregnancy was not without complications. However, there is no clear link between these problems and his later physical and mental condition. He was diagnosed as brain-damaged at the age of six weeks, and he was late in walking and talking. In addition, he has a minor speech disfluency which masked his early talent and still makes it hard for those not used to him to understand what he says. Throughout his childhood his mother and father, now both deceased,[1] fought strenuously for

Table 1 *Christopher's performance on formal psychological tests (Morgan et al., 2002a: 3)*

Raven's matrices [Administered at ages 14 and 32]	75	76
Wechsler Scale – WISC-R, UK [Administered at age 13.8]	42 (performance)	89 (verbal)
Wechsler Adult Intelligence Scale [Administered at age 27.2]	52 (performance)	98 (verbal)
Columbia Greystone Mental Maturity Scale [Administered at age 29.2]	56	
Goodenough *Draw a Man Test* [Administered at ages 14 and 32]	40	63

In a multi-lingual version of the Peabody Picture Vocabulary Test, administered at age 28, (O'Connor & Hermelin, 1991), Christopher scored: English 121; German 114; French 110; Spanish 89.

him to be accorded the special provision his talents and limitations required. His brothers and sisters have also systematically cared for him and provided an enriched and loving environment for him to live in. He regularly visits them in their homes and is taken on holidays both in the UK and abroad. Since 1988 he has lived in a Camphill Community home, where 'those with developmental disabilities can live, learn and work with others in an atmosphere of care and respect' (www.camphill.org.uk/) and where emphasis is laid on preserving the residents' human dignity and enhancing their quality of life.

1.2   Psychological profile

The most striking characteristic of Christopher's psycholinguistic profile is the asymmetry between his verbal and non-verbal abilities. As indicated in table 1 above (taken from Morgan *et al.*, 2002a: 3), there is a striking mismatch between these two halves of his performance.[2] The different figures show his performance on different occasions (the average is in each case 100).

An explicit indication of the interaction of his visual and artistic abilities is provided by his performance on the Rey-Osterrieth complex figure test of visual memory (fig. 1a). His copying of the figure was not without problem (his attempt is shown in fig. 1b), but his drawing of it from memory immediately afterwards (fig. 1c) was extremely poor.

A more intuitive idea of Christopher's artistic abilities can be derived from his picture in fig. 2 of two of the authors (reproduced from Smith & Tsimpli, 1995: 6).

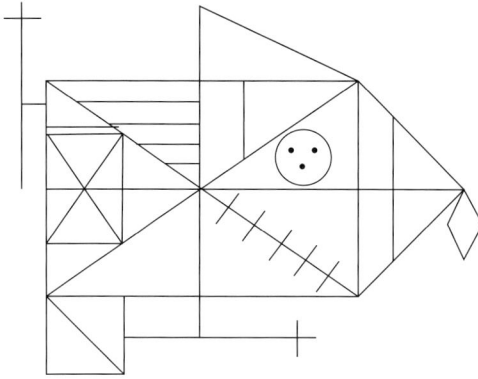

Figure 1a Rey-Osterrieth complex figure test of visual memory

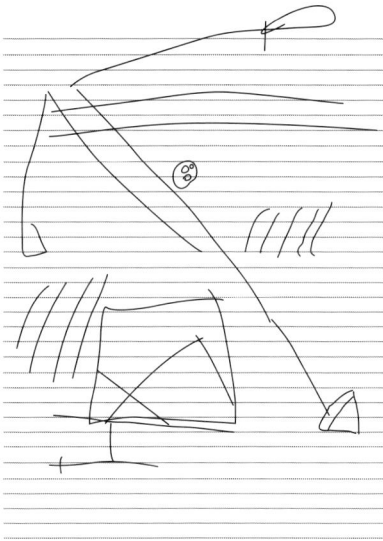

Figure 1b Christopher's copy of the Rey-Osterrieth complex figure test

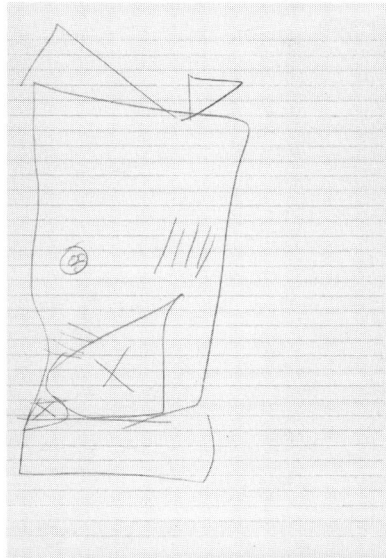

Figure 1c Christopher's drawing from memory of the Rey-Osterrieth complex figure test

Christopher's predilection for the verbal has previously manifested itself in his obsessive acquisition of a large number of spoken languages, but is borne out by two further tests. The first of these is a variant of the Gollin figures test (Smith & Tsimpli, 1995: 8–12) on which he was strikingly better at identifying words (in either Greek or English) than objects. The second is Warrington's (1984) test comparing ability to recognise faces and words. Christopher scored

Figure 2 Christopher's drawing of Ianthi and Neil

within normal limits on words, but performed too badly to score at all on faces (section 1.4 below). One of the major aims of the present book is to see if this verbal talent generalises to a signed language, but first we need to present a little more background material.

1.3   Medical background

Christopher's medical background is not as clear as one might wish. As mentioned above, he was born when his mother was 45 years old. Early in pregnancy she had contracted German measles, and towards the end of pregnancy she had a bad fall. Moreover, the delivery was long and difficult and the nurses sent for oxygen, presumably because of foetal distress, though this is not made clear in the records. Apart from the early suggestion that he was brain-damaged at birth, later institutional records suggest hydrocephaly (an abnormal build-up of cerebrospinal fluid in the brain), and an EEG carried out at age 13 revealed some oddities. A year later 'his intra-cranial pressure showed no abnormality but in 1982, at age 20, he was diagnosed as "possibly having hydrocephalic brain damage and severe neurological impairment of his motor coordination, amounting to apraxia" ' (O'Connor & Hermelin, 1991: 675). In 1993 he had an MRI scan which revealed 'moderate cerebral atrophy . . . and the cerebellar vermis [was] hypoplastic' (O'Connor *et al.*, 1994: 105). Such a configuration is not atypical of high-functioning autists, but there is no obvious connection between cerebellar hypoplasia and Christopher's unique combination of talents and disabilities. Indeed, while pathologies of various kinds can often be traced to particular patterns of neuro-anatomical abnormality, talents are generally unamenable to such explanation. Moreover, it seems unlikely that the range of characteristics found in the autistic spectrum is reducible to any single aetiology (see e.g. Happé & Vital, 2009). We return to the issue in ch. 5 where we compare Christopher with a number of other unusual cases.

1.3.1   *Autism and perspective*

In order to interact appropriately with other people, it is essential that you be able to adopt their point of view: saying 'Look at the picture' to someone whose line of sight is obstructed is an invitation to frustration. But this merely physical point of view is only a very small part of being able to appreciate someone else's point of view in the (more usual) metaphorical sense. If your partner agrees to fetch your keys from the kitchen, and you know that they are in the bedroom, you had better clarify the situation. Here the problem revolves around different assumptions about how the world is, and it is a commonplace that such disagreements are pervasive. But how do you interact with someone whose perception of reality differs from yours? The simple answer is that you entertain the relevant proposition and attribute it to them as a second-order representation or 'metarepresentation': 'I know that the keys are in the bedroom but Ann thinks the keys are in the kitchen.' What you do is then a separate matter: you can tell her, leave her to find out for herself, or whatever. This simple answer relies on your having a theory of (other) minds. But if you can't adopt someone else's point of view in this way, you have problems. There are two categories of people in this position: children up to the age of 3 or so,[3] and people with autism. The classic way of showing this is by tests in which the subject has to impute a 'false belief' to some individual.[4] This can be most simply illustrated by the 'Sally-Anne' and 'Smarties' tasks.

   In one version of the Sally-Anne test, the subject and another observer watch while the experimenter hides a toy. The observer is then sent out of the room and, in full view of the subject, the toy is moved from its first position and hidden in a new position. After ensuring that the subject was aware of where the toy was first hidden and of when the observer was last present, he or she is then asked where the observer will look for the toy on returning to the room. From about the age of 4, normal people indicate the first hiding place. Children under the age of 4, and autistic subjects, usually indicate the second hiding place, *where the toy actually is*. In the Smarties test, subjects are shown a Smarties container (a well-known chocolate candy) and asked what they think is in it. When they reply 'Smarties', they are shown that it really contains a pencil, and are then asked what their friends across the room will think is in it when they are asked. Again, very young children and autists typically reply 'a pencil'; older children, of course, reply correctly 'Smarties'. That is, young children, and autists, are unable to entertain the idea that someone else could have a representation of the world which deviates from reality, they cannot understand 'false belief'.

Christopher has never been formally diagnosed as autistic, but it is clear that he has a number of the characteristics of autism. Apart from his obsession with languages, a domain of interest which is markedly unusual, perhaps unique, for savants, he is extremely laconic in his interactions with other people, he is emotionally opaque – so that it is extremely difficult to gauge his feelings, and he is socially unforthcoming, typically failing to make eye contact and barely indulging in the normal rituals associated with meetings and leave-takings. More importantly, on formal tests of the ability to impute false belief to others, he shows a mixed profile, failing various forms of the 'Sally-Anne' test, but passing variants of the 'Smarties' test. In Tsimpli & Smith (1998) we pursued this issue in some detail and we return to it in section 1.4.4.1 below.

In addition to having problems with false belief, many, perhaps most, autistic children have impairments in the imitation of movements amounting to apraxia (see e.g. Baranek *et al.*, 2005). As a result, there are domains in which they are not good learners. As the acquisition of a sign language necessarily involves such imitation we would anticipate that autists should find the task more difficult than the general population.

1.3.2   Apraxia and the visuo-spatial

Some of the differences in Christopher's achievements on 'verbal' and 'performance' tests are a partial function of his mild autism, with his poor performance scores being exacerbated by a visuo-spatial deficit and apraxia. How far such impairments are independent is an interesting, if vexed, issue: Maguire (2008) notes that spatial navigation, the imagination of fictional states of affairs, and the prediction of future events (all of which cause Christopher problems) all involve the same neural substrate. Christopher is myopic and probably astigmatic; he has difficulty finding his way around and is quite severely apraxic. On an adaptation of the Boston Diagnostic Aphasia Examination (Goodglass & Kaplan, 1972, described in Poizner *et al.*, 1987), where the subject has to follow instructions such as 'show me how you chew something', 'wave goodbye', 'write your name', etc., Christopher scored twelve out of thirteen correct.

His one incorrect response was his reaction to 'move your eyes up', where he instead tilted his whole head back. However, on the Kimura movement copy test of non-representational gesture (Kimura, 1982), he scored extremely poorly, getting seven points (29%) with his right hand and none with his left hand. In this test, the subject has to imitate meaningless sequences of gestures involving only one hand and arm. For example, the first sequence begins with the arm positioned across the body with the hand in front of the opposite shoulder and the fingers spread apart. From this position the arm moves steadily across the front of the body to an outstretched position on the opposite side to the beginning of the movement. As the arm moves across, the fingers move from the spread position to touching each other. Two points are scored if the movement is copied correctly on the first trial; one point if it is copied correctly on the second trial, and no points if it is incorrect on both trials. A score below 90 per cent is considered apraxic. Comparable results were obtained in tests of motor coordination and praxis.[5] On tests of grip force Christopher performed normally, except that when the load force was increased unpredictably there was a delay in his latency increase. The tests involved holding an object such as a pen stable in a 'precision grip' between the thumb and the opposing index and middle fingers. It is plausible that this might be a reflection of cerebellar dysfunction, a conclusion compatible with the MRI results obtained some years previously (O'Connor *et al.*, 1994). On tests of praxis Christopher was able to recognise conventional movements (such as using a comb or scissors, or waving good-bye) at a normal level. In contrast, his ability to 'show how he would carry out a movement', such as using a comb or a teapot, (but without touching them) was impaired. With the actual use of the objects his performance was enhanced but there were still signs of object misuse. In the imitation of movements (such as blowing, shaving or smiling) his performance was very impaired. He was unable to reproduce the fine details of movement and there was considerable distortion, especially when the movements were complex, involving timing, sequencing and spatial organisation of the limbs. In addition, there was a marked lack of buccofacial expression. The results were even worse when it came to the copying of meaningless movements (touching his right hand to his neck, describing a circle with his foot, holding his hands parallel to the front while putting his right leg a step back). Altogether he scored nineteen out of a possible fifty-four, where this maximal higher score would normally be achieved by an adult of his age.

Christopher is a strikingly good learner when it comes to spoken languages, but his visuo-spatial deficit could affect his perception of sign, leading to incomplete or incorrect representation of signs; his autism could seriously limit his ability to imitate limb movements; and his severe apraxia would be expected to cause considerable problems in his production of a signed language. The auguries for the learning of BSL do not look very good.

1.4   Theoretical background

In order to make sense of Christopher's skewed abilities, we need to make a number of theoretical assumptions: about the nature of the language faculty; about the structure of the mind more generally, especially with regard to memory and general intelligence; about the 'theory of mind' which is standardly taken to underlie the problems shown by autistic subjects; about pragmatics; and about first and second language acquisition. We discuss each briefly in turn. More details are provided in some of the earlier work cited, especially Smith & Tsimpli (1995), and the references given there. In a nutshell, we adopt a broadly modular view of cognition and a Chomskyan approach to the language faculty. The details are sketched out immediately, beginning with memory. We have attempted to confront at least some of the technicalities of the relevant literature, so those prepared to take our conclusions on trust are invited to skim.

1.4.1   Memory

It is clear from his remarkable vocabulary in a large number of languages that Christopher must have an excellent long-term memory. He presumably also has a good phonological working memory as there is a correlation between this and native or foreign language vocabulary learning (Papagno et al., 1991; Ellis & Beaton, 1995; Masoura & Gathercole, 1999). Moreover, on formal tests of auditory recognition, visual recognition and temporal order,[6] he performed extremely well. The temporal order task involved us in presenting Christopher with a series of five pictures, each with an auditory label. Two of the five pictures were then shown or named and Christopher had to indicate which of the two he had seen or heard most recently. He made only one error across ten trials.

The test of auditory recognition followed the test of temporal order. He was asked to indicate whether or not he had recently heard each of twenty words, where ten of the words had been used in the previous experiment and ten had not. Christopher made his judgement by pointing to a YES-NO response sheet. He made no errors. The test of visual recognition was similar, but this time Christopher was shown twenty pictures, ten of which had been used in the temporal order task and ten of which had not. He made only one error on this task, failing to recognise the picture of a horse. Even this may not really be a mistake: the picture of the horse had previously been labelled by the experimenter as a 'mustang'. If Christopher was naming each of the pictures during the task and then matching his self-generated auditory label with the auditory labels given by the experimenter and held in memory, then the mismatch between 'horse' and 'mustang' might account for his error. Whether this explanation is correct or not, one error in twenty is very good.

So Christopher clearly has an impressively good memory, but, as with every-thing else about him, this initial characterisation turns out to be too simplistic. We wish to draw attention to two unusual and somewhat contradictory charac-teristics of his memory, as both have implications for the investigation of his linguistic and other abilities. The first is a 'delay' effect; the second is a 'speed' effect. The latter is simpler, so we discuss that first. On standard tests of digit span, Christopher tends to perform poorly if the stimulus rate is kept at the usual speed (roughly one item per second). If the stimulus rate is increased, his performance improves dramatically; indeed, to within normal limits. Specifi-cally, on forward recall with the items being read out at a rate of approximately one item per second, Christopher showed a digit span of 4.5; but when the speed was increased to approximately five items per second, his span increased to 8 digits. Presumably he is using a (somewhat impoverished) response buffer to store the information temporarily and the signal fades too rapidly for him to keep track of all the stimuli at the usual rate. This would follow from the kind of account provided by Alan Baddeley, where information from the phonological loop tends to 'fade and become unretrievable after about one-and-a-half to two seconds' (Baddeley, 1997: 52).[7]

More interestingly, on forward recall he sometimes got the order of the digits wrong but recalled them in their correct ascending order. For example, following the presentation of the items in (1a) he recalled them in the order in (1b):

(1) a   6 8 1 9 7 2   7 4 3 2 8 1
    b   1 2 6 7 8 9   1 2 3 4 7 8

This shows that he has remembered the items and sorted them into a coherent sequence, suggesting that a contributory factor in his behaviour is the semantic content of the stimuli. In tests of digit span there is, deliberately, no linking thread connecting the items to be repeated, whereas in the case of a text or discourse there is a semantic connection that can be retained subconsciously and exploited off-line. Christopher's performance on the digit span task would then appear to be an effect of redintegration[8] 'by which, before output, incomplete phonological traces held in STM [short-term memory] are reconstructed . . . by using knowledge relating to the phonological, lexico-semantic and conceptual properties of specific items' (Jacquemot & Scott, 2006: 482), and clearly shows the tight association but potential dissociability of phonological and semantic memory.

Given Christopher's talent for the verbal, we expected that his performance on a parallel 'letter span' task would show comparable effects of enhancement and redintegration. Accordingly we tested him on sequences of letters at two different speeds in three different conditions. The first series consisted solely of consonants with no obvious relation to a word of English; the second series

consisted of consonants arranged so that they could be easily associated with
a word of English; the third series consisted of consonants and vowels which
moreover formed an anagram[9] of a common English word. Each of the three
is illustrated in (2):

(2) a   F M H Z G C
    b   R P B L C N   (cf. 'republican')
    c   N E H S O T   (cf. 'honest')

His performance improved steadily on the three groups. At the slow rate
of one item per second his span was 4 for simple consonants as in (2a), 6
for 'associated' consonants as in (2b), and 7 for 'anagrams' as in (2c). At the
faster rate of four or five items per second the corresponding figures improved
to 6, 7 and 8 respectively. His mistakes in all conditions consisted typically
of transposing letters otherwise correctly remembered: e.g. repeating 'N C W
D P Y Q' as 'N C P W D Y Q'. He gave no indication of reorganising the
letters (into, say, alphabetical order) in the way he had regularised digits into
ascending order, and the only explicit indication of the facilitatory effect of the
use of 'anagrams' was his spontaneous reaction 'Bank' after he had correctly
repeated 'K B A N'.

The picture becomes murkier when we consider the results of a reading span
test[10] on which Christopher performed surprisingly badly. The test (adapted
from Williams & Möbius, 1997) requires the subject to read aloud sentences
that are presented on a computer screen one at a time. As soon as the subject has finished reading one sentence a new one is revealed. The stimuli are
grouped into sets of two to six sentences. At the end of a set (e.g. after having read two or three sentences) the subject is asked to recall the final word
of each sentence in the set in the correct order. Immediately after the recall,
the subject is presented with a yes–no comprehension question on one of the
sentences in the set. Christopher's score was below normal for a native speaker
of English and below average even for Chinese speakers of English as a second
language. He completed only one trial successfully at level 2, and recalled
the words correctly in a second trial but failed to answer the comprehension question. The discrepancy between this and the preceding tests may be a
result either of his wavering attention or of the delayed integration of meaning
from the sentence's component parts (see sections 1.4.4.3 and 1.5 below). The
results are also comparable with his extremely poor performance on tests of
digit span to signed input and of letter span to finger-spelt input (see ch. 2,
p. 46 below).

The second (delay) effect is less easily explicable and is in apparent conflict
with any model restricted to a phonological loop. On a number of occasions
we have observed that Christopher does better on a task after a considerable
lapse of time than on immediate repetition. The simplest example is provided

by the Warrington face/word recognition test mentioned above. When this test was run in the standard way, with the subject asked to identify which faces or words he had previously seen immediately after exposure to the whole series, Christopher scored 32 out of 50 for faces (too poor to be a given a percentile score) and 47 out of 50 for words (putting him in the 50th percentile). We then subjected him to a number of other quite different tests, allowed him to read some foreign language newspapers, and then we tested him again 50 minutes later (without, of course, showing him the initial sets again). On this occasion, he scored 27 out of 50 for faces (again unscorable), but improved to 48 out of 50 for words, equivalent to the 75th percentile. The normal expectation is that in the absence of rehearsal, or in the presence of interference from other material (in the same or a different modality), recall abilities deteriorate (Ebbinghaus, 1913; Kargopoulos et al., 2003). Normal subjects are expected to remember better shortly after exposure than in delayed conditions, especially if there are no semantic or phonological clues which can be used as an aid to processing the input.[11] Christopher's declining performance on faces was then expected: what is abnormal is that he was so poor in the immediate recall condition. The improvement[12] in his performance on words after a delay is also in need of explanation. We suspect that it may be because he is using the same language-learning mechanism that he deploys to remember new vocabulary items or morphological rules, rather than general short-term memory: perhaps the effect of redintegration again.

A similar delay effect was noted in his performance on certain act-out tasks. An experimenter[13] picked up an envelope and 'walked it around the room', starting from the table and going successively to the window, the door, the fireplace and the table again. When asked to imitate her immediately afterwards, Christopher simply walked to the door and returned in a curve to the table. Half an hour later he was asked if he recalled what he had been asked to do. At once he was able to say that the experimenter had visited each of the door, the table, the fireplace and the window, and (on prompting) recalled the correct order.

The most detailed example of such delayed recall was provided by his reproduction of a story read out to him (the Rivermead test, see Wilson et al., 1985). He was told that he would be read the following story (3) and that he would be asked to recall it both immediately afterwards and after some delay:

(3)   Mr Brian Kelly, a Security Express employee, was shot dead on
        Monday night during a bank-raid in Brighton. The four raiders all
        wore masks, and one carried a sawn-off shotgun. Police detectives
        were sifting through eye-witness accounts last night. A police
        spokesman said: "He was a very brave man. He went for the armed
        robber, and put up a hell of a fight."

Christopher's first (immediate) response is given in (4):

(4)   C: Well, how do I start?

K-S: As you like.

C: He went for a hell of a fight. And then the raiders wore masks. And then they had a shot – a sawn-off shotgun.

K-S: Anything else? Tell me the whole story.

C: Did they go by car? And then they went into a bank. And they nick – they stole some money. And then they went out.

He was given a number of other tests of memory and general knowledge, and half an hour later was asked what he could remember of the story. He responded as in (5):

(5)   C: There was a thief. And he had a shotgun and mask. And he also had, and he also went into a city, the city of Brighton. And he went into a bank. And what did he do? [inaudible] A police detective sifted, he took some eye-witness information. And they went home.

K-S: Do you remember what the name of the man who got killed was?

C: Brian Kelly.

K-S: And what did he do?

C: Security Express.

K-S: And what else can you remember about him?

C: He was shot dead.

K-S: He was shot dead, indeed.

C: On a Monday.

K-S: Excellent. And where was the bank-raid?

C: In the city.

K-S: Which city?

C: Brighton.

K-S: And how many raiders were there?

C: Four.

K-S: And what did the policeman [sic] say at the end?

C: I, I dunno.

K-S: He said something about the man?

C: He was a brave man.

K-S: Good, and why was he brave?

C: He put up a fight.

K-S: Do you remember what they said exactly? They said it in a very strong way.

C: Hell . . . of a fight.

In order to have any hope of accounting for such effects we need a more sophisticated fractionation of memory. We need to distinguish not only *long-term (encyclopaedic) memory* (LTM) from *short-term memory*, but both of these from *working memory*, viewed as 'an integrated system for holding and manipulating information during the performance of complex cognitive tasks' (Baddeley, 2000b: 78; see Daneman & Carpenter, 1980). LTM manifests a difference between episodic memory ('explicit', conscious, specific and personal – e.g. when one got married) and recognition memory ('implicit', unaware, general – e.g. what trees are, what *giraffe* means).[14]

In addition to this ontology we need to distinguish at least three stages in the operation of memory: *encoding*, *storage* and *retrieval*. Encoding and retrieval may be accompanied, and facilitated, by rehearsal: 'maintenance' rehearsal (for encoding operations) versus 'elaborative rehearsal' (for retrieval operations), where 'successful retrieval depends on the similarity of encoding and retrieval operations' (Brown & Craik, 2000: 99).

Even assuming agreement on this fractionation, there is still disagreement on at least two issues: first, is memory 'unitary' or 'multiple' (for discussion see Tulving, 2000: 41); second, is memory best characterised in terms of 'gateway' or 'parallel' systems (McCarthy & Warrington, 1990): i.e. whether 'there is a serial relationship between short- and long-term memory so that information must be initially held in short-term memory if it is to reach long-term memory' (Mayes, 2000: 428).[15] We think that Christopher's case provides some evidence on both issues. First, his asymmetrical behaviour on STM and LTM tasks provides evidence against a unitary memory system. In particular, it seems incompatible with the (reductivist) claim that STM and LTM are distinguished only by 'differences in the dynamics of activation within the same neocortical memory circuits' (Ranganath & Blumenfeld, 2005: 378). Second, he provides evidence against the 'gateway' model which has no means of attributing the 'delay' effect to encoding, storage or even retrieval. (He may also provide evidence for the information processing framework. Here information enters the processing system through modality-specific sensory stores and then proceeds to a limited STM store before entering LTM. The difference in Christopher's performance on faces and words shows that some modality-specific storage is necessary, the former not being amenable to 'deep' processing.)

This evidence is suggestive, but we still need an account of the 'delay' effect. In particular, it is not even clear yet whether the consolidation[16] process – the transfer from STM to LTM – reflects difficulty with encoding, with storage or with retrieval. The basis for an explanation may come from Baddeley's model of *working memory* (WM) which contrasts two (later crucially, three) 'slave' systems and a central executive: (see fig. 3, reproduced with permission from Baddeley, 2000a):

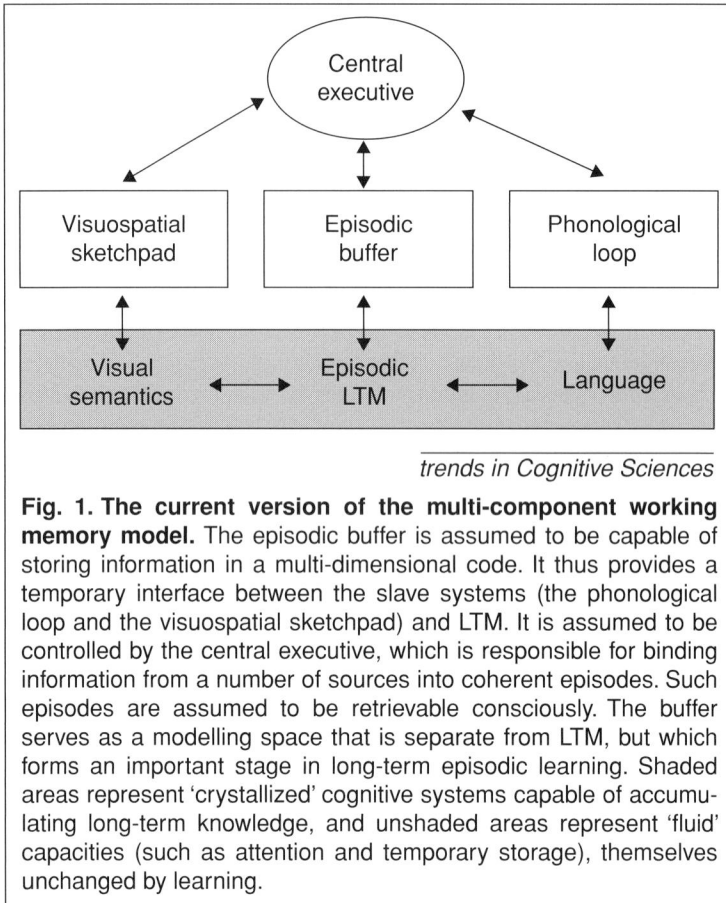

trends in Cognitive Sciences

Fig. 1. The current version of the multi-component working memory model. The episodic buffer is assumed to be capable of storing information in a multi-dimensional code. It thus provides a temporary interface between the slave systems (the phonological loop and the visuospatial sketchpad) and LTM. It is assumed to be controlled by the central executive, which is responsible for binding information from a number of sources into coherent episodes. Such episodes are assumed to be retrievable consciously. The buffer serves as a modelling space that is separate from LTM, but which forms an important stage in long-term episodic learning. Shaded areas represent 'crystallized' cognitive systems capable of accumu-lating long-term knowledge, and unshaded areas represent 'fluid' capacities (such as attention and temporary storage), themselves unchanged by learning.

Figure 3 Baddeley's model of working memory (reproduced with permission from Baddeley, 2009)

The *central executive* (see Norman & Shallice, 1980/1986) comprises com-ponents able to focus, switch and divide attention (Baddeley, 2007: 138). The 'slaves' are: the 'visuospatial sketchpad', including a kinaesthetic component, the 'phonological loop' and latterly the 'episodic buffer'. The *visuospatial sketchpad* is a 'storage system capable of integrating visual and spatial infor-mation, whether acquired from vision, touch, language or LTM, into a uni-tary visuo-spatial representation' (Baddeley, 2007: 64). The *phonological loop* comprises 'a phonological store and an articulatory rehearsal mechanism'. The *episodic buffer* is a limited-capacity temporary storage system that is controlled by the central executive and is capable of integrating information from various sources. Baddeley argues that the episodic buffer is preferentially dedicated to the consolidation of stimuli into LTM, (there is a distinct, privileged, path from the episodic buffer to episodic LTM), while the phonological loop and visuospatial sketchpad are preferentially dedicated to STM. He further suggests (Baddeley, 2007: 147) that there may also be bidirectional paths linking the visuospatial sketchpad and the episodic buffer, and the episodic buffer and the phonological loop.

This parallel model with different (but overlapping) resources for STM and LTM provides a basis for describing Christopher's delay effect. Informally, it appears that he has problems both with the encoding of events and the consolidation of the associated memories. On the one hand, it takes him an unusually long time to encode information represented in a linguistic format. For instance, encoding the semantic relations inherent in a visual sequence of events such as the act-out task, carrying out the reading span task, comprehending written text, processing sentences with some complexity (e.g. ambiguity), are all delayed, as becomes more obvious when integration of information (meaning) is required. On the other hand, in laying down memories, Christopher needs time for these memories to be consolidated, as though the processing mechanisms are operating off-line, and relatively slowly, perhaps in the same way that he rehearses dialogues until they become 'routinised' (Smith & Tsimpli, 1995: 167). Although not conscious, these processes must be built on a subconscious linguistic analysis of the relevant stimuli, a procedure he is unable to carry out with faces or visual figures, suggesting that it is the visuospatial sketchpad slave that is affected. A further implication is that the visuospatial sketchpad should make provision for two different pathways from the 'visual semantics': one for letters (graphemes) and one for shapes. Clearly, Christopher has no problems with the former (other than the delay effect in meaning integration from visually presented language), but the other pathway operates sub-optimally. There is also evidence from Christopher's performance on digit span that there must be two different pathways from 'language' to the other slave systems, the phonological loop and the episodic buffer. Despite the fact that no effect of meaning is supposed to be involved, he clearly subjected the sequence of digits to some semantic analysis to provide an ordering which was stored in the episodic buffer and then consolidated.

The central executive and the various slave systems can all dissociate. Christopher's central executive is impaired and his attentional resources cannot be focused sufficiently fast to encode a trace of an event for it to be immediately available – i.e. without consolidation. His phonological loop is intact but limited – witness his improved digit span at speed. The semantic interference seen in (1b) can be attributed to the intrusion of the episodic buffer, either directly (as in the 2007 version of Baddeley's theory) or indirectly through the central executive (in the 2000 version). Although the evidence is not conclusive, and we exploit both possibilities below, we prefer the more parsimonious earlier system with no direct link between the episodic buffer and the phonological loop. The evidence for such a link that Baddeley presents (2007: 172–3) is the following. There are data which suggest a role for both the central executive and the phonological loop in subjects' immediate recall of 'constrained' sentences,[17] but a role only for the phonological loop in their performance recalling unrelated words. Experimentally disrupting the central executive during auditory presentation of stimuli had the same effect on both kinds of material, suggesting that the episodic buffer has unmediated access to the phonological loop. However, we know independently that Christopher's central executive is slow, so it seems that having necessarily to go through the central executive in all cases might be sufficient to account for his performance.[18]

The Warrington word recognition test obviously requires more resources than just the digit span capabilities of the phonological loop, and if consolidation to LTM has to go through the central executive as well as the episodic buffer it would take more time than is available under immediate recall conditions. Similarly, the story reproduction test involves an interaction between the phonological loop and the central executive, mediated by the episodic buffer. If there is a direct link between the episodic buffer and the phonological loop it seems likely that the transfer to LTM is direct *and* indirect, rather than just indirect: that is, the phonological loop and the episodic buffer would work in parallel to convey information via the central executive to LTM, with the contribution of the episodic buffer being invoked twice.

Christopher's visuospatial sketchpad is impaired. Moreover, the sub-parts of the visuospatial sketchpad themselves dissociate. Both the visual and the spatial components are limited but, on testing, the spatial appears to be better than the visual (contrast his improvement on the 'act-out' test and the degradation in his performance on the 'face recognition' test). However, there are at least two complicating factors. First, face recognition is special in that it is underpinned by dedicated neural architecture and so can be differentially impaired with respect to other visual stimuli, as in prosopagnosia; so it may be that it is just Christopher's face recognition component which is affected rather than the visual system more generally (see e.g. Kanwisher & Moscovitch, 2000). Second, the delayed 'act-out' task was not really an 'acting-out' but a verbalisation of the events, so Christopher's improvement may be due to the fact that in the time that elapsed between his watching the experimenter and describing what she did he was able to integrate a verbal description of the events in the central executive so that he could access them more successfully in the delayed condition. This possibility suggests that simple asymmetry between the visual and the spatial is not the correct explanation of Christopher's behaviour. It is significant that in his BSL he performed worse on classifiers than other parts of the morpho-syntax (see ch. 4.6 below), and here the extra difficulty resides precisely in the spatial component – the visual element is equally essential for all aspects of BSL. An alternative possibility might be that the episodic buffer interfaces better with the spatial component than the visual, allowing usable consolidation for the former but not the latter; but we think the crucial contrast can be related to Christopher's verbal talent. Both objects and faces have visual and spatial properties, but the former also have labels, i.e. names in language, whereas the latter do not. Obviously, faces can be associated with the names of their bearers, but this strategy is excluded under the experimental conditions of the Warrington test. The asymmetry in Christopher's performance can then plausibly be attributed to the fact that the spatial can be semantically characterised through language, whereas faces cannot be. Recall that a major dissociation in Christopher's performance concerns the kinds of visual stimuli involved: written words versus pictures on the one hand, and between pictures of objects and pictures of faces on the other. Objects have names, but faces don't and, in keeping track of objects in the 'act-out' description, he performed better than with faces. Verbalisable information – i.e. information that can be recast in verbal-propositional form – can be easily stored and retrieved 'centrally'. Without special training faces cannot be verbalised, and objects – while verbalisable – are not already available as words are, so there is a hierarchy in his performance, with words handled better than objects and objects better than faces. Accordingly, we propose that the asymmetrical delay effect in Christopher's reactions arises in part from the mediocre capabilities of the visuospatial sketchpad allied with the intact status of the episodic buffer, in part from the time it takes him to encode a stimulus into the 'deep' semantic form that is linguistically accessible, but most importantly from the facilitatory effect of the language faculty and the central executive. The episodic buffer allows for efficient transfer to LTM, but the links between the episodic buffer and each of the sub-components of the visuospatial sketchpad may be defective (in the 2007 version) or missing (as in the 2000 version). But the core of our account of his poor ability to perform immediately after exposure to the stimuli invokes the links to the central executive and the relative ease of verbalisability of different types of stimuli.

Assuming that this application of Baddeley's model works (Baddeley himself describes an earlier version of it as 'ambitious but not entirely convincing' – p.c.) we need to integrate it into a model of the mind. We attempt this in ch. 6.7.1.

One further relevant consideration may be the consciousness of the thought processes involved. It seems that Christopher reflects consciously only when drawing on information from long-term memory (as in the case of the Rivermead story in (3) above), and here prompting is useful to him, showing that he does not memorise without understanding. In different tasks he can be prompted not only by semantic or conceptual properties but also by phonological and morphological patterns and by the existence of orthographic cognates. This means that he can be primed effectively depending on how he has analysed and stored the information through the operations of his central executive and episodic buffer. In brief, the apparently contradictory speed and delay effects in Christopher's performance are attributable to the respective absence and presence of conceptual or propositional content. If correct, this analysis should generalise to characterise a contrast between quantitative and qualitative aspects of his performance. On the one hand his performance on some tasks (face recognition, false belief and so on) is qualitatively different from the norm, and this is attributable to deficits in the conceptual systems involved (for instance, a defective theory of mind). On the other hand, his poor abilities in language tasks which involve increased cognitive complexity, such as the parsing of garden-path sentences, the processing load associated with negation and Wh-movement, and the production of coherent or appropriate word or text translations, are all quantitative in nature. These are due to the reduced capacity of a functioning central executive, or impoverished links between the natural language and the language of thought.

1.4.2   Modularity and modality

We adopt a view of cognitive architecture on which the mind is pervasively modular, but modular in Chomsky's (1975, 1984) sense, rather than in the sense of Fodor's (1983) now classical position. Fodor differentiates the central system, which is responsible for higher cognitive activities, such as general problem solving and the fixation of belief, from the input systems, which provide grist for the central mill. He then argues that these input systems, which correspond in the first instance to the sensorium, but crucially also include the language faculty, share a number of further properties, and any component with these properties is then, by definition, a module. For instance, modules are domain-specific, in that their operations are sensitive only to a subset of impinging stimuli – light waves for vision, sound waves for audition, and likewise for the other senses. They are relatively fast, in that it takes minimal time to see a person as a person, but much longer to decide what to buy him or her as a birthday present. Modules operate mandatorily: you have no choice but to see a face as a face, or to understand a sentence of your native language; but you may choose to ignore what you have seen and heard. They are ontogenetically deterministic, in that their development typically unfolds in the same way across the species without the benefit of overt instruction. The visual systems of children from all over the world appear to grow in much the same way, irrespective of culture; and their linguistic systems characteristically

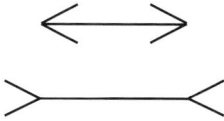

Figure 4 The Müller-Lyer optical illusion

go through comparable stages at comparable ages, irrespective of the language being acquired. Modules are subject to idiosyncratic pathological breakdown, in that brain damage in the auditory cortex can cause deafness, in the visual cortex it can cause blindness or, in the left temporal lobe, it can cause aphasia. That is, it is brain damage, not 'external' damage to the eyes or ears, that typically results in pathology. Finally, the operations of modules seem to be largely impervious to the influence of the central system; they are 'informationally encapsulated'. The classic example is provided by the Müller-Lyer optical illusion, in which two lines, flanked by inward or outward pointing arrow-heads are displayed, as in fig. 4.

The visual system makes you perceive the lower line as longer than the upper line. Even if you take a ruler and convince yourself that the two lines are indeed of identical length, your eyes still interpret them as being different. That is, the working of the visual system is impervious to the explicit knowledge provided by the central system. All of these properties are, of course, the subject of debate and controversy (as is the whole notion of modularity; for discussion, see Ingram, 2007), but it is generally agreed that the most important of them are domain specificity and informational encapsulation (Carston, 1996; Coltheart, 1999).[19] As it is a position with which we shall disagree, it is also worth noting Fodor's early claim that the central system is largely inaccessible to scientific investigation, although he later (Fodor, 1992) admitted some structure into the central system as well.

For Chomsky, the language faculty cannot be a Fodorian module, for two reasons. First, we use language to speak as well as to understand, and if Fodor is correct in identifying modules with 'input systems', then language, which is also an output system, cannot be a module. Second, and more importantly, the language faculty must in some respects be 'central' to accommodate the basic fact that it is (or includes) a system of knowledge. Moreover, this knowledge constitutes a common store which is neutral as between speaker and hearer. That is, we draw on largely the same knowledge whether we are producing an utterance of our own or interpreting that of someone addressing us. If understanding (parsing) and production deployed different systems, we would expect it to be the case that someone could speak one language and understand only a different one. Moreover, Chomsky does not share Fodor's pessimism that the central system is essentially inscrutable, suggesting that a range of functions from moral judgement to the number sense fall within its purview, and that language is just one such domain, albeit the one about which we know most (for discussion, see Levy & Kavé, 1999; Smith, 2003, where schematic flow diagrams of Fodor's and Chomsky's models are suggested, and Smith, 2004).

Building on both Fodor's and Chomsky's work, we adhere to a conception of *modified modularity*. The language faculty is clearly domain-specific[20] and it is, at least in part, independent of other aspects of mind. But it is not just an input system in Fodor's sense, and it is furthermore necessary to attribute greater structure to the 'central' system than Fodor allows for, so we need a more subtle ontology than one that just differentiates modules and the central system. Accordingly, we have suggested that it is desirable to draw a distinction between modules and what we have labelled 'quasi-modules' (Tsimpli & Smith, 1998; they were called 'central modules' in Smith & Tsimpli, 1995). Like Fodorian modules, quasi-modules are domain-specific, fast and mandatory, but they are not informationally encapsulated and their vocabulary, which may differ from case to case, is conceptual not perceptual. We have argued extensively elsewhere (Tsimpli & Smith, 1998) for the claim that theory of mind is a quasi-module in this sense. Other domains which partake of at least some of the same properties include moral judgement, music, common sense, the number sense, the senses of social structure and of personality structure, and perhaps folk physics and folk biology. In addition, it is still necessary to maintain the notion of the 'sub-modular' structure characteristic of the language faculty (and other domains) in which, for instance, we have Chomskyan modules[21] of Theta-theory, Binding theory, Case theory and so on. We have modules within modules.

In every case where a module or quasi-module is postulated, there should arise the possibility of (double) dissociation. Concentrating on the case of Christopher, we can indeed see a number of such dissociations. Christopher illustrates the situation in which linguistic ability is generally spared and general intelligence is impaired, while some aphasics provide evidence for the converse – impaired linguistic ability and spared general intelligence. A developmental parallel to such aphasias, where aspects of the language faculty are impaired but general intelligence is within the normal range, is provided by specific language impairment (SLI; for an overview, see Joanisse and Seidenberg, 1998). In this condition children fail to develop age-appropriate knowledge of language despite being cognitively normal in all or most other respects. In fact, this simple characterisation is itself controversial: many researchers have claimed that the deficit is *not* language specific but is rather a reflex of a general deficit in the processing of rapid auditory sequential information (Tallal, 1990). Although some SLI subjects may show such deficits in addition to language problems, it has been suggested that there is a population in whom the only difficulty is linguistic (Bishop, 1997; van der Lely, 1997; van der Lely &

Stollwerck, 1997), where moreover the epidemiology shows that the deficit is (at least in part) genetically determined (Gopnik, 1997). Such cases provide an interesting contrast to that of Christopher, both in the double dissociation of the deficits involved, and also in the details of the putative linguistic problem. We also think that our framework is capable of dealing with the phenomena accounted for by the 'limited core language system', that Talmy proposes as a substantive modification of the 'Fodor-Chomsky model' (Talmy, 2003: 194). While acknowledging the existence of a common linguistic core to spoken and signed languages, Talmy argues that it is significantly less extensive than is claimed by the modularity hypothesis and has to interact with other cognitive subsystems. We develop precisely such an interactive model below and claim that the differences between signed and spoken languages that Talmy identifies are best handled in terms of a common system with different interactions with other (modular) components of the mind.

Given the notion 'modularity' and the double dissociations that partly define it, one would expect that the modality (auditory or visual) of linguistic – and other – inputs would have a crucial and differentiating effect on people's (hence Christopher's) ability to cope with particular phenomena. That is, given that Christopher has an established talent for mastering *spoken* languages, and an established apraxia that gives rise to problems of hand–eye coordination and spatial awareness, one might expect that his talent for second language learning would not generalise to the signed domain, and/or that his mastery of the intricacies of a signed language would be dramatically worse than that of a comparator group. One of the more striking conclusions of our investigations has been precisely that these tacit predictions have in general not been fulfilled.

1.4.3   The language faculty

We assume that a significant part of the language faculty is innately determined, comprising a lexicon and a computational system or syntax, the 'computation for human language' (C_{HL}) (Chomsky, 1995: 221). The lexicon consists of lexical items characterised by sets of features, especially morphological features; the syntax consists of computational operations such as Merge, Move and Agree. Representations produced by the language faculty have to be accessible to and 'legible' by other cognitive systems, both conceptual and sensori-motor, with which they interface. We further presuppose that this internal structure is as hypothesised in current work in Principles and Parameters theory, as elaborated in the Minimalist Program (Chomsky, 1995). We elaborate on this general framework in ch. 6.7.1 below (for elementary introductions, see Smith, 2004; Roberts, 1997; Chomsky, 2000: ch. 1. The clearest statements of Chomsky's recent position can be found in his 2002a, 2009a, 2009b).[22]

1.4.3.1 Principles and parameters   The innate endowment of the child which enables it to acquire its first language is referred to as 'universal grammar' (UG). It consists of a number of general principles accounting for the common properties of all human languages, and a set of parametric choices which accommodate the differences between languages. The origins of the theory reside in the tension arising from the conflict between achieving descriptive and explanatory adequacy: languages are complicated and necessitate complex descriptive devices, but children learn them with little effort at an early age. This tension is often referred to as 'Plato's problem'. The solution is to remove the complexities from individual grammars and 'attribute them to the genetic endowment of the child' (Chomsky, 2002a: 152). As Chomsky puts it elsewhere:

We can think of the initial state of the faculty of language as a fixed network connected to a switchbox; the network is constituted of the principles of language, while the switches [= parameters] are the options to be determined by experience. (Chomsky, 2000: 8)

At first, parameters were associated directly with the principles of UG. For instance, the X' (X bar) theory of phrase structure, which guarantees that all structures are headed, had an associated parametric choice determining whether the head preceded or followed its complement (head-first, as in English, versus head-last, as in Hindi). Similarly, the 'extended projection principle' which guarantees that all clauses have subjects, had an associated parameter – the 'pro-drop' or 'null-subject' parameter – determining whether that subject could be empty (as in Greek and Italian), or was necessarily overt (as in English and French). Parametric values were then set for the language as a whole, with the major advantage that they gave rise to 'cascade effects'. By *learning* that verbs precede their complements (as in 'see Mary') the child *comes to know*, without exposure to any data, that prepositions (as in 'with Mary') do too. By learning that its language has null subjects (as in the Spanish for 'he/she dances well' – *baila bien*), the child comes to know that it will *not* show 'that-trace effects' (*¿quién dijo que baila bien?* – 'Who did he say [that] dances well?'), it *will* have postposed subjects (*baila Juan* – 'John dances'), and so on. The cascade effect produced by parameter-setting went a long way to solving Plato's problem, but it encountered two serious problems: 'dissociations' and 'inconsistencies' (for useful discussion, see Biberauer, 2008).

The triple of properties supposedly definitional of the 'pro-drop' parameter (null subjects, *that*-trace effects, postposed subjects) dissociate. For instance, Portuguese and the Camerounian language Denya allow null subjects but disallow inversion; the Trentino and Florentine dialects of Italian disallow null subjects but allow inversion. To compound the problem, some languages are 'inconsistent': Farsi has SOV and prepositions, making it look as if some parameter would have to be set in two contradictory ways in the same language.

As a result of such findings, parameter values came to be associated with lexical items, not principles of UG. This may seem an unfortunate development, but it has advantages. The first and major advantage is that parametrisation can be restricted to the lexicon (Borer, 1984; Chomsky, 1995: 131). A minor one is that this resolves a problem in bilingual (first) language acquisition, where children appeared to have to make conflicting choices. Building on the advantage of restricting parametric choices to the lexicon, subsequent research has led to a situation where parametric variation has been constrained to refer only to functional categories,[23] and within that, only to the value of the feature [± strong]. Functional categories are those which have no substantive content, such as determiners, complementisers, tense and agreement, as opposed to the lexical categories noun, verb and adjective. The feature [± strong] is a somewhat arbitrary means of coding a variety of different properties in a single simple element. For instance, English (interrogative) C is strong (hence Wh-movement is overt, whereas it is covert in Japanese), but I is weak (hence main verbs cannot raise, though auxiliaries can; whereas in German both can move). We return to the implications of this view of parametric variation for first and second language acquisition below.

In our discussion of modularity we emphasised the possibility of dissociations. When we look at the linguistic domain, similar 'sub-modular' dissociations within the language faculty are also manifest, providing corroborative support for any linguistic theory that postulates the kind of structure characteristic of most versions of the Principles and Parameters model. The most obvious of these dissociations is between the lexicon and the computational system (Clahsen, 1999).

Christopher's first language, English, is entirely normal, but it is striking that his talent in his numerous 'second' languages is restricted largely to mastery of the morphology and the lexicon, whilst his syntactic ability rapidly peaks and then plateaus. This dissociation is significant for the light it casts on the structure of the language faculty. The computational basis of syntax is universal, allowing a small range of possible operations (Merge, Move, Agree), whereas the feature-values associated with functional categories are parametrised. Particular features trigger these universal operations and different spell-out effects are found, depending on morpho-phonological properties which vary from language to language. Christopher's command of English demonstrates that the computational part of his syntax must be intact, but his problems with other languages indicate that he is unable to associate appropriate feature-values with novel functional categories or with functional categories activated in his first language (L1) but with feature-values different from the second language (L2) target. In other words, he cannot re-set parameter values. Parameter-setting is most likely to unfold during a particular 'critical period' (Tsimpli, 1996; Smith, 1998), and if Christopher's 'second' languages have all been learned after the end of this critical period, when 're-setting' is impossible (Tsimpli & Roussou, 1991; Hawkins & Hattori, 2006; Tsimpli & Dimitrakopoulou, 2007), it suggests that his talent, while remarkable in the domain of second language vocabulary and morphology, is necessarily flawed in the domain of syntax. It also suggests that in interesting respects, Christopher's abilities are only partly linguistic.

Unlike first language acquisition, second language learning may crucially involve the deployment of general learning strategies which are ultimately correlated with attributes of the central system (Tsimpli & Smith, 1991). In Christopher's case this suggests that while he is able to 'relexify' the particular syntactic template of his first language, he cannot modify that original template itself – a large proportion of his second language activity consists in introducing items of vocabulary from a wide variety of languages into English syntactic structures. This makes Christopher strikingly different from talented second language learners whose 'ultimate attainment' is close to that of native speakers (Birdsong, 1992), as well as from the average L2 learner who, with increased exposure to and use of L2, will generally approximate the input, with varying degrees of success, more and more closely (Hawkins, 2001; White, 2003). Assuming nonetheless that there is an obvious linguistic component to Christopher's learning of 'second' languages, it is worth highlighting the dissociation between morphology and syntax. Christopher's mastery of morphology combined with severe limitations in syntax is the mirror image of the reverse dissociation found in children with spinal muscular atrophy, who seem to develop a proficient syntactic rule system but have greater difficulty with lexical development (Sieratzki & Woll, 2002).

1.4.3.2 Morphology as an interface   The above account of Principles and Parameters theory is standard and widely accepted; though the framework is itself the subject of ongoing heated debate (see, for instance, Tomasello, 2000 for an alternative position, and Culicover, 2004, Newmeyer, 2005, Biberauer, 2008, Smith & Law, in press, for discussion). The next strand in our framework is more controversial. As argued in Smith & Tsimpli, 1995 (and Tsimpli & Smith, 1998), we view the language faculty as being partly modular and partly central, with the link between the two being provided by the morphology. For reasons of compositionality and learnability (see Cormack & Smith, 2002) we think that the relation between the representations in natural language and the language of thought (Fodor, 1975, 2008) must be close to isomorphic, and the morphology constitutes a natural bridge between the two. Although morphology and syntax show specific correlations and, in the Minimalist Program, syntactic operations are driven by the need to satisfy morphological conditions (of agreement and tense for instance), the two are in principle independent and subject to different constraints (see Tsimpli, 1996). Crucially, the morphology is accessible both to functional categories – e.g.

tense – within the grammar, and to substantive categories – e.g. time – within the central system. Moreover, morphological features have a role both in the derivations within 'narrow syntax' and in mapping the output of the syntax to PF (phonetic form), where this mapping is mediated by language-specific morphological properties and constraints. Further, in first (and perhaps second) language acquisition the two may follow parallel but not identical developmental paths. Children's mastery of parametric choices such as verb-movement, which is based on feature-specification on functional heads, seems to be achieved earlier than their mastery of the full range of corresponding morphological forms (see e.g. Borer & Rohrbacher, 2003). This different pattern of development in the two components is further evidenced in second language acquisition (Lardiere, 2000, 2006) and in various pathologies,[24] acquired or developmental (Leonard, 1998; Clahsen & Almazan, 1998). We shall trade on the interface status of morphology in our model of the mind in ch. 6.

1.4.4   Theory of mind

In section 1.3.1 we described some of Christopher's autistic traits and tentatively attributed them to a defective *theory of mind* (quasi-)module. We now return to the main evidence for this characterisation.

1.4.4.1   False belief and the language faculty   Christopher has problems with the imputation of false belief to others. It is important to note that it is false *belief* that is problematic for him. Some of our earlier work had involved him in remembering and/or inferring the identity of different symbols on flash cards, of which he could see only one side. The results suggested that he 'has no difficulty in adopting a perspective different from his own; in recalling past, currently invalid, states of affairs; and in projecting hypothetical states of affairs' (Smith & Tsimpli, 1995: 178; see work on the development of deaf and autistic children in de Villiers *et al.*, 2000).[25] Moreover, like most autistic subjects (see for example Nichols *et al.*, 1996), he performed correctly in a version of the Zaitchik (1990) photograph task. In this test, a photograph was taken of a doll wearing a pink dress. While we waited for the photograph to develop, the doll's dress was changed for a blue one, and Christopher had to 'predict' the colour of the dress that would appear in the photograph. His response was confident and appropriate, showing that tasks which require no ascription of belief are systematically within his capabilities. However, he finds tasks which necessitate the imputation of false belief to others difficult or impossible, though here his performance is interestingly inconsistent. As mentioned in the earlier discussion of autism (section 1.3.1 above), he systematically failed the 'Sally-Anne' test but passed the 'Smarties' test. If autistic behaviour is correctly viewed as being partially a function of an impaired theory of mind, and if failing such tasks is correctly attributed to such impairment, then these

results are problematic. There is some scepticism about the use of the false-belief task as a measure of theory of mind (see e.g. Bloom & German, 2000), in part because of the differential behaviour of normal 3-year-olds and autistic subjects; in part because of the kind of results achieved by Baillargeon and her colleagues (see note 3 on p. 191). Be that as it may, it is clear that Christopher's performance is anomalous, is correlated with his (mild) autism, and may be because he 'lack[s] the capacity to acquire a theory of mind' (Bloom & German, 2000: B29).[26] We had further argued that the reason why Christopher was successful on Smarties, but not on Sally-Anne, was because the Smarties test could be solved by having recourse to encyclopaedic information and without the necessity of ascribing a mental representation to another individual. We had also surmised (Tsimpli & Smith, 1998) that Sally-Anne would be differentially difficult for Christopher depending on a number of factors: specifically, the familiarity of the participants involved, the medium – spoken versus written – in which the test was presented, and the spatial or temporal nature of the crucial false belief. To determine whether these hypotheses were correct, we tested Christopher on a number of variations of both tests. First, in view of our explanation for the mismatch between his performance on the two tasks, we conducted a Smarties-type test in which the help of encyclopaedic information was factored out. For instance, the box contained a dead scorpion and there was no indication as to the content on the box itself. Thus, the initial answer to the question 'What do you think is in the box?' should be a guess or 'I don't know'. Second, in view of our earlier characterisation of theory of mind representations as involving a modal predicate embedded under a verb of thinking (Smith &Tsimpli, 1995: 185), we tested to see whether Christopher could recall and report on his earlier beliefs when these contradicted his current ones; whether he could systematically control the difference between the use of *say* and *think* in the test questions; and finally, whether there was a difference in his performance depending on the modality – written versus spoken – in which the material was presented.

For the Smarties variants there were three relevant dimensions of variation. First, Christopher was consistently able accurately to recall and repeat his own initial suggestions, whether correct or incorrect. Second, in the absence of clear-cut encyclopaedic clues, he was inconsistent in reporting the potential responses of a third person, answering apparently at random. Third, questions with *say* and *think* received identical answers when they were about Christopher himself; they received apparently random answers when they were about a different referent.

The Sally–Anne variants involved three modifications to the previous tests. First, in view of Christopher's obsession with language and his superior performance on verbal as opposed to performance IQ tests, we devised variants in which the scenario was read as a story instead of being acted out. The tentative hypothesis to be tested was that such verbalisation would exploit his linguistic abilities to the maximum, and minimise the use of abilities in which he is putatively defective. Second, in view of the facilitatory effect of encyclopaedic knowledge on the Smarties test, the stories were controlled for the familiarity of the characters depicted. The hypothesis to be tested here was that familiarity might reduce the cognitive complexity of the task and simultaneously render it easier for Christopher to identify with what was going on.[27] Third, the content of the proposition for which the false belief was supposed to be held alternated between the temporal and the spatial. Here the idea, prompted by Christopher's established difficulty with spatial orientation and hand–eye coordination, was that temporal variation, especially when linguistically encoded, might be less difficult for him to manipulate than visuo-spatial variation. That is, where the false belief pertained to the time at which something happened, as conveyed by the tense system, rather than the place where something was located, as conveyed by a combination of the visual and the lexical, Christopher should perform better. In each case the hypothesis was confirmed (see Tsimpli & Smith, 1998 for the details). To summarise, Christopher is an atypical autist not only as regards his linguistic abilities, including enhanced lexical and encyclopaedic knowledge, but also with respect to his inconsistent performance in false-belief tasks. Given his varying performance when variables such as the medium, the temporal versus spatial dimension, and familiarity were controlled for, we argued that Christopher can compensate for his deficit in theory of mind through strategies involving the use of language. In fact, his performance on theory of mind tasks has proved disconcertingly inconsistent. In an informal test carried out in October 2005 he failed 'Smarties' and passed 'Sally-Anne', an apparent reversal of his previous behaviour. Given the relative consistency of his previous performance we leave this as an aberration, probably explicable on the grounds that he was performing under stress in front of strangers and was anyway only given a single traditional example of each test.

1.4.4.2   Theory of intelligence and the executive   In previous work we have exploited Anderson's (1992) theory of intelligence, and we continue to use a radically modified version of it here. Despite sustained criticism of the validity of any notion of 'general intelligence' (g), Anderson attempts to 'make[ ] plausible the psychological reality of general intelligence' (1992: 24). The core of his theory is a *knowledge store* (encyclopaedic memory) built up on the basis of input from Fodorian modules and a *basic processing mechanism*, responsible for psychometric g, and probably to be equated with some form of executive.[28] A final crucial element is a set of *specific processors* dedicated to manipulating incoming data in particular formats – minimally 'visuo-spatial' and 'verbal-propositional' (see fig. 5).

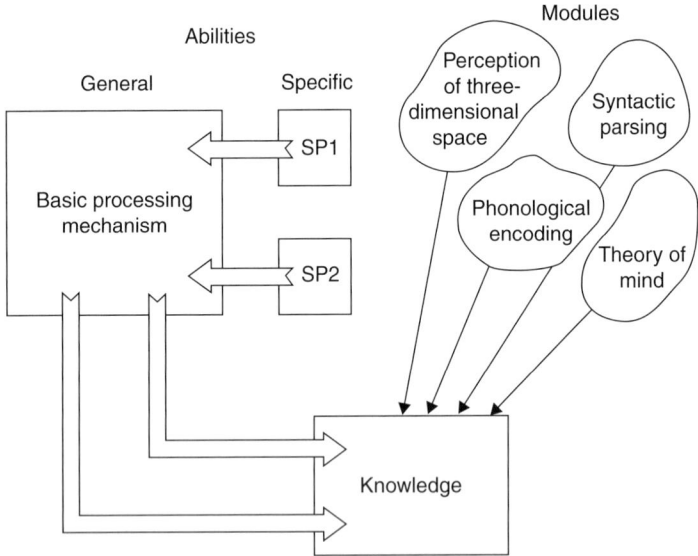

Figure 5 Anderson's (1992) model of the mind (reproduced with permission from Smith & Tsimpli, 1995: 32)

Christopher's linguistic and other behaviour led us to sketch his mental (dis)abilities as including a deficit in the visuo-spatial processor and the basic processing mechanism. However, the various peaks and valleys in Christopher's performance led us to considerable modifications of Anderson's model. The most radical revision involves the abandonment of the basic processing mechanism as a separate entity. As we hinted in earlier work (Smith & Tsimpli, 1995: 213–14) we think that postulating some form of 'executive' (akin to Baddeley's central executive discussed above) may be independently necessary, and the basic processing mechanism should be viewed as a 'horizontal' faculty (Fodor, 1983: 11) 'which crosses content-domains, and hence acts as a constraint on the operation of other parts of the system, rather than being any kind of module in its own right'. This is probably not as alien to Anderson's original conception as may appear. In his introduction of the notion of a basic processing mechanism he talks of there being 'low-level cognitive processes that underlie intelligent thinking. Let me gather these processes together and locate them in a particular mechanism: the *basic processing mechanism*' (Anderson, 1992: 58). We are not convinced that this reification is justified: the kind of asymmetries seen in *savant* abilities seems to us to argue against any such gathering together. Savants' isolated talents imply that they have one preserved domain – visuo-spatial, mathematical, musical or whatever. This intact domain allows the construction of one class of cognitive representations that work efficiently, and anything that can be recast in terms of these representations operates effectively. In contrast, what is seen in Asperger's individuals is that one domain (theory of mind or social affect) is defective while speed of processing, the overall capacity of the memory systems and the central executive are normal or enhanced. In Christopher's case, and perhaps in that of other savants, we have a combination of quantitative and qualitative deviations from the ordinary, predicting that outside the domain of their exceptional talent savants should show problems with increased computational load rather than just a complete inability to cope with domains in which they do not excel. In Anderson's theory the spared component could either be one (sub-part) of the specific processors (a qualitative problem) or the basic processing mechanism they feed into (a quantitative problem). In intellectually typical subjects the cognitive system operates with equal efficiency on any kind of representation, but in savants it can only make optimal use of what is intact – in Christopher's case linguistic representations, because the other components are not working properly. If we assumed that Anderson's basic processing mechanism equated to working memory this would imply that (for Christopher) it should operate preferentially on linguistically representable entities. However, it seems more plausible, and more parsimonious, that the locus of Christopher's unique combination of abilities should reside not in the basic processing mechanism but should result from the properties of the specific processors, together with the reduced capacity of his central executive. This interaction results in his cognition being qualitatively characterised as exhibiting 'weak central coherence', to which we turn in the next section.

Our reinterpretation of Anderson leaves us with the problem of explaining why in most people the various cognitive abilities cluster: if you are good (or bad) in one domain you are likely to be good (or bad) in the rest. At this level of abstraction the reason is probably physiological – synaptic efficiency, something that follows automatically from the postulation of a basic processing mechanism. As *savants* show, however, such uniformity is not necessary, and we return in ch. 6 to further discussion of Anderson's model in the light of our results on Christopher's learning of BSL.

1.4.4.3 Central coherence Uta Frith (1989/2003) and her colleagues have suggested that the typical characteristics of autistic behaviour can be described, and explained, in terms of the notion 'central coherence': the ability to gain an understanding of the overall coherence of a scene rather than being sidetracked by details. Autistic subjects have weak central coherence in comparison with the relatively strong central coherence of the normal population.[29] This manifests itself in a variety of ways: good rote memory combined with poor ability at extracting the gist of a complex narrative; good ability at identifying hidden figures combined with failure to integrate details into a whole; good ability at noticing typos but poor ability at detecting ambiguity. In a nutshell, the drive for coherence can be attributed to Sperber and Wilson's (1986/1995: 260) cognitive principle of relevance (see section 1.4.5 below), with its dependence on the successful exploitation of context. 'Weak central coherence' would then be a reflection of a problem with the principle of relevance. The simplest manifestation of this difference can be shown by reactions to 'Navon' figures (Navon, 1977) of the kind shown in (6), where a large letter (or other figure) is composed of a number of smaller letters of a different kind:

(6)   n   n
        n   n
        n n n n n
        n   n
        n   n

In the example illustrated, the overall gestalt of the letter H is composed of a large number of n's. If asked to identify what they see, or to respond as quickly as possible to the presence of a particular letter, autists (see e.g. Frith, 2003: 155; cf. Tammet, 2006: 45) typically see the 'n' rather than the 'H' – the detail is more salient for them than the 'big picture'. Christopher's immediate response to (6) was 'It's an "n" '. On subsequent testing with different combinations (an E made of s's, an H made of c's and a T made of u's) he responded instantaneously 's, c and u; e, h, t spells "the" '. That is, he seemed to perceive both the gestalt and the detail essentially simultaneously: he noted the relatedness of e, h and t and correctly identified the word, but explicit awareness of the detail nonetheless had priority and so was reported first.

Even though (as noted above p. 9) Christopher performed 'logically' in digit span tests, suggesting strong central coherence, the notion of weak central coherence may cast some light on his inconsistent behaviour with false-belief tasks. For instance, his problems with the spoken versus the written modality may be a joint function of weak central coherence and some impairment to his theory of mind. In terms of the model developed in ch. 6 (especially fig. 30) this would suggest that the primary deficit was in the integration provided by the central executive. That is, any particular perceived inadequacy of performance can be attributed either to the failure of some input system or module (e.g. the language faculty, theory of mind, moral judgement, or whatever), or to a failure to integrate such preserved input into a coherent system.

It may be helpful to recapitulate the interplay between qualitative and quantitative deficits in Christopher's abilities. We have argued that the central executive and episodic buffer are characterised by a capacity which is (quantitatively) reduced in his case. At the same time his performance is circumscribed by a (qualitative) pragmatic deficit which inhibits the integration of information from various cognitive systems to provide enriched representations. The properties of the central executive and pragmatics jointly define the notion *central coherence*. Christopher's weak central coherence is shown with *complex* linguistic input (multiple embeddings, garden-path structures, semantically complex or discourse-marked structures such as topicalisation and dislocation) and with *any* non-linguistic, e.g. visuo-spatial, input. That is, although his linguistic representations are spared in the computational sense, the reduced capacity of his central executive together with his impaired pragmatics results in weak central coherence. When the linguistic input is simple, Christopher shows normal central coherence, even when some pragmatic inferencing is involved (see the discussion of modus ponens, etc. in section 1.4.5) since this is within the central executive's capacity. Discourse-marking however requires the integration of linguistic information provided by the language faculty with contextual information from higher levels of representation. This integration may be affected either by the reduced capacity of the central executive, by defective pragmatics (specifically the principle of relevance) or by both.[30] In contrast, non-linguistic input is systematically inadequately processed because of the limitations of, for example, the visuospatial sketchpad, which means that what reaches the central executive is an inherently deficient representation. To the extent that the input can be encoded linguistically, as in some false-belief tasks, Christopher is able to process, store and access it when prompted. We suspect that his various behaviours with their indication of autism argue for both a theory of mind deficit and a problem with the executive, and that his problems with discourse-marked linguistic structures indicate that his pragmatics is affected as well.

An impairment to his executive would also go some way to explaining Christopher's difficulty with the Hayling sentence completion task (Smith & Tsimpli, 1995: 171f.) where the subject has to inhibit a natural response in order to produce an anomalous completion (for instance, completing 'I went to the post office to post a —' with *kettle* rather than *letter*). This is probably both a 'capacity' and an 'inhibition' problem: he cannot retain the stimulus for long enough while entertaining the normal completion, which he has to inhibit, and the anomalous one which he has to produce. We return to the relevance of inhibition in section 1.6.3. In brief, our discussion of central coherence suggests that Christopher has problems with the (central) executive, which has an essential role in both licensing and inhibiting verbal and non-verbal actions, and with the pragmatic operating principle responsible for linking seemingly unrelated information.

Although Christopher may be an atypical autist, his communication skills, eye-contact and social interaction are clearly all impaired. Moreover, the acquisition of most of his (second) language skills has been based on the written form (reading and writing) due, at least in part, to his general unease with direct human interaction. From this perspective, we expected his progress in learning BSL to be negatively affected more than his progress in learning any spoken (or written) language. This prediction turned out to be only partially accurate as his deficit in social affect did not significantly impair his ability to learn a signed as opposed to a spoken language.

1.4.5   Relevance, and Christopher's pragmatic ability

Somewhat surprisingly in view of his other limitations, some aspects of Christopher's pragmatic ability are generally good. His spontaneous speech tends to the monosyllabic, but it is generally coherent, even if it sometimes demonstrates the effect of rote memorisation. In tests of his inferential ability, he demonstrates normal mastery of modus ponens and related devices; he uses implicated assumptions and conclusions in essentially normal fashion, and he shows adequate performance in tests of discourse structure involving non-truth-functional connectives such as *anyway, after all*, etc. To illustrate, in examples like (7), Christopher correctly replied 'No' to the question in (7b) following the dialogue in (7a); in (8), he correctly replied 'Yes' to the question in (8b) following the dialogue in (8a); and in (9), he correctly supplied the sequence 'After all' to fill the gap left in the mini-story. (See Smith & Tsimpli, 1995: 67ff.)

(7) a   Michael said: 'If George comes I shan't be able to play.'
          Fred said: 'George is coming.'
   b   Do you think Michael will be able to play?

(8) a   Bill said: 'Do you speak Portuguese?'
          Fred answered: 'I speak all the European languages.'
   b   Do you think Fred can speak Portuguese?

(9)   Jill was waiting for her boyfriend in the park. She was very
          depressed and miserable — she'd just lost the pet dog her boyfriend
          had given her.

This indicates that at least in some instances he is capable of enriching a purely linguistic representation to derive an 'explicature' (what is explicitly conveyed by a speaker; Sperber & Wilson, 1986/1995: 182) in conformity with the principle of relevance. There are nonetheless serious gaps in his ability. Although he is excellent at giving grammaticality judgements (see below), he is often unable to carry out the inferential operations which would tell him whether the interpretation of the sentences he is judging is coherent. Thus he fails to differentiate possible and impossible interpretations of negative sentences, claiming for instance that (11) allows the same ambiguous interpretation as (10). That is, (10) may be construed as asking when the asking took place or when the buying took place, but (11) allows only a construal on which the (non-)asking took place yesterday, and not one on which the taking to the cinema took place yesterday:

(10)   When did Susan ask Bill to buy the book?

(11)   It was yesterday that Mary didn't ask Bill to take her to the cinema

More strikingly, he appears to be quite unable to use sentences 'interpretively'[31] (Sperber & Wilson, 1986/1995: 228), with the result that the meta-representational usage found in jokes, irony, rhetorical questions, and so on is beyond him (see Smith & Tsimpli, 1995: 74ff.). Similarly – and in blatant contrast to his apparent inferential abilities – he fails to notice the anomaly present in garbled texts of the kind found in nth order representations of English (or other languages), finding nothing wrong with texts where for example five words were given, five omitted, five were given, and so on (Smith & Tsimpli, 1995: 73).

This highlights a general, and intriguing, analytic problem in that, despite his verbal sophistication in some areas, he seems to have serious difficulties with some fairly basic notions. For instance, he is always anxious to please, with the resultant failure on occasion to give straight answers, as illustrated in (12):

(12) a I   Do you like being called 'Christopher' or 'Chris'?
      C Both.
   b NS Which is easier Turkish or Portuguese?
      C Both.
      NS How can both be easier?
      C Because I studied them.

It may be that this is a reflection of his mild autism if, like children at the age of 3 or so, he does not wish to reveal himself as liking one or the other. Alternatively, it may be that he doesn't understand the concept of the comparative (or of disjunction) in relation to adjectives that require epistemic modification (e.g. 'easy for X') as opposed to descriptive ones. Indeed, we also suspect that modal notions such as possibility are beyond his understanding, as he fails to differentiate between 'possible' words and 'extant' words in a language, even though tests more subtle than simply asking him for judgements reveal that he has such tacit knowledge (see again, Smith & Tsimpli, 1995: 20).

Further corroboration of this defect in modal reasoning comes from his identical treatment of the predicates *guess* and *know*. Presented with examples like those in (13) his response was uniformly 'Yes', even though he was alert enough to answer 'No' appropriately to distractors such as (14):

(13) a   John guessed that his visitor was Albanian
          Can you be sure that the visitor was from Albania?
     b   Fred knew that the boy was 11 years old
          Can you be sure that the boy was 11 years old?

(14) a   Mary knows that Celia is either Chinese or Japanese
          Can you be sure that Celia is Chinese?
     b   Edward guessed that his friend was French or Swiss
          Can you be sure that his friend was Swiss?

Such examples highlight the problem of disentangling pragmatic considerations from purely linguistic ones in accounting for Christopher's behaviour, so we turn next to his processing difficulties.

1.5   Linguistic processing problems

As should be clear from our Chomskyan perspective, we subscribe to a view of language in which it is essential to differentiate competence and performance: knowledge of language and the use of that knowledge in speaking and understanding, in communicating, thinking, making judgements of well-formedness, translating, interpreting and so on. It is nonetheless a truism that separating out the respective responsibilities of the two domains is far from trivial, and this is nowhere more apparent than in the case of sentence processing. Above, we mentioned Christopher's difficulty with negative sentences, but it is not clear whether this difficulty is due to a defect in his knowledge of grammar, specifically the blocking effect of adjunct extraction across negation, or to difficulty with carrying out the relevant inferences or with interpretive use, to short-term memory limitations, or simply to parsing difficulty. As we shall see in the discussion of his acquisition of BSL, all of these factors may contribute to the overall picture, as may the emphasis on the written form of the language which has been characteristic of much of his learning.

What is clear is that certain structures, which we have independent reason to think should be within Christopher's grammatical competence, cause him difficulty, even distress. The most notable of these are centre-embedding sentences and garden-path phenomena, mostly exemplified by sentences which are locally ambiguous (see Smith & Tsimpli, 1995: 57ff.). Presented with examples like that in (15a), Christopher typically gave an anomalous response in which Fred hired a story, as was confirmed by his translation of it into Greek in (15b).

Pursuing the matter proved impossible as he became upset and the test had to be cut short.

(15) a   Fred told the man that he hired a story
   b   O Friderikos ipe ston anthropo oti proselave mis istoria
      = Fred told the man [that he hired a story]

Similarly, he was puzzled by the garden-path example in (16a), refusing to judge it correct or incorrect, but his well-formed Greek translation in (16b) again indicated that he had indeed been garden-pathed to arrive at the impossible interpretation on which 'her friends' is a constituent. Moreover, he rejected the parallel grammatical example in (17a), recasting it as the ungrammatical (17b), and translating it incorrectly into Greek as (17c). Interestingly, the Greek translation indicates that he had identified the correct reading of (17a):

(16) a   Susan convinced her friends were unreliable
   b   I Susana pistike oti i fili tis itan anaksiopisti
      (Susan was convinced that her friends were unreliable)

(17) a   John persuaded him friends were unreliable
   b   John persuaded his friends were unreliable
   c   O Yanis ton – tu epise oti i fili itan anaksiopisti
      the Yanis him – his persuaded that the friends were unreliable

All subjects find these and comparable examples problematic, but normal controls can usually backtrack and compute an acceptable interpretation. On most processing accounts, backtracking is not automatic (Phillips, 1996), but involves a post-syntactic level which integrates information from various sources: syntactic structure, subcategorisation properties, semantics and pragmatics. Christopher seemed to be quite incapable of such backtracking, presumably because memory limitations and his weak central coherence inhibited the necessary integration. Thus, his performance on locally ambiguous structures indicates that his syntactic processing is restricted to the first parsing option which is accessible (Ferreira & Clifton, 1986; Mitchell, 1987).

This account would also explain his performance in detecting lexical ambiguity in isolation as opposed to within sentences. Specifically, he does have access to the two readings of an ambiguous word, but he can identify them only when this is the only thing he has to do. When the word is included in a sentence, his performance drops because of his difficulty integrating different types of information. A striking example was provided by his rendering of the Hindi *magar* as 'but' instead of the contextually appropriate 'crocodile' (see Smith & Tsimpli, 1995: 86).[32] All of these aspects of his performance point to a deficit in higher processing which requires the executive to integrate information from a variety of sources and inhibit information which is activated but which is contextually inappropriate. It may even be that his failure to cope with 'interpretive use' – e.g. his difficulty in understanding figurative speech – is ultimately attributable to weak central coherence stemming from a defective executive. If this is correct, it confirms the claim that 'the root of his anomalous responses lies in performance limitations rather than in a deficiency of his language module itself' (Smith & Tsimpli, 1995: 60).

1.6   L1A versus L2A

One of the major asymmetries in Christopher's language learning is that between his first language, English, and his numerous 'second' languages, with the former being essentially flawless, but the latter decidedly flawed.

1.6.1   Christopher's English

Christopher's knowledge of English is virtually indistinguishable from that of other native speakers; and where there do appear to be some differences, they can usually be attributed to problems of a non-linguistic kind. He has normal command of English syntax, as tested in production, comprehension, and well-formedness judgements of examples including: relatives, clefts, questions, negatives, *that*-trace effects, control relations, parasitic gaps, etc. His only problem areas are topicalisation and dislocation, and sequence of tenses. We have attempted to explain these (Tsimpli & Smith, 1993; Smith & Tsimpli, 1995) in terms of the need to access a level LF',[33] strictly outside his (intact) language faculty. That is, his difficulties in these domains reflect not deficiencies in his syntax, but problems with interpreting syntactic structures beyond the grammar at the interface between syntax and the language of thought. This account is supported by Christopher's problems with pronominal reference in cases where pragmatic considerations cancel the default subject-prominence of the antecedent. Thus, in the sequence *John telephoned Bill. He refused to talk to him* Christopher interpreted the subject pronoun *he* as coreferential with *John* despite the pragmatic implausibility of this reading. It seems that his syntactic parser operates in terms of default strategies which, in this case, opt for the subject *John* as being the most prominent antecedent for the subject pronoun (Brennan *et al.*, 1987; Grosz *et al.*, 1995; Carminati, 2002).

In sum, Christopher's problems processing locally ambiguous structures, his failure to accept dislocation or topicalisation structures whose interpretation is largely dependent on syntax–discourse interface constraints, his discoursally blind assignment of pronominal reference, his responses to garden-path structures, and his inability to backtrack, indicate that he cannot make on-line use of the context to arrive at an appropriate interpretation of the input. In other words, his parser is restricted to using default (first-pass) options. Our characterisation of Christopher's problems in terms of weak central coherence with a reduced capacity of the central executive accommodates all these problematic aspects of his native language. As becomes clearer when we look at his numerous 'second' languages, Christopher's delight in language and languages is more for their inherent, formal, properties than for their use as a tool for communication. He treats pairs of languages like input-output devices linked by a particular operation corresponding to choice of language. Given *sheep* and the operation 'French' he provides *mouton*; given the same input and the operation 'German' he provides *Schaf*, and so on. Like many (autistic) *savants* he appears to illustrate Baron-Cohen's notion of 'systemising' (e.g. Baron-Cohen, 2002, 2008).

1.6.2   *Christopher's 'second' languages: lexicon–syntax asymmetry*

Christopher first came to attention because of his remarkable prowess in apparently mastering a wide range of second languages. It is accordingly somewhat ironic that, on analysis, these second languages reveal problems quite distinct from anything in his first language. As outlined in section 1.4.3.1 above, Christopher's second language ability seems rapidly to reach a plateau beyond which he is unable to proceed. A simple example is provided by his (lack of) mastery of the range of phenomena associated with the null-subject parameter.

We pointed out there that a number of syntactic properties typically cluster with the possibility of having null subjects. We also observed that these properties may dissociate, indicating that they are not the product of a single parametric choice. Nonetheless Christopher's performance across this range of examples is interesting irrespective of whether they reflect the functioning of a single parameter or (as we believe) fall out from a set of partially independent choices. Although there are problems accommodating languages with virtually no morphology (like Chinese), it is usually the case that the existence of null subjects correlates with a rich verbal morphology (see Neeleman & Szendrői, 2005). In this respect it is notable that, presumably on the basis of its rich morphology, Christopher treated Berber as a null-subject language – spontaneously producing example sentences with no subject, despite their absence from the input (see Smith & Tsimpli, 1995: 126). Similarly, he over-generalised object agreement in the artificial language Epun, on the basis of the morphological properties of object elements and the verbal morphology observed in the input. This in fact reflects the generalisation that he is extremely sensitive to properties of the morphology and lexicon, picking up new paradigms and new lexical items with remarkable facility. This might be viewed as just association, as the patterns are reminiscent of Spanish, Italian and other languages he knows. However, simple associationism is an implausible hypothesis when one appreciates that his performance on what can be viewed as purely syntactic constructions is dramatically less proficient. Although he was exposed to numerous examples of inverted subjects in all of Greek, Spanish and Berber, for instance, he never accepted them as well-formed and never produced them in his own speech. That is, even in the presence of overt evidence his linguistic talent seems to be (largely) restricted to the morpho-lexical at the expense of the syntactic. As we shall see below, this syntactic asymmetry was in part belied by his limited ability in BSL where, surprisingly, he used non-English word-order in a range of constructions.

1.6.3   Inhibition and weak central coherence

Christopher's performance in his 'second' languages is surprising in another respect: although his lexical acquisition is exceptionally fast, his use of this knowledge in translating text is rather poor. His translation is basically word-for-word and there seems to be no filtering of the output in terms of coherence or cohesion. It should be pointed out that translation is one of his favourite activities, as he seems able to translate from and into his native language fast and without showing signs of fatigue. However, it is during translation that his lexical knowledge appears pragmatically most impaired. In particular, Christopher's inability to evaluate the pragmatic well-formedness of his translation output, to produce the appropriate lexical item when the source word is ambiguous, and to produce the appropriate target item when the source word is phonologically or orthographically similar to a word in the target language, indicate that he is unable to suppress activated but inappropriate lemmas.[34] An early example of his performance in Spanish is given in (18) (Smith & Tsimpli, 1995: 161, where further examples from other languages are also provided):

(18)   Visiblemente complacido, Carmelo se ajustó las gafas, dio media
         vuelta y entrabrió las puertas correderas que communicaban con la
         pieza inmediata . . .

         (Looking satisfied, Carmelo adjusted his glasses, turned round and
         half opened the sliding doors that led to the next room . . .)

         Christopher's translation: 'Visibly pleased, Carmelo adjusted his
         glasses, put on a full speed and open windows which communicated
         with the immediate piece . . . '

Given that in other language tasks Christopher seems to be able to select appropriate lexical items, e.g. when producing written text or word lists within the same language, it is possible that in translation tasks, which are more demanding due to the activation of two languages, his weak central coherence is more evident, leading to his inability to inhibit the production of a lexical item that has been activated during the search for a candidate word.

This behaviour falls out naturally from Green's (1998) 'inhibitory control' model for word production. This assumes that there is a central control system, the 'supervisory attentional system' which monitors the construction and modification of mental schemas with respect to certain goals, including language goals (see Shallice & Burgess, 1996). On the basis of neuropsychological evidence (Paradis *et al.*, 1982), Green assumes that spontaneous language production and translation are functionally distinct activities belonging to different task schemas, and he suggests that word selection involves the inhibition of other activated lemmas. During translation the activated source word has to be linked with the word in the target language. This linking is checked by inhibitory control whereby activated but non-optimal lemmas – for instance, those with an incorrect language tag (i.e. from the source language) – are suppressed. The linking is based on conceptual similarity: the two words are defined as translational equivalents. It is well known, however, that translation is also affected by factors such as orthographic or phonological similarity and not just conceptual identity. Indeed, in the case of *false friends* there may even be no conceptual similarity at all (Smith & Tsimpli, 1995: 87f.). Christopher's performance on translation tasks, as well as his inability to backtrack and reanalyse garden-path sentences, indicates that his power of inhibition is impaired, ultimately for reasons independent of his language abilities.[35]

On this last point it is important to note that the supervisory attentional system is responsible for controlling behaviour in general and not just language behaviour. It has been shown that frontal lobe patients have a poor supervisory attentional system and so perform badly on language tasks such as the Hayling sentence-completion test which requires them to inhibit automatic responses (Burgess and Shallice, 1996; see also Smith & Tsimpli, 1995: app. VI). In this respect, the role of the supervisory attentional system is essentially equivalent to our central executive, which oversees the control of behaviour. It is then plausible to assume that it is the faulty operation of this system that leads Christopher to react in an automatised fashion in other aspects of his non-verbal behaviour, such as his commitment to everyday routines. For instance, when he was being filmed for Dutch television he was asked to do some gardening (specifically, pushing a wheelbarrow) so that an impression of his everyday life could be conveyed. But it was the weekend and his normal routine had no place for gardening on a Saturday, with the result that he became somewhat upset. Fortunately, the tact of those filming and Christopher's desire to oblige resolved the brief contretemps.

If Christopher has problems inhibiting natural responses, as evidenced by his performance on the Hayling test, we would expect him to have considerable difficulty with Stroop tests (see Perret, 1974) where, for instance, the subject has to report the colour in which a word is written, rather than read the word itself. It is typically much harder to identify the colour of an incongruent stimulus (e.g. 'blue' written in red) than of a congruent stimulus (e.g. 'blue' written in blue). Accordingly, we tested him on a range of examples: a standard basic Stroop test, an animal Stroop test, and variants of our own devising which used Greek and English stimuli. Full details are provided in app. 1 (pp. 185–9), but the generalisation we arrived at was that the high incidence of mistakes he made constitutes evidence for his having problems with inhibiting the incorrect response.

This completes the presentation of Christopher's background and of our theoretical assumptions. We turn next to the predictions these gave rise to.

1.7   Summary and predictions

The asymmetries revealed in our previous work left us with as many questions as answers, and inspired us to arrange a variation on Nature's experiment by setting up a hypothetical conflict between Christopher's talent and handicap. He is superbly gifted at learning new languages, but his apraxia means that he is seriously impaired in his manual dexterity and hand–eye coordination – hence the disparity in his results on various IQ tests; and his mild autism means that he typically fails to make eye-contact or engage appropriately with his interlocutor. So what would happen if he were required to learn a language which crucially exploited the visual and manual modality rather than the auditory medium, and which relied on the necessity of looking and interacting with people face-to-face: social abilities that seemed to be so lacking in him? British Sign Language (BSL) should be simultaneously both congenial and uncongenial for him. It falls within the domain of his obsessional talent, but it exploits the visuo-spatial medium which causes him difficulty in performing everyday tasks.

We expected that Christopher's linguistic talent would enable him to acquire competence in BSL with some of the same facility he had shown in mastering spoken languages, as well as with some of the same asymmetries that appeared in his spoken language proficiency. We predicted that Christopher would be able to learn to sign but we suspected that his performance would fail to live up to his previous superlative abilities with spoken and written languages.

On standard assumptions about competence and performance, one would not expect either knowledge or comprehension of BSL to be affected by apraxia. Indeed, we reject any framework, such as the motor theory of speech (or sign) perception, on which it *would* be affected. Accordingly, Christopher's severe limb apraxia led us to predict that his production skills should be considerably worse than his comprehension. However, his representational ability in BSL and hence his comprehension of it could be adversely affected by his visuo-spatial deficit. This is because the (visual) linguistic input has to be transduced by a system which, in non-linguistic tasks, appears to affect both his perception and production. It is thus plausible to predict that the visual modality of

BSL would affect Christopher's perception of the sign and, indirectly, its representational properties. Despite this possibility, Christopher's near obsessional preoccupation with languages, and language in general, led us to predict that his linguistic talent should outweigh the disadvantages of the medium, and his ability in BSL should mirror his mixed abilities in spoken languages. We thus expected a parallelism between his attested performance in spoken languages and BSL with respect to the characteristics in (19):

(19)   he should make rapid initial progress with the learning of vocabulary;
        his morphology and vocabulary should be better than his syntax;
        Syntactic properties, such as word order, that differentiate BSL from
        spoken (or written) English, should occasion him considerable
        difficulty.

   Given the different properties of BSL compared to the languages Christopher speaks, our predictions had to extend to domains for which we had no direct previous linguistic parallels. Starting with his visuo-spatial deficit, we predicted that his comprehension skills would not be as impressive as those found in his spoken languages, partly because more exposure to the input in the same modality would be required for him to extract the relevant linguistic information from the visual signal, and partly because acquisition of this information could not be reinforced by exposure to a written representation of BSL. With the exception of his native language, the written form has been the primary medium underpinning his linguistic obsession in nearly all the spoken languages he knows. Having said that, it is worth noting that he often becomes really excited when listening to any language other than English. His interest in foreign languages also involves listening to someone reading text aloud or attempting to do so himself. It therefore seems that it is mostly his lack of interest in discourse interaction that focuses his attention on the written language. Be that as it may, his learning and consolidation of knowledge in a large number of his non-native languages, although not structured in the usual classroom sense, is largely based on reading diverse material in various registers. We thus predicted that the absence of a written version of BSL would prevent Christopher from showing the rapid and morphologically sophisticated acquisition of the sign lexicon and morphology which characterised his learning of spoken languages.

   Further, as is documented in the next chapter, BSL systematically coordinates manual and non-manual signs, requiring signers to look at each other and identify facial expressions which carry important morpho-phonological information. Two aspects of Christopher's psychological make-up might affect his processing of this property. The first is his autistic profile, characterised not only by his avoidance of eye-contact and his insensitivity to extra-linguistic features such as prosody and intonation, but also by his lack of interest in facial expressions, body language and ordinary discourse interaction. Nevertheless, we predicted that when he realised that looking at the addressee gave him linguistic information, Christopher would be able to modify his autistic behaviour enough to exploit it. The second is Christopher's weak central coherence which led to his inadequate performance on tasks involving higher levels of language processing. Activities which require the integration of information from outside syntax proper and thus exert pressure on memory and processing abilities, e.g. translation, ambiguity resolution, garden-path structures and discourse-related grammatical phenomena, are performed considerably less well than tasks having to do with the form of the language. Given the simultaneous expression through manual and non-manual signs of morphological, syntactic and phonological information, we predicted that Christopher would show reduced or delayed performance in the acquisition of BSL in comparison with spoken languages, where extra-linguistic features may largely be ignored in decoding linguistic meaning.

These various predictions derive on the one hand from the linguistic structure of BSL and Christopher's uneven learning of different properties of language and, on the other, from the putative effects of his deficits in motor coordination, social interaction and spatial processing. These impairments have effects that extend beyond the language faculty but we expected that his success in learning BSL would be a function of how far he could overcome these challenges.

In order to put Christopher's development of BSL in context we recruited a comparator group of 'talented' hearing second language learners with no physical or mental disabilities. Our prediction was that, although individual variation in successful BSL development was expected, no systematic asymmetries between production and comprehension, or between the acquisition of the lexicon and morphology versus syntax would be found. The comparator group's intact motor coordination, social interaction and spatial processing skills should result in their scores on tests of vocabulary, morphology and syntax revealing normal development of BSL as a second language.[36] One area where, initially at least, controls are more likely than Christopher to misinterpret BSL is in the mastery of vocabulary. Given Christopher's difficulty with gesturing, he is less likely than members of the comparator group to assign gesture status to lexical signs, something that is typical of non-native signers (Pizzuto & Volterra, 2000; Boyes-Braem *et al.*, 2002). This led us to predict that the comparator group would show improved performance in the understanding and production of BSL signs with a high degree of iconicity as opposed to non-iconic signs. Christopher's performance, on the other hand, was not expected to differ on the basis of the iconicity of the sign. As we shall see, these predictions were in large measure fulfilled, but not quite as clearly as we had anticipated. Before discussing them we turn to an overview of BSL.

2   British Sign Language

An overview

2.1   Introduction

This overview of sign language with specific reference to British Sign Language (BSL) aims to provide the linguistic background for the language learning part of the study. With this intention, our description and analysis is biased towards those aspects that will be the most relevant for our exploration of Christopher and the comparator group's signing. For a more detailed description of BSL see Sutton-Spence & Woll (1999); for a detailed theoretical account of American Sign Language (ASL) see Neidle *et al.* (2000); for a more universal perspective, see Sandler & Lillo-Martin (2006).

The structure of the rest of the chapter is as follows. In section 2.1 we look at the fundamental nature of signed languages as 'natural' (human) languages, and begin the discussion of 'sign space'. In 2.2 we explain how the basic building blocks of BSL can be analysed as 'phonologically' organised. We summarise current theory on how sign languages are structured at this most fundamental level, and then describe how the modality of sign language presents the learner with specific problems of articulation and perception. This allows us to present a preliminary proposal for how signs are represented in the lexicon of the signer, a proposal which raises issues to do with iconicity in sign languages. We suggest that there are radical differences between child and adult sign language learners to do with the role of a sign's iconic elements. This difference is captured in our model of the mind, as spelt out in detail in ch. 6 and summarised in outline below. In section 2.3 we give an overview of the morpho-syntax of BSL, including word-order and topicalisation, negation and question marking, verb agreement, pronominalisation and anaphora. For all these domains the importance of 'facial action' is emphasised. We devote section 2.4 to our current analysis of classifiers in signed and spoken languages, with special reference to their relation to topographic space. In section 2.5 we return to the issue of modality and discuss the most salient differences between signed and spoken languages.

2.1.1   Sign languages as natural languages

It is now universally accepted in the linguistic community that sign languages such as ASL (American Sign Language), BSL (British Sign Language), CSL (Chinese Sign Language) and so on are indeed natural languages with comparable expressive power to that of spoken languages. Indeed, the realisation that signed languages are true languages is one of the great linguistic discoveries of the twentieth century. Although more and more signed languages around the globe are being systematically documented, the original insight that signed and spoken languages were comparable was based on ASL, and most research on signed language continues to rely on findings from the study of ASL.

However, in the last forty-five years, research on many different languages has revealed profound and reassuring similarities in the structure, acquisition and processing of signed and spoken languages. There has recently been a recrudescence of interest in the Sapir-Whorf hypothesis of linguistic relativity: briefly, that the properties of the language you speak have a systematic effect on your thought processes (see e.g. many of the papers in Bowerman & Levinson, 2001), but there is no suggestion that being a (native) signer rather than a (native) speaker has any negative effect on your ability to communicate or think. To the contrary, as a result of their language's use of rotation and manipulation in the formation of signs it may be that native signers have better visual and spatial abilities than their hearing peers (Bellugi *et al.*, 1990; Emmorey *et al.*, 1993, 1998; Bavelier *et al.*, 2006a; Keehner & Gathercole, 2007).

The difference in modality notwithstanding, it also seems to be the case that the parts of the brain responsible for the acquisition and representation of knowledge of (spoken) language in hearing individuals is essentially the same as the parts of the brain responsible for knowledge of (signed) language in deaf individuals. This is seen most clearly in cases of aphasia where, as a result of damage to particular parts of the brain, individuals may suffer from a range of different problems. Spoken language is characteristically the major responsibility of the left hemisphere (with all sorts of caveats)[1] and visuo-spatial abilities are largely dependent on right hemisphere function. Lesions to different parts of the left hemisphere then produce characteristic patterns of language breakdown: Broca's and Wernicke's aphasias, for instance.

Despite the medium in which it is conveyed, sign language seems also to be largely the responsibility of the left hemisphere (MacSweeney *et al.*, 2008b). For the normal signing population, MacSweeney *et al.* (2002) have shown, using fMRI evidence, that there is no difference in lateralisation as between those processing topographic sentences[2] involving spatial verbs and those processing non-topographic sentences. However, Atkinson *et al.* (2005) have demonstrated that fluent signers with right hemisphere lesions have problems using classifiers with spatial verbs, and it is generally accepted that processing such constructions crucially exploits both hemispheres when there is a need to link linguistic structure with the real world.

Further evidence comes from deaf signers with aphasia who show patterns exactly parallel to those of speakers with comparable lesions (see Hickok *et al.*, 2002, for a summary). Indeed, pathological dissociations between different linguistic functions and different visuo-spatial functions seem to pattern similarly in deaf and hearing subjects, providing some support for the claim that the mind-brain includes a linguistic module with a dedicated architecture for language. (Whether this functional architecture is localised or distributed is a separate issue.) The conclusion that they come to is that 'different neural modules process visual inputs in different ways. For example, visual inputs that carry linguistic information would be translated into a format optimized for linguistic processing . . . But visual stimuli that carry a different kind of information – such as the features and contours of a drawing – would be translated into a format that is optimized for, say, carrying out motor commands . . . ' (Hickok *et al.*, 2002: 53).

This separation of sign language processing abilities and other visuo-spatial processing tasks is of course, not complete, since intact perceptual abilities are a pre-requisite for processing linguistic and non-linguistic materials. The difficulties of right hemisphere lesioned signers with topographic sentences may reflect a visuo-spatial 'bottleneck' blocking access to an intact linguistic system where, for example, the materials of the experimental stimuli are pictorial. Similar observations may be made in relation to Christopher. The fact that constructing the Rey-Osterrieth figure and coping with classifiers both presented him with serious problems suggests some overlap in the different types of processing required. In each case, using sign space requires the ability to hold in memory spatial locations and rotate them while keeping Euclidean relations constant. It is not clear whether this requirement is part of the linguistic or interface representation, but a deficit in visuo-spatial cognition seemed to hamper Christopher's use of signing space. His difficulties may derive in part from the fact that he is not a native signer but an adult L2 learner of BSL, whereas the studies referred to above report on fluent deaf signers. Nonetheless, the differences in his performance seem to reflect whether he is carrying out a purely linguistic task, such as manipulating sentences, or a task embedded in real-world activity.

With their basic equality established, more recent investigation has turned to how signed and spoken language may diverge. While it is uncontroversial that the expressive power of the two kinds of language is essentially the same, the two modalities may give rise to differences in use and learning because of physical constraints on their perception and processing (Meier *et al.*, 2002). This research provides evidence for the nature of the human language faculty, and casts some light on the use of this knowledge in communication. Two areas that are relevant for our work with Christopher pertain first to the organisation of signers' short-term memory and second to the role of iconicity in lexical processing.

A number of studies focusing on ASL have found a persistent difference between signers' and speakers' average short-term memory capacity as measured by digit span. While speakers can remember 7 ± 2 items, signers typically remember 5 ± 2 (Boutla *et al.*, 2004; Bavelier *et al.*, 2006a). Moreover, Bavelier *et al.* (2006b) have shown convincingly that these differences cannot be attributed to phonological factors, item duration or inferior memory abilities in deaf individuals. STM is assessed by measuring subjects' ability to rehearse ordered phonological representations – sequences of digits. In comparison with speakers, signers appear to be more retentive of the individual features of what is being encoded and the context associated with those features, rather than the order in which items appear. When order is not required in recall, differences between signers and speakers disappear. This suggests that remembering sequences of signs is a skill which is less dependent on rehearsing order in a phonological loop and more on recalling the individual features of the items in different spatial arrays, presumably involving the episodic buffer. It is interesting in this context to recall (see section 1.4.1 above) that Christopher sometimes reproduced sequences of digits in ascending order rather than in the order given (though there was no comparable effect in his letter span). To see if there was any effect of modality, we tested Christopher's digit span and letter span in BSL. To avoid the problem of interpreting his somewhat apraxic output, all tests were conducted with a signed (or finger-spelt) stimulus and Christopher had to respond in spoken English. His digit span (to signed input) was limited to two or three items and even there his responses were characterised by mistakes and repeated examples of his responding before the signer had finished. His letter span (to finger-spelt input) was equally minimal and he again got sequences of only one or two letters correct. He seemed typically to conjecture a word of English on the basis of his recognition of the first stimulus letter and guess at random thereafter.

Christopher's tendency to re-order spoken digit span stimuli – presumably for better storage and recall – allied with his poor performance in both digit span and letter span in BSL, indicates that his talent relies heavily on the linear presentation of linguistic elements or features. As this linearity is of differing importance in signed and spoken languages, we would expect it to have an effect on Christopher's perception and analysis of signed sentences. This suggestion is corroborated by the 'processing overload' account of Christopher's problems with perceiving, analysing and storing elements of BSL in short-term memory that we discuss in section 6.3.

We turn next to the role of iconicity in lexical processing. Vinson and colleagues (e.g. Vigliocco *et al.*, 2005; Vinson *et al.*, 2009) have explored the processing of signs which reflect the motion involved in the relevant action (e.g. the sign HAMMER which simulates hammering), comparing the performance of English speakers and British Sign Language (BSL) signers in tasks involving judgements of similarity of meaning. In one experiment (Vigliocco *et al.*, 2005) they found that BSL signers used iconic properties in making judgements of similarity of meaning differently from English speakers. BSL signers judged tool-actions as more similar to tools than to body-actions; in sharp contrast, English speakers judged tool-actions as more similar to body-actions than to tools. They argued that this was because signs for tool-actions resemble signs for tools more than they do body-actions. Whether these differences reflect anything profound is unclear as, in a second experiment, they found that English speakers behaved more like BSL signers when asked to develop mental images for the words before performing the same task.

These investigations raise the vexed issue of the relationship between sign language and non-linguistic gesture. It is clear that signers gesture while they sign (Emmorey, 1999; Sandler, 2009), but how far gesture is incorporated into sign language and how far it stays as a non-linguistic accompaniment to language (as in spoken languages) is still under debate. A related issue concerns how much more, or how differently, deaf signers gesture as an effect of sign language; and how much more, or differently, bimodal bilinguals (deaf signers who speak too) use gesture while they speak ('co-speech gesture'; Casey & Emmorey, 2009). One example of this complex web of issues can be seen in the different analyses proposed to account for the extent to which BSL recruits non-linguistic gesture to describe space via the classifier system (Emmorey, 2003; Morgan & Woll, 2007). A second example can be seen in how much the morphological structure of pronouns and verb agreement is influenced by the interaction between sign and gesture (Lillo-Martin, 2002; Thompson *et al.*, 2006). The putative conflation of sign and gesture in particular aspects of sign language use will be an important issue when we discuss the learning of BSL by Christopher. In this context it is worth noting that gesture may be 'linguisticised':[3] while all signers and sign learners may recruit gesture in particular contexts, there are differences in how this gesture is used, depending on the person's age of acquisition of BSL as well as the stage of BSL development the non-native signer is going through. We return to a discussion of this issue in the section on iconicity (section 2.2.2 below). For the moment it suffices to note that the process of linguisticisation is idiolectal rather than dialectal.

2.1.2   Sign space

Throughout the book we make repeated reference to the notion of *sign space*, so it is necessary to specify exactly what is meant by the term. In much of the linguistic description of different sign languages sign space has been identified as the area of space around a signer including his own body (Sutton-Spence & Woll, 1999). The sign space is sometimes even depicted in written transcriptions (e.g. Bellugi *et al.*, 1990), and it has been proposed that it is the area within which all signs are articulated and where referents are assigned specific locations. The need to postulate 'sign space' has probably been overstated, as the spatial limits of sign space are largely those imposed by the 'phonetic' constraints of human movement (see e.g. Rathmann & Mathur, 2002, and the discussion of 'whisper' below). Moreover, although sign space does not normally extend below the waist or behind the back, Warlpiri sign language, a secondary sign language used by mourning (hearing) women, has signs located on the thighs and knees (Kendon, 1980). There is also a problem in identifying exactly where the sign space is, since many signs (e.g. index-setting or pronominals) pick out end points that are beyond the limits of the arm's movement. This means that locations exploited for reference are often set up beyond the restricted sign space in front of the signer. Nonetheless, a restricted sign space does appear to be consistently used for some purposes. For instance, an imaginary flat surface at around waist height is used both when signers are assigning fixed index points to non-present referents and when moving the subject and object of agreeing verbs (see below) between these locations. Further, when signers provide topographic descriptions with classifiers, that is, when they are talking about space, they use this type of sign space, as is shown in fig. 11 on p. 72. Exploiting an abstract sign space containing non-present referents proved problematic for Christopher, whose anchoring in the concrete here and now was similarly reflected in his inability to refrain from touching objects when referring to them.

The proposal that there is some restricted area for the articulation of grammar may have arisen because of the emphasis on contrasts between sign language and non-linguistic communication, for example, pantomime, where communication can involve walking, turning around, etc. Now that all linguists agree on the status of sign languages, it is no longer necessary to suggest that sign languages exploit a restricted sign space, and the importance of describing the dimensions of sign space as a preamble to linguistic description is being abandoned (see e.g. Lillo-Martin, 2002). Nevertheless, the use of a restricted area for signing has implications for sign form – signs obey constraints on location despite the resulting decrease in iconicity, and spatial relations are mapped onto the restricted space available, despite the resulting inconsistencies of scale. The use of gaze in conjunction with pointing means that the points used for reference can be well outside areas that can be reached by the hands. Agreeing verbs use a restricted sign space in that the signs' movement is limited, but the possible locations acting as indices need not be, as signs may be moved towards a location indefinitely far away. That is, signers point straight in front of them towards an area which would correspond to the location of the addressee if one were present and agreeing verbs may be inflected towards these locations. This point has been made forcefully by Liddell (e.g. 2003), and we agree with his observation, encapsulated in his term 'surrogate space', that signers use areas beyond the fixed space surrounding the signer, though we disagree with his linguistic analysis of these uses of extended sign space. It is of course the case that there are constraints on a sign's production, with some logically possible combinations being linguistically impossible (Sutton-Spence & Woll, 1999: 5), just as in spoken languages some sequences are (universally) impossible or unpronounceable for physiological reasons, and some sequences are (parochially) impossible because of language-specific phonotactic constraints.

2.2   Phonology: the lexicon

We have not investigated Christopher's phonological abilities in either signed or spoken languages in great detail, but the difference between the two modalities is so stark that we need to outline the nature of sign language 'phonology'. In earlier work we described his pronunciation of his various 'second' languages as 'schoolboyish' (Smith & Tsimpli, 1995: 22), but he seems generally to have no difficulty perceiving the relevant contrasts in a variety of languages. As an example, we tested his ability to discriminate tonal minimal pairs in Cantonese (a language of which he is ignorant) such as [hai] (on a low fall) ('shoe') and [hai] (on a low rise) ('crab'). His performance was mixed: he almost certainly perceived the words as different but, when asked to identify repetitions of the members of the minimal pairs uttered, his responses were random, as he refused ever to give the same answer twice running. Interestingly, when presented with the pair [foŋ] (on a high level) ('wind') and [foŋ] (on a low level) ('phoenix') he immediately volunteered *feng shui* for the former: his general knowledge in the linguistic domain continues to impress us.

While utterances in signed languages are obviously not composed of sounds, the level of linguistic organisation labelled 'phonology' is as applicable to sign languages as it is to spoken languages, despite the word's etymology. Although it is now agreed that there are shared phonological categories and processes between signed and spoken languages (e.g. Corina & Sandler, 1993; Morgan, 2006), and imaging studies suggest that the two phonologies are similar in neural localisation (MacSweeney *et al.*, 2008a, 2008b), how these are instantiated across the two modalities may be radically different (see Brentari, 2002). An indication of the close parallelism between the analysis of sign and sound is that with the development of phonological models of signed languages, especially ASL (e.g. Liddell & Johnson, 1989; Perlmutter, 1992; van der Hulst, 1996; Brentari, 1998), sign language phonology has been assimilated into spoken language phonological theory and has stimulated changes in that theory.

The classic view of sign language phonology was that a sign could be decomposed into three major parameters or parts: hand configuration, movement and place of articulation (Stokoe, 1960; Stokoe *et al.*, 1965), though subsequent research has often not discriminated the relative importance of each of these parts (Brentari, 2002: 39). Importantly, there is a further parameter of accompanying facial action, where we use 'action' to refer to the use of the face for linguistic functions, as opposed to facial 'expression' used to refer to the use of the face for extra-linguistic functions. A small number of lexical signs require specific facial actions (for example, the BSL signs BOSS and GOD are distinguished only by eye-gaze). However, most treatments of facial actions do not handle them within phonology,[4] as they are more crucial for the description of morpho-syntactic processes (see 2.3.2 below). One exception is mouth action, where two distinctive uses of the mouth have been described. As Lewin (2006: 7–8) puts it: '"mouthings" describes the voiceless mouth patterns, either fully or partly articulated . . . derived from the dominant spoken language . . . "Mouth Gestures" . . . describe[s] the mouth patterns which have no relation to the spoken word of the dominant language.' Some manual homonyms are disambiguated only by mouthings (e.g. UNCLE and BATTERY), and in 'echo phonology' (Woll & Sieratzki, 1998; Woll, 2001) mouth gestures are obligatory at the lexical level.

Hand configuration describes the particular shape the hand makes, including the extension or flexion of the fingers and position of the wrist as well as the orientation of the hand relative to the body (that is, whether the palm is facing the torso or another direction). This part of the sign is often labelled simply 'handshape'. The hand configuration can be described in terms of a hierarchy of complexity, where the 'simplest' handshapes involve the fewest number of features (selection of fingers, contact between fingers, etc.). It is also the case that these 'simple' handshapes appear most often in the language's lexicon: thus the handshapes, 'B', '5', 'G' and 'A', are found in 50 per cent of all BSL signs (Sutton-Spence & Woll, 1999: 162) and have been termed 'unmarked'. These are shown in figs. 6a–6d.[5]

Hand configuration is the most contrastive of the three parameters within and across signed languages (Brentari, 1998). Most sign languages share a core set of common handshapes (typically those shown in fig. 6) but individual signed languages may differ on the basis of some particular phonological parameter. Comparing BSL and ASL we see that the handshape 'middle finger extending' appears in BSL signs (HOLIDAY, IDLE) but not in ASL. However, it is striking that sign languages do not differ as much in their phonological inventories as

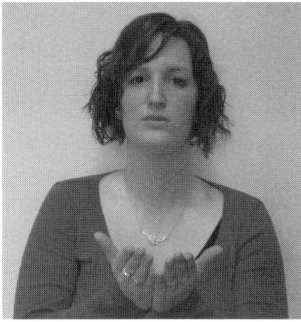

Figure 6a 'B' – BOOK

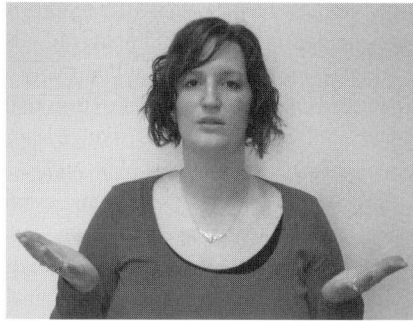

Figure 6b '5'- WHERE

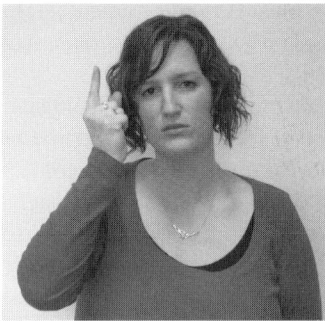

Figure 6c 'G' – UNDERSTAND

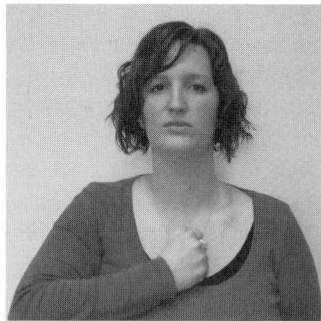

Figure 6d 'A' – MY

spoken languages do, perhaps because the phonetics of sign production is more restricted than in spoken language production.

All signs in BSL are constructed on the basis of strict well-formedness conditions at the phonological and at the morphological level, determining how different parts of the sign may be combined. Possible signs follow language-specific rules for the movement and posture of the hands, arms and upper body. An example of a phonologically possible but morphologically impossible BSL sign would be the sign KNOW + HEAD-SHAKE 'don't know'. The correct sign is KNOW-NOT where negation is incorporated into the sign. By way of comparison, Greek Sign Language (Antzakas, 2006) allows examples of negative incorporation that don't appear in BSL. Zeshan (2004a) compares and contrasts negation in a wide variety of sign languages.

Less is known about the phonological organisation of movement. As a marker of aspectual choice, signs can differ in the path of movement (e.g. straight versus arc) and in their local or secondary movement, such as finger-wiggling or opening and closing of the hand during its movement across or along a path.

Signs may be further classified according to their form, as one- or two-handed. Two-handed signs can either have symmetrical movement, or one hand (the dominant one) can move while the other serves as a fixed location. While some signs are one-handed there are no constraints on which hand (right or left) the signer should use. However native signers are consistent in which hand they use as dominant (Battison, 1978; Klima & Bellugi, 1979).

Two further constraints on hand configuration and movement at the phonological level, which appear to be universal, have been proposed for two-handed signs (Battison, 1978). The Dominance constraint states that if a two-handed sign has different handshapes, the non-dominant hand may have only a limited number of handshapes (the unmarked set) and forms the location for the whole sign. The Symmetry constraint states that if both hands move independently, both must have the same location, handshape and movement (either simultaneous or alternating), and the hands' orientation must also be symmetrical. In this case, there is no dominant hand. As will become apparent, classifiers may violate these principles.

Signs may also differ in their place of articulation. A sign's phonological representation determines whether it is produced in the vertical, horizontal or sagittal planes in signing space (Brentari, 1998).[6] Some signs make contact with the signer's body (e.g. MY), arms, head or face, while in other signs the hands touch each other (e.g. BOOK). In first language acquisition these phonological factors can predict order of acquisition of signs and also error types. Signs that are located on the body (including the arms and head) are mastered first, followed by signs which involve contact between the hands, and lastly by signs which involve no hand or body contact. Children frequently make errors by adding body and hand contact to signs (Meier, 2000).

In learning a sign one must therefore form some phonological representation of the sign's configuration, how it moves, its place of articulation and the accompanying facial action: the mouth can be used phonologically (obligatorily in some signs), or morphologically (as in some adverbials). Some signs are articulated with all these parameters produced simultaneously. But as Liddell & Johnson (1989) point out, phonological and phonetic processes in sign languages are also linear: a sign is produced with a sequence of moves and holds. Knowledge of the various components of a sign is obviously important, as the lexicon exploits them systematically. For example, movement can be used productively to make the categorial distinction between nouns and verbs, where typically the movement of the noun reduplicates and shortens the movement of the verb: e.g. TELEPHONE (noun) has minimal movement at the cheek while TELEPHONE (verb) moves away from the signer. Movement can also be used morpho-phonologically to mark aspectual contrasts. The situation is parallel to the multi-functionality of 's' in English which is sometimes phonological

Figure 7a – NAME   Figure 7b – AFTERNOON

and sometimes morpho-phonological. Movement is a property of lexical signs (either a movement or hold is required to fill that slot in the sign's phonological description) but that movement can be systematically altered for morphological purposes – to show reduplication, etc.

As in spoken languages, evidence for the phonological status of the different components of the sign comes from examples of minimal pairs where only one parameter differs but meaning is contrasted. For example, the signs NAME (fig. 7a) and AFTERNOON (fig. 7b) have identical handshape (H), movement (twist at the wrist), orientation (palm faces down) and facial action (neutral), but differ in location (forehead and chin, respectively). The difference in the orientation of the head is not significant in this example, though it could be in others (e.g. SLEEP (head tilted) versus CHEEK (head upright)).

2.2.1   Modality effects

We have emphasised the similarity between signed and spoken language phonology but there are also important differences. Thus while there is general agreement that '[t]he burden of evidence suggests that there is an amodal language processing component supported by frontal regions including the left inferior prefrontal cortex, the left premotor region and the supplementary motor area . . . [nonetheless] working memory for sign language and working memory for speech each have at least one function that is not shared with the other language modality' (Rudner & Rönnberg, 2006: S184). One therefore expects to find both commonalities and systematic difference between the modalities. As regards the former, it seems that age of acquisition is a reliable predictor for visual word recognition by the hearing and the deaf alike (see e.g. Barry et al., 1997; Vinson et al., 2009). For the latter, it is significant that more than one part of the morpho-phonology of a sign, as well as more than one sign, can be produced and perceived simultaneously (see Vermeerbergen *et al.*, 2007). Although more than one phonological property of a word can be pronounced simultaneously (e.g. voicing and nasality), spoken languages do not allow two words to be articulated simultaneously. Accordingly, it may be that the definition of phonological 'word' (and of word boundaries) is different in sign language. Crucially, whereas the articulation of a spoken word or sequence of words is linear, the linearity of signs is accompanied by the simultaneous expression of morpho-phonological features in the manual and the non-manual space: for instance, the movement of a sign changes to express aspect; the direction of movement changes to reflect semantic roles; negation may be marked entirely non-manually, e.g. by facial action. Such facial action has a grammatical function and serves in part the same role as is played by intonation in spoken languages. Simultaneously, facial expression may be used for affective functions, playing the same role as intonation and voice quality in spoken languages.[7]

Further, the movement of different articulators leads to a radically different phonetics of sign languages. This obviously affects sign production (for instance, in the coordination of articulators and the speed of articulation) as well as sign perception (in visual tracking and visual contrast detection). The average number of words per second in running speech is about four to five, compared to two to three signs per second for fluent signing (Bellugi & Fischer, 1972). The slower rate of sign transmission is due to the arms and hands being bigger than the tongue and lips and thus slower movers. In terms of processing, signs can be recognised more quickly than words (Grosjean, 1981; Grosjean & Lane, 1981; Emmorey & Corina, 1990). Although signs are much longer than words in duration, Emmorey & Corina (1990) observed that only roughly the first 240 msec, or 35 per cent of a sign, had to be seen before it could be correctly identified, whereas Grosjean (1981) found that the first 330 msec, or 83 per cent of a word, had to be heard before it could be identified. It's not entirely surprising that signs can be recognised fairly early, since most signs are monosyllabic so that all of the relevant phonological material is available at the beginning of the sign except where there is a change in movement, handshape or location. The implication is that there would be significant differences in speed of identification of words in typologically different languages, making comparison with sign languages somewhat opaque.

This difficulty is compounded by the fact that signers use multiple articulators to encode meanings. This is useful as the temporal resolution of signs – the speed at which transitions between parts of signs as well as between whole signs are made – is much slower in sign than temporal resolution of words in speech. Additionally, the position of the articulators is visually salient in sign languages, while it is mostly hidden in speech. In a nutshell: sound has

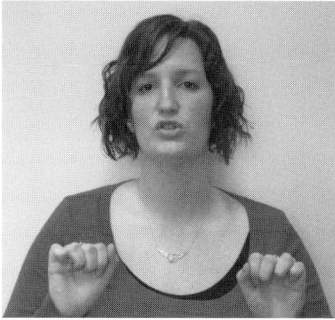

Figure 8 – NOT-YET

great temporal resolution, but poor spatial resolution, vision has great spatial resolution, but poor temporal resolution. We will return to possible implications of modality differences for sign learning in section 2.5.

2.2.2   Iconicity in the sign lexicon

In spoken language, Saussurean arbitrariness is the norm, while in signed languages there is a somewhat greater correlation between concepts and their form (Trask, 1996: 131).

In learning labels for concrete nouns in any spoken language some sensory element may be encoded in the learner's cognitive representation (e.g. perceptual or functional features based on experience). Examples include a small number of onomatopoeic words and 'baby talk' items such as 'choo-choo' for *train*. However, even in such cases the form of the label is retained only as encyclopaedic information in the conceptual lexicon.

An important aspect of the sign lexicon is the relationship of a sign's form to the real world object or concept it expresses: its iconicity. Many BSL signs exhibit an arbitrary mapping between their form and meaning (e.g. NOT-YET in fig. 8). Many signs, however, are more or less iconic, with general agreement among signers as to the nature and degree of their iconicity. That is, they are consistently able to judge signs on a continuum from 'not at all iconic' to 'highly iconic'. While NOT-YET is not at all iconic, an example of a sign at the 'highly iconic' end of the spectrum is TELEPHONE in fig. 9.

A recent study (Vinson *et al.*, 2009) derived iconicity, familiarity and age of acquisition ratings from twenty native signers for a set of 300 signs. An interesting result was that many of the most familiar signs were rated as extremely low in iconicity, e.g. BOY, EASY, IMPORTANT and RIGHT ('correct') (Vinson *et al.*, 2009: 1084). This highlights the fact that although iconicity is pervasive in signed languages, many arbitrary (non-iconic) signs are highly familiar and

Figure 9 – TELEPHONE

frequently occurring: that is, iconicity and frequency are orthogonal properties. The putative advantage of iconicity depends on metalinguistic inferencing, so young deaf children will rely on it minimally in learning their first language, since their meta-language skills don't develop until late in lexical acquisition. In contrast to the independence of iconicity and familiarity, age of acquisition does correlate with familiarity, making it a good predictor in both signed and spoken languages for the success of word recognition across a number of tasks: object naming, word naming and lexical decision (see Barry *et al.*, 1997).

Although iconicity plays a minimal role in the first stages of sign acquisition in child learners (Meier, 1982, 1987; Tolar *et al.*, 2007), it probably plays a major role in second language learning: adult learners of sign language may begin with conscious links between conceptual representations and their labels (Campbell *et al.*, 1992; Morgan *et al.*, 2002b), and there is experimental evidence (Lieberth & Gamble, 1991) that hearing adults remember iconic signs better than non-iconic signs.

Several caveats about iconicity need to be made: most importantly, that it is often culturally determined (Boyes-Braem *et al.*, 2002). Thus signs for the same referent may be iconic but entirely different from each other: e.g. signs for 'woman' represent long hair, lips, earrings, smooth cheeks, breasts, etc. in different sign languages. An iconic link inevitably relies on only part of an object's visual appearance, so some abstraction may be required to see the link with the concrete object in the real world. Children who acquire a sign language as their first language seem blissfully unaware of the 'etymology' of a sign such as MILK (it imitates the action of milking a cow by hand) (Orlansky & Bonvillian, 1984; Sutton-Spence & Woll, 1999). Only later, once the core grammar has been mastered, is it likely that young children return to the language forms they have learned previously and carry out a metalinguistic analysis. Such a progression is akin to what happens when hearing children discover explicitly the segmentation properties of their language during the development of literacy. The link between a sign and its iconic root enters the child's encyclopaedic knowledge only after the sign's phonological and grammatical properties have been acquired.

Although there has been little research into second language acquisition of sign (see Campbell *et al.*, 1992; Marshall *et al.*, 2004), it is plausible that adults learning a new sign use whatever world knowledge is available, including any iconic properties the sign may have, in guessing its meaning. Adult learners may be highly motivated to create such links between form and meaning, as BSL has no written script and forming an imagistic representation may be a useful learning or memorisation strategy. In the evolution of many signs there has probably been a process of the linguisticisation of gestures, (see this chapter, note 3 and p. 107 below) so it is not surprising that sign languages show considerable iconicity, even if child learners do not yet have the metalinguistic ability to take advantage of it. For example, the sign for PARIS in BSL refers to the shape of the Eiffel tower, but information of this kind is not available to the young child.[8]

Even if this knowledge were available to young deaf children, it is an empirical question whether at an early stage they could understand the link between a building somewhere and the name of the whole city where this building is situated. Hearing children tend to associate the name of a city with the area or the house they live in, rather than the city itself. This suggests that, for both signed and spoken languages, identifying conceptual boundaries for word meanings necessitates going through a process of *overextension* or *underextension*. As with the example of MILK, even if the deaf child was living on a farm, linking the action of milking the cow with the result requires some inferencing between action (verb) and product (noun). Moreover, as mentioned above, iconicity in sign language seems to be a gradient phenomenon: there is not just a difference between iconic and non-iconic signs, but also a difference of degree between iconic signs such as TELEPHONE and MILK. The first is more iconic than the second because the sign is closer to the physical properties of the object, whereas the second requires more inferencing if the sign's form is to facilitate its conscious learning (see Taub, 2001; Demey & van der Kooij, 2008). Iconicity could play a role in non-native acquisition of the sign lexicon either because it helps storage of the sign on the basis of a conscious inferential link or because it licenses an abstract representation of some physical properties of the object represented. In contrast, in children acquiring their first language, vocabulary acquisition is more automatised (the property of 'fast mapping'). Also, the physical properties of an object (shape, size, texture, etc.) that children pay attention to are not necessarily the same as those depicted as more salient by the adult, hence the examples of 'overextension' in child language data (see Bloom, 2000).

In sum, iconicity is often apparent only with hindsight. Once adult learners are told the English equivalent for a sign, forming an iconic connection becomes simpler: the image associated with the particular concept can be compared with the sign they are trying to learn. Of course, in the context of first language acquisition, whether signed or spoken, providing translations into other languages is not available to facilitate learning. The real contrast is between first and second language acquisition. In this respect L2 learning of a sign language is no different from that of a spoken language, as in both cases the lexicon is built up on the basis of a linking between the form and the meaning via the L1 form and meaning (de Groot, 1993; Kroll & Stewart, 1994). When adult English speakers learn BSL, for example, the English translation of a BSL sign may activate some image related to the relevant concept (perhaps inevitably, if it has a high degree of iconicity). They then perform a metalinguistic analysis, comparing some of the physical properties of the sign that can be inferentially related to the image. With advanced learning of BSL, the automatisation of lexical knowledge presumably reduces the activation of the iconic aspects of the sign. Children learning their first language, on the other hand, build a direct mapping between the sign and the concept without the need to mediate this relation through a metalinguistic analysis of the link.

2.2.3   A preliminary model

Such differences between first and second language learning can be captured in our model of the mind and the position of the language faculty within it. Detailed discussion will be postponed to ch. 6 but we introduce the elements here. Our account of the faculty of language crucially distributes different aspects of it between the central system, which includes the conceptual lexicon, and a quasi-modular 'input' system, which includes the UG lexicon (see Smith & Tsimpli, 1995: 29). This latter contains categorial and selectional information of the kind that tells us that *eat* is a verb and *chocolate* a noun; that *eat* selects a direct (DP) object, and has a particular phonological form (/iːt/); that *chocolate* can be count or mass and is phonologically /tʃɔklit/. This part of the lexical entry is linked to a concept whose detailed properties are given in the conceptual lexicon: for instance, that the object of *eat* is edible and its subject is typically animate; that chocolate is sweet, addictive, made from cacao, is etymologically from Aztec and so on.[9]

Given the simplified diagram of the faculty of language in fig. 10, a child would hear the word or see the sign for (e.g.) 'Paris', and set up a representation in the UG lexicon linked to some minimal conceptual information – e.g. that it denotes a place or a town. In the case of a signing child the sign would be as

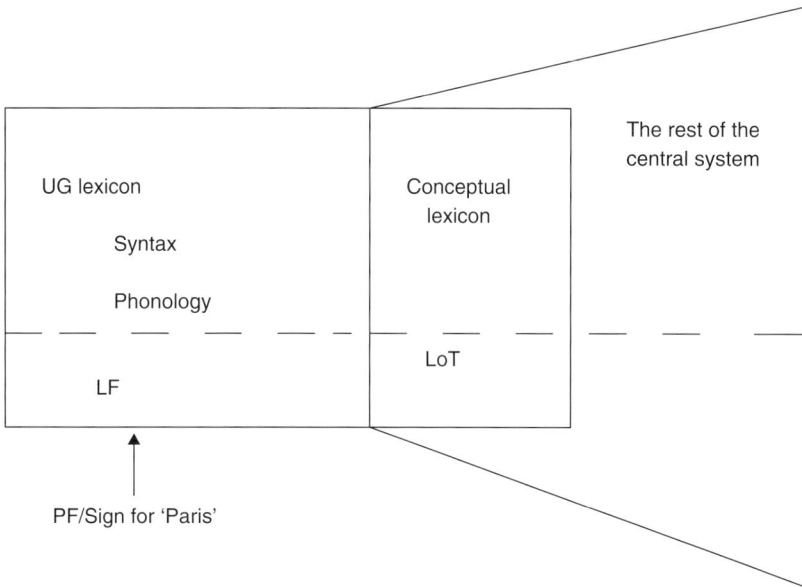

Figure 10 The position of the language faculty in cognition

arbitrary as the corresponding phonological form would be for the hearing child. Later, with the acquisition of appropriate encyclopaedic knowledge (about the Eiffel Tower) the sign would become associated or linked with this information, retrievable if required, but this could have played no role in the acquisition of the sign itself.

In adult L2 development of a sign language, however, the link between a word in the spoken L1 and what the sign represents is mediated by extensive world knowledge, e.g. what the sign looks like as an iconic element and hence how it is linked to that object or entity in the real world. In this way encyclopaedic knowledge may be involved in the learning and storing of signs and, as a result, it may partially determine the learner's mental representation of the sign's phonological structure. If you know what the Eiffel Tower looks like in the real world it affects what handshape, movement and location you use when trying to recall the sign. There may also be concomitant differences of mouthing. For instance, the signs for BLACKPOOL and PARIS which are manual homonyms, are differentiated by mouthing, not by changes in the form of the manual part of the sign.

This interaction of linguistic and encyclopaedic knowledge entails that some-one learning a sign language as an L2 may make use of the four elements in (1a–d) and links among them:

(1) a   the concept;
    b   the stored visual representation of the concept associated with the L1 entry and its imageability;
    c   the iconic properties of the sign (in the event that there are any);
    d   the formal (phonological, categorial, morphological and syntactic) properties of the sign.

We assume that adult L2 signers do not, in the beginning, form associations between concept and sign (1a and 1c), but between concept and image (1a and 1b), producing or interpreting the sign as gesture. We have evidence for this from the pre-test we did on iconicity (see section 3.1.2), before the subjects knew any sign language. In other words, (1b) is what makes L2 signers different from native signers in the acquisition of iconic signs. Native signers link the (visual representation of) the sign as a lexical element (1d) directly with a concept (1a), without the mediation of any other encyclopaedic, metalinguistic, or decompositional analysis of the sign. As Atkinson *et al.* (2005) have shown, in general iconicity gives no privileged access to the semantic content of signs: (1d) may also be directly associated with (1a) in the case of the L2 learning of signs that have minimal or no iconicity.

Deaf children may later associate their sign with an image from encyclopaedic knowledge, but only for some (iconic) signs, and not always then: compare the behaviour of hearing speakers who may only infrequently make iconic associations in their native languages – when uttering an onomatopoeic word or a conventionalised metaphor. What seems to be more difficult is how experience of the language makes it possible for a motivated gesture to become a lexical item used automatically without activating world knowledge. That is, how does the L2 learner move from a gestural representation of an iconic sign to a pure sign representation, gradually inhibiting the conceptual associations that originally motivated the sign? The simple answer is 'with practice'. When the L2 learner becomes more adept, the use of the sign in fluent production can help diminish the gestural representation. Additionally, some of the morphological processes which signs undergo conflict with a simple iconic interpretation. For example, the verb TO-TELEPHONE (someone) (see fig. 9) involves movement of the hand away from the ear, which does not directly represent the action of making a telephone call iconically, even though the movement may itself be iconic. As well as suggesting that at this later stage iconic signs do not activate (or activate less strongly) the link with the encyclopaedic and visual image of the signed concept, this discussion also supports the view that some aspects of the acquisition process are idiosyncratic and result in knowledge that is part of an individual's idiolect rather than being a dialectal feature.

There are nonetheless certain areas of BSL where iconicity has a direct impact on the formation of lexical items. Signed languages allow for the possibility of referring to spatial or formational contrasts (the size, shape, location or path of an object's movement) in a much more detailed and direct way than in spoken language. Accordingly, the model in fig. 10 will have to be refined to include an interface level for language and the visuo-spatial processor, as shown in fig. 30 in chapter 6, where the input to the UG lexicon is mediated either through 'audition' or 'vision'.

In sign language, this interface is active in native signers right from the start, precisely because shape, size, location, path of movement and so on are grammaticalised. Evidence for this claim comes from errors that children make in first language acquisition: for instance, decomposing movements so that they no longer map on to real-world representations (Morgan *et al.*, 2008). Classifier constructions provide the clearest example in that to interpret or produce a classifier you need to be able to form a complex iconic representation with both visual and linguistic properties. However, iconic signs are not necessarily evidence for the interface as such, as iconicity crucially involves pragmatic knowledge. The image of the concept we activate is part of our 'central' system of knowledge. So, iconicity in non-native signers involves a link between an abstract conceptual representation and a visual image provided by the visuo-spatial processor.

Objects, scenes and pictures can obviously elicit linguistic representations for everyone: seeing a penguin may evoke the word *penguin*. However, for someone with a spoken first language learning a signed second language, the interface between the visuo-spatial processor and language is initially less active than in a native signer. Until it becomes more active, the learner may be able to use compensatory mechanisms based on encyclopaedic information associated with stored images of words in the first language. It may be that morpho-phonological features such as path, size, shape and movement are perceived as iconic because we, as speakers, view them from a non-native perspective. Although there are no relevant acquisitional studies, the prediction is that for a deaf child these features will be perceived and acquired much earlier than for a hearing child. This is especially the case as path and movement may also represent morpho-phonological features associated with grammatical categories such as aspect. Even if this prediction is confirmed, the interpretation of the result would be far from straightforward, as sign language vocabulary tests (e.g. Kirk *et al.*, 1990) have shown that where items are iconic, hearing non-signing children, who already have a spoken language, can sometimes guess the answers correctly using gestures. Presumably the relevant interface is not active for these children and their performance indicates that they behave similarly to adults, exploiting their knowledge of symbolic gesture but not grammar.

The conclusion is that care needs to be exercised in talking about 'iconicity', as the situation may be radically different for different populations: child versus adult, first language learner versus second language learner and so on. The issue arises particularly starkly in the description of topographic space through the classifier system, which we explore in more detail in section 3.5.

We turn next to aspects of core BSL grammar. BSL has a complex morphology and syntax. We describe those aspects of most relevance to the learning of BSL by Christopher and the comparator group: word-order, the marking of negation and questions, and processes of verb agreement.

2.3   Morpho-syntax

The complex morphological structure of BSL often makes it hard to decide whether sequential constraints are a property of the morphology or the syntax. The problem is made particularly difficult by the pervasive importance of facial action – the prosodic result of morpho-syntactic triggering – as when a Yes-No question is signalled by raised eye-brows simultaneously with the sequence of manual signs.

Assuming that it is possible to effect an appropriate demarcation, we begin with the syntax and the putative existence of a 'basic' word-order, and how that order may be perturbed by processes such as topicalisation. It should be borne in mind that in spoken and signed languages alike it is not necessarily the case that the 'basic' word-order is the most frequent one. There could still be a basic word-order even if it were used in only a minority of sentences, where rhetorical and stylistic factors are reduced to a minimum.

2.3.1   Word-order and topicalisation

Even though there has been little systematic work on establishing a basic word-order for the language (Deuchar, 1983; Saeed *et al.*, 2000), it is clear that word-order in BSL is much freer than in spoken English. Of most relevance to us are the surface regularities for questions and negation, as documented in Sutton-Spence & Woll (1999). For example, in Wh-questions the Wh-word typically occurs clause-finally, but there is still little agreement on whether this reflects the basic word-order, or even whether there is such a thing. If there is, the most likely candidates are SVO, SOV and OSV, with OSV being statistically the most common and SVO feeling very 'English'. But whichever pattern is assumed to be basic for BSL, much observed signing will deviate from it, even in simple declarative sentences.

The general flexibility of BSL word-order is licensed by a variety of factors, of which the most notable is the topicalisation of subject, object or predicate. Topicalisation is marked through one or more facial actions: widening of the eyes, a head nod, a pause after the sign, or the topicalised sign may be held while the other hand carries on signing (Sutton-Spence & Woll, 1999: 60–1). The topic marker may also be temporally extended so that it varies in duration across the manual sign or signs it is highlighting. Topicalisation is also subject to somewhat idiosyncratic constraints, with some native signers finding sentences with verb and object topicalised to give VOS word-order as in (2), 'unusual', or at best highly marked.

(2) a   _____t
           BITE BOY GIRL
           'As for the biting of the boy it was the girl who did it'

Such preferences support the assumption that there are constraints on syntactic form, including word-order, while simultaneously raising the issue of what is syntactic, what is pragmatic and what is 'prosodic'. By hypothesis, topicalisation is pragmatically triggered – that is, there is always some pragmatic or discourse reason for selecting a particular word-order and associated prosody. However, the fact that the range of possible orders is not unconstrained indicates that there are syntactic conditions on what can be pragmatically triggered and how that syntactic structure can be associated with specific facial action. Further, the particular facial action involved may in turn be grammaticalised for a specific function. Topicalisation is then a pragmatically controlled syntactic process with prosodic (facial) repercussions.

The syntax may itself be complex. For instance, when a subject or object is topicalised, a pronominal copy may appear on the verb. Thus, 'GIRL BITE BOY' is a relatively neutral order for 'The girl bit the boy', but when BOY is topicalised one likely (but not necessary) form is 'BOY IX GIRL BITE-HIM'.[10] That is, the 'doubling' of the topicalised element with the pronoun is an indication of topicalisation as a syntactic process (similar to left-dislocation structures in English). The topicalisation of BOY could also be accomplished with a different structure (2b) to produce a rhetorical question. In this case, as well as the sign WHO, there is non-manual topic marking and a pause before GIRL, serving to make GIRL prominent.

(2) b   _____t
           BOY IX BITE WHO GIRL
           'Who bit the boy? The girl'

When we turn to morphology intuitions about structure are in general more robust. This can be shown by reference to example (3) where the incorporated negation seen in verbs like KNOW, WANT, and HAVE (a rotation of the wrist and an opening of the hand at the end of the sign's articulation) is used incorrectly with the verb EAT. Native signers immediately reject this sign (see section 4.4.2.1).

(3)   *EAT-NOT

There are similarly clear intuitions about the position of the question or negation morpheme in relation to the verb. For example, native signers have no problem making the judgements about sign-order in Wh-questions in (4), immediately rejecting the first two and accepting the latter two:

(4) a   *WHEN PROFESSOR LECTURE
   b   *PROFESSOR WHEN LECTURE
   c   PROFESSOR LECTURE WHEN
   d   WHEN PROFESSOR LECTURE WHEN
     'When does the professor lecture?'

Other factors associated with the flexibility of word-order in BSL are the availability of subject and object agreement, allowing for the omission of the subject or the object or both; pronoun copying (ME ICE-CREAM LIKE ME ('I like ice-cream' – with the pronoun in both initial and final position)); and the existence of classifiers. The presence of a classifier characteristically gives rise to a subject-predicate configuration in which the two syntactic categories – for instance, the noun represented by the classifier and the verb it is incorporated into – are signed simultaneously. Classifiers usually serve to mark anaphoric reference and in example (5) ('The car hit the man') the classifier predicate [CL-B-HIT-CL-G] relies on the previous mention of a man and a car: MAN CL-G_L CAR. The verbal predicate (shown in square brackets) includes information about the path the vehicle takes in hitting the person (towards the left side of sign space, shown by the subscripted L):

(5) a   MAN CL-G_L CAR [CL-B-HIT-CL-G_L]

We explore the analysis of classifiers in detail in section 2.4, but for now are concerned only with whether there is a linguistically determined order of elements in the verbal predicate [CL-B-HIT-CL-G_L]. Example (5a) presents them sequentially, but (5b) is a more normal representation:

(5) b[11]   left hand: MAN CL-G_L CAR [CL-G_L ....]
          right hand: CAR [CL-B-HIT-(CL-G_L)]
          'There was a man and a car, [the car hit the man]'

If we then consider the minimally different sentence in (5c), 'There was a man and a car, [the man hit the car]' we can also see how the distinction between subject and object is encoded:

(5) c   left hand: CAR [CL-B_L ....]
        right hand: MAN CL-G_L CAR [CL-G-HIT-(CL-B_L)]
        'There was a man and a car, [the man hit the car]'

2.3.2   *Negation, questions and facial action*

Both signers and speakers use facial expressions and movement of their heads to convey emotions and attitudes. Signers can also use movement of the head and face to convey linguistic contrasts. In section 2.2 above, we referred to this property of signed languages as *facial action*, to be contrasted with *facial expression*. Facial action is usually distinguished from facial expression in two main ways. Linguistic markers (grammatical facial actions) have a clear onset and offset and a precise coordination with the manual channel (as described for topicalisation above). In contrast, affective facial actions are relatively inconsistent in production and do not have precise coordination when combining with signs or syntactic constructions (Baker & Padden, 1978; Reilly, McIntire & Bellugi, 1991). In fact, the contrast may not be as clear as this description suggests. Antzakas (2006) has shown that in Greek Sign Language there is a very variable relationship between the onset and offset of facial actions and manual elements in negation: the actions are tied to the manual part but not precisely.

Grammatical facial action is crucial for several syntactic constructions in BSL, such as conditionals, subordination, aspect and adverbial contrasts. We focus on the role of the face and head in two syntactic contexts: negation and questions.

2.3.2.1   Negation   There are three main markers of negation in BSL: facial action, which can vary in intensity, head movement and manual negation signs, or signs with negation incorporated into them. Each marker can occur in conjunction with the others except that Neg incorporation doesn't co-occur with manual negation signs. Negation is often accompanied by specific mouth actions (see Boyes-Braem & Sutton-Spence, 2001; Atkinson *et al.*, 2004) which are not independent but must co-occur with the negation head movement. These head movements (specifically a head-shake or a slight turn of the head to the side) may be single or repeated and can serve on their own to negate a sentence, without any accompanying manual negator. As with the topic marker the head-shake (hs) can vary in the extent to which it is spread across a sentence, as indicated by the horizontal lines in (6) and (7).

(6)   _____hs
         BOY MILK DRINK
         'the boy does not drink milk'

(7)   _____hs
         BOY MILK DRINK
         'It was not the boy that drank milk'

This variation functions to negate different parts of the phrase: that is, to mark the scope of negation. Thus BSL allows constituent negation with, for example, only the subject negated. Manual negators normally occupy a position following the verb, as in (8):

(8)   _____hs

       BOY MILK DRINK NOTHING
       'the boy does not drink milk'

There are several manual negation markers – NOT (B hand); NOTHING (F hand, often interchangeable with NOT); NOT-EXIST; and other signs which include negation, such as NEVER, NOT-YET, WILL-NOT, WHY-NOT and SHALL-NOT. These signs must be accompanied by negation head movements. Finally, some signs, usually verbs of experience or sensation, have their own negation form, such as KNOW-NOT, LIKE-NOT, WANT-NOT and BELIEVE-NOT. In these forms the negation is incorporated into the sign (the status of the negator as an affix or clitic has not yet been resolved (see Zeshan, 2004a)). The interpretation of these forms is always such that the negative has scope over the predicate, as in '~[know]', rather than '[know]~'. Morphologically, the negation element (NOT) of these forms is transparent, but the affixation of negation to the lexemes KNOW, BELIEVE, etc. gives rise in some instances to morphophonemic changes which render them opaque. Thus, the forms of BELIEVE and LIKE remain unchanged by the addition of negation, but KNOW and WANT undergo some change. The situation is comparable to the affixation of the plural morpheme in spoken English, where the plural marker is itself systematically transparent, but where the stem to which it is affixed may change, as in the contrast between *cuff/cuffs* and *leaf/leaves*. As indicated above, signed sentences often contain multiple negation markers, as shown in (9):

(9)   _____hs

       MAN_a IX_a KNOW-NOT NOTHING
       'I really don't know the man'

In such cases, the presence of a negation sign (i.e. NOTHING here)[12] is optional, its effect being mainly to add emphasis to the negative meaning of the sentence.

The syntax of negation in BSL is strikingly parallel to that in other sign languages, for instance, Greek Sign Language (GSL), as described by Antzakas (2006). Just as negation in BSL is typically head-final, Antzakas says that in GSL there is a negation marker which usually comes at the end of the sentence; the only case when it may change its position in his data is if the signers code-switch and are affected by the word-order of Greek. So, negation in GSL is head-final and negative signs such as 'nothing' also come in final position. Moreover, even the presence of a negative element such as NOTHING is optional in the same circumstances as in BSL. There are of course minor differences: for instance, the backwards tilt of the head found in Greek Sign

Language has not been reported as a marker of negation in other sign languages. Antzakas also observes that in GSL the optionality of the head-shake is found only with verbs with incorporated negation or in an embedded negative clause. In fact, optionality in both BSL and GSL (and presumably all sign languages) affects any negative marker (facial, manual or head-shake) *additional* to the basic sign as, for reasons of 'full interpretation' (Chomsky, 1995: 151), there must be at least one marker of negation to enable the sentence to be interpreted as negative.

2.3.2.2 *Questions*   Questions in BSL have one or more of three features: a question sign, a characteristic facial action and a characteristic sign-order. The two question types in BSL we describe here are Wh- and Yes-No questions. Wh- questions are formed with a question sign such as WHAT, WHO, WHERE, WHY or HOW. Question signs most often come at the end of the sentence but, in apparent free variation, the Wh- sign sometimes appears both at the beginning and at the end of the questioned clause as, for example, in WHERE CAT WHERE ('Where is the cat?') (see example (4d) above). Such Wh-copy has been reported in other sign languages (Zeshan, 2004b). There is no special manual Yes-No question sign at the beginning or end of an interrogative clause in BSL.

Facial action, as the prosodic reflex of a syntactic choice (the [Q] feature), is generally obligatory. With Wh- questions, the brows are furrowed, the eyes are slightly closed, and the head is thrust slightly forward or tilted to one side: the symbol 'bf' is used to refer to this combination of actions. Yes-No questions are also signalled by facial action: usually raised eyebrows, opened eyes and a slight backwards thrust of the head and shoulders: the symbol 'br' is used to refer to this combination of actions. The choice of lowered or raised brows seems to be driven by speaker attitude (e.g. a Wh- question about something unexpected will have raised brows; a Yes-No question where the speaker is puzzled will have lowered brows (see Campbell *et al.*, 1999). The two uses of the brow in Wh- and Yes-No questions are shown in (10 a and b):

(10) a   _____bf
         BOOK WHERE
         'Where's the book?'
      b _____br
         DEAF YOU
         'Are you deaf?'

The extent of the non-manual element in the question does not always affect the scope of the question, as is shown in example (10c), which has different morphological marking but does not differ in meaning from (10a):

(10) c   _____bf
     BOOK WHERE
     'Where's the book?'

This overview of the role of non-manual mechanisms highlights the importance for signers of looking at each other's faces during interaction. A further issue to consider is the coordination of the manual and non-manual channels. Evidence from first language acquisition suggests that combining both elements in the sentence is subject to a complex process of linguistic and motor control (see Anderson & Reilly, 2002). Further, BSL differs from English in the position of the negative and interrogative elements: head-initial in English, head-final in BSL. In English negation a contracted or uncontracted form is attached to a finite auxiliary or positioned between the infinitival marker and the verb. Wh- questions, on the other hand, are marked sentence-initially. In BSL, both question markers and negators are typically sentence-final. There is some discussion in the literature on the correct analysis of these phenomena (see e.g. Sandler & Lillo-Martin, 2006, for an extended discussion of rightward versus leftward movement of Wh).

The most striking parametric differences between English and BSL are the existence of non-manual signs (with their scope-marking potential), the possibility of Wh-copy in initial position, and the doubling of negation for emphasis. These differences are interesting for our predictions regarding Christopher's learning of BSL. For instance, Emmorey (see Pyers & Emmorey, 2008) recently presented research on bilingual hearing adults who used ASL facial actions when they were speaking English. Apparently they come across as angry!

2.3.3   Subject-object agreement

On more than one occasion we have mentioned the existence of 'agreeing' verbs and their implicit contrast with other categories. In order to underpin the discussion of agreement, and to introduce the account of classifiers in the following section, it is now time to elaborate on this classification. There are three basic classes of verbs in BSL and other European sign languages: 'plain' verbs, 'agreeing' verbs, and 'spatial' verbs, where this last is the domain in which classifiers are found. We provide a brief introduction to all three types.

Plain verbs undergo relatively little modification (normally only for aspect and manner) and do not move through space to show grammatical information. Semantically, they express agentive functions and cognitive and sensory experiences. Examples in BSL include: RIDE-A-BICYCLE, LOVE, RESEARCH, RUN, SMOKE, THINK and UNDERSTAND. Many plain verbs are made using the body as the location and are referred to as 'body-anchored'.

Agreeing verbs semantically often represent 'transfer'. Information about who is carrying out the action, and who or what is affected by the action is shown by changes in the movement and orientation of the verb. The start and end locations of the verb 'agree' with the locations assigned to the person and number of the agent/subject and/or the patient/object. In general, subject agreement is optional, object agreement is obligatory. Examples of agreeing verbs in BSL are: ASK, GIVE, TELL, TELEPHONE, TEASE, CRITICISE, BLAME, FILM(-by-camera) and SAY-NO-TO.

Agreeing verbs can be modified to show, as well as manner and aspect, the person, number and class of the subject and direct object. As an example, nominals introduced for the first time into discourse may be accompanied by a point to a location in sign space, and verb signs move between such points to specify the verb's subject and object. Subsequent re-pointing to a previously established location in sign space functions as a pronominal reference to the earlier articulated nominal, as illustrated in (11). In extended discourse a point towards one of the locations can act as anaphoric reference.

(11)   BROTHER IX$_b$ MAN IX$_{a\,a}$TELEPHONE$_b$ **PRON**$_b$ NOT-HAVE
        WORK
        'The man telephoned his brother, but he wasn't there, he was
        working'

Agreeing verbs may also be used in conjunction with referents present in the context. When such referents are present, they are used as the syntactic locations of the subject and object: e.g. I-ASK-YOU or YOU-TELL-HER, where the sign begins at the signer and moves in the direction of the 2nd person, or from the 2nd person towards the location of the 3rd person. As described previously in the discussion of sign space, signers are more likely to use other means for establishing the location of subject and object arguments in a sentence with an agreeing verb. Where there are two 3rd person referents, the signer often represents one of those, using his or her own body. A slight shift in the eye-gaze shows that the subject is not the signer himself or herself but another NP. In example (11) above this would be achieved by the signer signing MAN but omitting the IX$_a$. The agreeing verb then moves from the signer's own location (representing MAN) towards the location previously indexed for BROTHER.

As we shall see, this use of sign space caused Christopher some difficulty. Whether (11) involves indexing to two arbitrary points in the sign space, or to the signer and a second arbitrary point, is a matter of choice. You can do either and still produce a grammatical sentence, but Christopher mastered neither option. This indexing is reminiscent of hearing people's co-speech gesture, where both types of referential location can be used. Sign learners frequently use these devices when they start learning the basics of the agreement system in BSL even though Christopher didn't do so. From this brief description it is clearly important that the learner develop an initial tacit understanding of sign space. However, as indicated in sections 1.3.1 and 1.3.2, Christopher was unable to abstract away from real locations, objects or individuals. The implication is that understanding and using sign space is inherently demanding, perhaps involving theory of mind. Christopher's flawed performance on agreement (and the comprehension of classifiers) is then attributable to his problems in interpreting spatial relations. These problems derive from his visuo-spatial deficit and his inability to imitate abstract spatial movements, due ultimately to his apraxia and autism.

The final category of 'spatial verbs' includes verbs of movement and location. These are sometimes called 'classifier verbs' because they provide information about the class of noun moved or located by means of classifiers which comprise the handshape element in these verbs. They use topographic space, and rather than inflecting for person or number they give information about path, trajectory, speed and location. The movement and location of these spatial verbs are isomorphic with the disposition of the participants in the real world. Examples in BSL include RUN-DOWNSTAIRS, GO-TO, DRIVE-TO, PUNCH-(someone), SHAVE-(someone), CARRY-BY-HAND, or PUT-(somewhere). In all examples of spatial verbs, information is provided obligatorily about the location of a referent, where it moves from and to (or where it is located), and what semantic class it belongs to.

2.4   Classifiers and topographic space

In this section we outline the linguistic and interpretive properties of classifiers in both spoken and signed languages. We begin with a brief overview of classifiers in spoken languages, proceed to a discussion of classifiers in signed languages, especially BSL, and conclude with a comparison of the two, highlighting similarities and differences. Our discussion of classifiers in spoken languages will of necessity be only representative, but for classifiers in BSL we hope to be exhaustive of the various possible types.

2.4.1   Classifiers in spoken languages

Classifiers are a lexical device used to differentiate classes of noun according to perceived properties of their typical referents. They are found only marginally in English when we distinguish 'lumps' of sugar, 'head' of cattle, and 'pieces' of paper, but are widespread elsewhere. Using a database of some fifty (spoken) languages, Allan (1977) suggested a division into classifier languages, such as Thai, Assamese and Navajo, and non-classifier languages, such as English. Within the classifier half of this basic dichotomy he distinguished 'numeral', 'concordial', 'predicate' and 'intra-locative' classifiers. For all types, the general consensus is that such classifier systems are based on human perception of entities in the world. He writes (Allan, 1977: 285) that 'classifiers have meaning in the sense that a classifier denotes some salient perceived or imputed characteristic of the entity to which the associated noun refers (or may refer)'. According to Anderson (1978: 344) the primary classifier distinction to be made is that between animate and inanimate, with further categories dependent on shape (especially, round, long and flat). Similar conclusions are reached by Adams & Conklin (1973), Bisang (1999) and others. Syntactically, classifiers may be words or particles, and are characteristically used with numeral-noun combinations, with certain types of verbs, and with both of these in 'concordial' systems. In the relatively rare 'intra-locative' type, they occur embedded in locative expressions. Of most relevance to us are 'verbal classifiers' (sometimes referred to as predicate classifiers) which categorise the referents of their arguments according to their shape, consistency, size, etc., by means of agreement markers (see Aikhenvald, 2000). It is often asserted that classifiers have a discourse function (see e.g. Daley, 1998), but we are not convinced that such a function is distinct from normal anaphora.

2.4.2 Classifiers in signed languages

Classifiers in the sign linguistics literature (e.g. Supalla, 1986, Sutton-Spence & Woll, 1999) are broadly considered to be handshapes which occur in spatial verbs (verbs of movement, location and existence) and which represent class properties of nouns. They have traditionally been divided into anything from two to seven groups; we follow Schembri's (2003) tri-partite classification. 'Entity classifiers' are used to classify referents as geometric objects, for example long thin objects (a person walking, or a pencil located in some designated position), flat objects (vehicles moving along a road, tiles on a wall, piles of papers), and so on. 'Handling classifiers' classify referents in terms of how they are held or used by agents, for example curved objects (holding a cup), thin objects (holding a certificate, holding a needle), etc. 'Size and shape specifiers' describe referents by 'drawing' salient features found on the surface of members of the class (for example, having stripes or having a flat surface).

The first class of classifiers (entity classifiers) were a main focus of the current study. These signs are verbal classifiers: they provide the surface realisation of handshape in spatial verbs and incorporate several layers of information. They specify a referent as belonging to a particular class of animate or inanimate nouns, where this classification is based on perceived physical characteristics: in particular, the number of dimensions identified. For example a noun from the class of long thin objects, such as a person, can be described as moving rightwards in a zigzag manner by selecting a G handshape classifier (with the

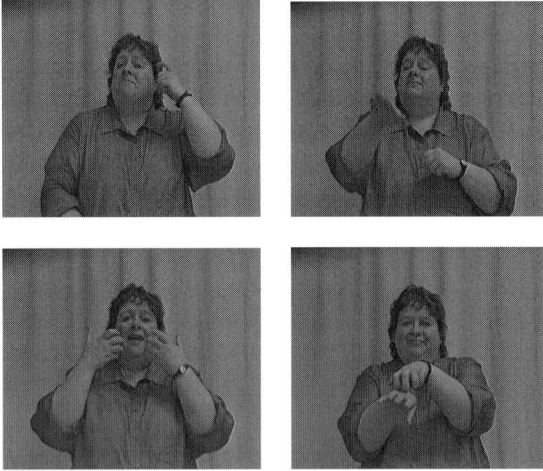

Figure 11 Topographic function of classifiers in BSL (reproduced with permission from M. MacSweeney; see: www.ich.ucl.ac.uk/macsweeney/jocnstimuli/)

index finger pointing upwards to indicate vertical orientation) and articulating a zigzag path through sign space.

To summarise: classifiers resemble agreement in that they refer to already established entities. Subject agreement, however, does not provide such rich information as a classifier because it provides the index of the antecedent but no physical properties of the antecedent. The morphology is determined by verb class: plain verbs allow neither agreement nor classifier insertion; agreeing verbs require (subject and object) agreement; spatial verbs (verbs of movement, location and existence) require classifiers. In addition, classifiers can describe spatial relations in terms of a correspondence between real-world topography and an array represented in sign space as a spatial map. An example of the topographic function of classifiers is given in (12), where the signer is describing the relative locations of two objects (a cat on a bed) as schematised in fig. (11). The handshape '3-claw' is a variation of '3' with fingers curved.

(12)   BED CL-B (flat object)RIGHT HAND CAT CL-B (flat object)RIGHT HAND
        CL-3-CLAW(small animal)LEFT HAND (ABOVE RIGHT HAND)
        'The cat sat on the bed'

The signer (who is left-handed) first signs BED, followed by a classifier (B handshape) representing BED. She then signs CAT followed by two classifiers, a B-handshape representing BED (with the right hand) and then, while maintaining the right-handed handshape, a 3-CLAW classifier representing a small animal (with the left hand). The 3-CLAW handshape is placed on top of the left hand, isomorphic to the real-world layout: 'cat on top of bed'.

If the addressee is asked to repeat this description he will normally use the same relative locations, but from his own perspective rather than that of the original signer. Spatial mapping is therefore speaker-orientated. When native signers produce descriptions of spatial relations other than from their own perspective they indicate this with a pronoun to signal 'from my/your point of view'. Close equivalents in spoken English are provided by the contrast between 'to John's right' and 'to the right of John', as used in describing a picture, or the differing exploitation of deictic perspective seen in the appropriate use of 'take' and 'bring'. In signing, the location of the sign relative to the current signer is held constant and thus shifts in terms of where it is located in sign space depending on the perspective of the present signer: that is, the addressee mentally reverses the relative locations (see Emmorey, 2002).

The use of sign space in (12) has been described as involving topographic space, in contrast to the movement of agreeing verbs in non-topographic or syntactic space. However, while topographic information is conveyed in spatial verbs, it is not purely spatial but is linguistically encoded, i.e. it has been linguisticised. That is, we assume that everything signed is in syntactic space, and that classifiers encode spatial features which have a morphological and phonological realisation. Classifiers in signed languages can encode all the features that spoken language classifiers do but, because of the advantage of the visual modality, they have developed to convey extremely detailed spatial and geometric information via linguistic structure (see Emmorey, 2003). Moreover, classifiers in signed languages convey this linguistic information simultaneously with other information, i.e. in the same complex sign, whereas in spoken language classifiers are subject to the linear restriction of spoken production.

To summarise, classifiers are used first for syntactic functions such as anaphoric reference and pluralisation; and second for indicating the verb's spatial mapping, as in describing the layout of objects on a table. Thus there is a distinction between a signer's use of classifiers in sign space for conveying syntactic information and the use of classifiers in sign space for mapping topographic information. Both usages are linguistically encoded. However, the first uses classifiers to encode morphological information (e.g. plurality), which is not topographic; the second uses classifiers to describe locational relations between entities in real space by specifying their relative positions in sign space, without further lexical or morphological marking. These relative positions are abstractions from the topographic representation. As mentioned above, it is significant that Christopher's disabilities, especially his apraxia and autism, meant that he had problems even with the syntactic use of space to show subject and object agreement if the two entities were not visible.

2.4.3   *Parallels between classifiers in spoken and signed languages*

We turn now to the similarities and differences between classifiers in the two modalities. Aikhenvald (2003; see also Schembri, 2003) observes that all signed languages investigated to date have classifier constructions comparable to those known as 'verbal' classifiers in various spoken languages. These classifiers characteristically appear on the verb and categorise the subject of an intransitive or the object of a transitive verb in terms of its orientation or stance in space, in addition to specifying its inherent properties. She further claims that there are 'striking differences' (2003: 89) between classifier constructions in spoken and signed languages. In particular, while in spoken languages deictic and locative classifiers are extremely rare, in all sign languages classifiers appear to have at least some of the semantic properties of locative classifiers, since they usually serve to locate a referent in space as well as indicating shape and other properties (Aikhenvald, 2000). We consider that what is really unusual in sign languages as compared to spoken languages is the identification of classifiers just with the class of spatial verbs.

   While doubtless in need of explanation, the comparative rarity of locative classifiers in spoken languages seems to us to be less important than the fact that they do occur in languages in both modalities, affording yet another example of where UG provides the same apparatus to be exploited in the two domains. Thus, Aikhenvald (in press: 22) describes Palikur, a Brazilian Arawak language, as having 'locative classifiers' which occur 'fused with locative adpositions . . . and characterize the head noun in terms of its animacy or shape', a description which carries over directly to signed languages. There are further parallels: in both modalities one finds languages exemplifying multiple uses of classifiers; the range of semantic and syntactic possibilities seems to be closely comparable in both domains, and so on.

   Emmorey (1996) has suggested that signed languages are unlike spoken languages in requiring that a cognitive representation of a spatial array is embedded within a linguistic system itself based on space. More recently, (Emmorey & Falgier, 1999; Emmorey, 2002) she has described this as 'talking about space with space'. The influence of spatial cognition on the processing of classifiers is then supposedly greater in signed languages than in spoken languages. There is an element of truth in this claim but we think that the differences between the two modalities are less drastic than she suggests, and that the use of spatial deixis in spoken language is sufficiently close to what is found in signed languages to make the contrast less absolute than it might at first appear. Nonetheless, there is a significant difference in the case of 'incorporated prepositions' (see e.g. Emmorey, 2002: 91) where information about the fine detail of the location of some entity is incorporated into the classifier, rather than being spelt out by the use of a separate preposition as in spoken languages.

Given the focus of this study, it is also relevant to note that autists frequently have problems with deixis in spoken languages.

Although the linguistic representations may be similar, it is a separate question whether the psycholinguistic processing of space as described using English prepositions or using BSL classifiers is identical or even closely comparable. For instance, Christopher had much greater problems with understanding and describing location in BSL than in his spoken languages (see Morgan *et al.*, 2007). That the shape or size features of a referent can be encoded in the classifier of a spoken language does not entail that the link is at the same interface as with a signed language. It is likely that the link between image and descriptor is indirect, as is the case where the spatial relations between objects are described using prepositions. Moreover, neuro-imaging studies (e.g. MacSweeney *et al.*, 2002) also indicate different regions of activation for BSL sentences with classifiers and their English translations. We return to this issue when we discuss the role of the language/visuo-spatial interface, which is more active in signed than in spoken languages.

2.5   Cross-modality effects: space, gesture and iconicity

The modality differences discussed in earlier sections and their potential effects on learning can be summarised as follows. The phonetic properties of sign languages are radically different from those of spoken languages as they involve the movement of different articulators, both manual and facial. That is, the articulation and perception of BSL involve different sensory and motor apparatus with different performance implications from what is found in spoken language. This means that learners need to pay attention to manual and non-manual movements as well as to develop different coordinated motoric processes. Most strikingly, more than one part of a sign, as well as more than one sign, can be produced and perceived simultaneously. Further, it is easier to express spatial or formational contrasts (the size, shape, location and path of objects' movements) in BSL than in spoken languages, and there is a more direct possibility of combining gestures with signs than with speech. As a result, the sign lexicon may more easily exploit iconicity via world knowledge than may the spoken lexicon. Finally, BSL has no conventional written script, thus removing completely one source of information for the learner.

2.6   Conclusions

Signed languages, hence BSL, are natural languages with both the richness that this implies and the systematic differences in attainment by children versus adults, and by first versus second language acquirers. Signed languages also appear to be neurologically parallel to spoken languages in terms of cerebral dominance and patterns of pathological breakdown, though this does not deny the possibility of systematic differences in the memory structure and some aspects of processing by sign language users. Despite this similarity, there is a systematically greater role for iconicity in signed languages than in spoken languages.

The phonology is radically different in its outward manifestation, especially when one considers the importance of facial action in the formation of signs, but even here the parameters of variation seem to be comparable across modalities. The most salient differences are again iconicity and the possibility of simultaneous articulation, but even the greater role for iconicity is largely irrelevant in the acquisition of a first (signed) language. Our preliminary model of cognitive architecture can remain essentially neutral as between the signed and spoken modalities.

As a consequence of this commonalty the morpho-syntactic structure of BSL can be described in the same terms and using the same theoretical devices as a spoken language. This is true in general and, a fortiori, for the phenomena we chose to concentrate on: word-order (including topicalisation), negation, questions and classifier constructions. These all illustrate BSL's rich agreement morphology but, except for the role of facial action, none of them manifest anything which would be alien to spoken languages.

The major exception to the parallelism between signed and spoken languages resides in the interaction of sign space and topographic space, an area that caused Christopher considerable difficulty.

3 The programme

3.1 Preliminaries

3.1.1 *Methodology of data presentation and analysis*

A qualified Deaf BSL tutor taught Christopher a conventional (Signature Level 1)[1] BSL class once a month for a year, concentrating on the core grammatical properties of the language. Over twelve months, there were accordingly twelve hours of formal teaching, which was supplemented by conversation with a native (Deaf) signer, who went over the same material in a less formal context between classes.

The total amount of BSL contact (formal teaching and informal interaction) was therefore about twenty-four hours. Although the curriculum was divided into formal lessons and informal discussions, the teaching was sufficiently flexible for both types of session to contain both types of material. By way of comparison, this is more than twice as much as Christopher's exposure to each of Berber and Epun,[2] the other (spoken) languages we had taught him previously (see Smith *et al.*, 1993; Smith & Tsimpli, 1995). In teaching Christopher these new languages we had left him with tape-recorded and written versions of the material he had been exposed to, and homework exercises to complete and post back to us. There were no further texts or documentation in these languages.[3] In teaching him BSL we could not leave him any written material, but we did provide him with a BSL dictionary and some video material. He used these sporadically, but he never mastered the transcription used in the dictionary, and soon broke the video machine. In fact his use of any of the material for spoken or signed languages appears to have been minimal. It is important to emphasise the difference between BSL on the one hand and Berber and Epun on the other. If his excellent memory is devoted largely to the written form of language, we would expect him to have greater difficulty learning BSL than languages with a written mode.

All classes and discussions were video-recorded. Coding and transcription followed conventional sign language research protocols (see Brennan, 1990, 1992; Sutton-Spence & Woll, 1999). All transcriptions were checked with two fluent signers, and reliability was established at above 90 per cent. All of Christopher's spontaneous signing which showed any use of negation, questions, person agreement and classifiers was transcribed. We took a random ten-minute sample from each hour of exposure for closer scrutiny, recording his gaze behaviour and his improving mastery of sign phonology. Christopher and some of the comparator group also had opportunities to practise their BSL through informal conversation with their tutors and other Deaf people although this aspect of their learning was not controlled for.

The twenty-four hours of BSL exposure were divided for the purposes of analysis into five stages: four periods of five hours, and a final period of four hours. During the five periods of exposure we assessed Christopher's and the comparator group's uptake, using translation tasks from BSL to English and from English to BSL as well as analysing spontaneous and elicited use of sign in conversation. In addition, as documented above, we carried out a variety of tests of Christopher's general cognitive abilities, such as the apraxia test, the Rey-Osterrieth test and so on.

3.1.2   Iconicity

The detailed contents of the course that Christopher and the members of the comparator group were taught are given in section 3.2. However, before we embarked on the teaching, we thought it necessary to accommodate explicitly one special characteristic of sign languages – their greater iconicity vis-à-vis spoken languages, to see if this had a significant effect on the acquisition of BSL. To do this we subjected Christopher and the comparator group to a number of preliminary tests: specifically, we first asked them to guess the meaning of a number of BSL signs, and we then asked them to invent signs (or appropriate gestures) for particular meanings. Such tests could not be carried out with learners of a spoken language, as what we were asking them to do was not to use their spoken language ability to guess sign meanings or to produce appropriate gestures, but to exploit the partially iconic basis of sign language to infer interpretations. This exploitation of iconicity crucially proved significantly more difficult for Christopher than for the comparator group, a matter of some importance when it comes to the interpretation of the respective results of their learning of BSL.

Part of the rationale for this part of the investigation was to see whether the initial ability to guess meanings of signs or to invent possible gestures for concepts would be related to eventual attainment of BSL. For hearing people without knowledge of sign language to guess the meanings of signs involves their using world knowledge to make links between the form of signs and their possible meanings. This interaction among cognitive systems, especially in the context of language learning, is a central concern of this book.

In order to make iconic links between signs and the real-world referents they are used to pick out, sign learners need to be able to reflect on what visual properties of the referent determine why a sign is formed in a particular way. Often these links are far from obvious but with hindsight and world knowledge they can be a powerful memory aid at the start of sign language learning. For example the sign SHEFFIELD resembles a person using a knife and fork which a learner could associate with 'knives and forks are made in Sheffield'. Learners do not need to know that Sheffield is or was the centre of cutlery manufacture in England to use and remember the sign but information of this kind might be useful for recalling signs.

In the first hours of his exposure to BSL Christopher's behaviour was interestingly unexpected. Despite his apraxia and his resultant problems in forming and moving signs in sign space, he was very keen to gesture, and spontaneously offered a variety of arbitrary gestures for novel objects and concepts. As mentioned above, BSL has many iconic signs, and Christopher's enthusiasm suggested that there should be some intuitive transparency in the gestures he invented in lieu of signs. Accordingly, we attempted to discover how many signs both Christopher and the comparator group could guess, without any knowledge of BSL, by giving them a sign-to-picture matching test before their sign courses started. The results of this test are given in ch. 4.2.

3.2   The curriculum and other interactions

The contents of the twelve sessions of the course that Christopher and the comparator group followed consisted of the topics in (1):

(1) a   Introduction to signing. Vocabulary, standard questions (such as 'Are you deaf?', 'What's your name?', etc.) and fingerspelling.

 b   Wh- and Yes-No questions. Simple naming questions ('What is this?'), asking about work, family, foods. Vocabulary and practice.

 c   Negation markers in different syntactic constructions (different markers of negation, e.g. manual, affixal, incorporated, negative quantifiers, facial negation) and their combinations.

 d   Verb agreement for present referents through different morphological and phonological modifications of the sign. Indexing referents. Indexing with plain verbs. Vocabulary and practice.

 e   Simple narratives. Marking questions and negation using facial action.

 f   Review of previous topics and practice.

 g   Using topic markers in simple sentences. Using aspect morphology.

 h   Questions and negation with new verbs, fingerspelling.

i   Person–verb agreement with abstract locations for absent referents in sign space.
j   Narratives with two characters; classifiers, sign space and role shift.
k   Narratives with three characters.
l   Complex sentences using topic markers.

At each stage we assessed Christopher's and the comparator group's progress before increasing the complexity of the material they were exposed to. The formal classes exposed all the learners to the grammatical structures of negation, verb agreement, questions and sign-order, as well as aspectual morphology, classifier constructions, non-manual modifiers and spatial location setting. Throughout the teaching programme we focused on three main aspects of Christopher's and the comparator group's acquisition of BSL, as shown in (2):

(2) a   the production and comprehension of lexical signs;
    b   the production and comprehension of manual grammatical devices;
    c   the mastery of facial action and facial expression accompanying manual signs.

3.3   Christopher and the comparator group

There has been very little research on the learning of signed languages as second languages, so it was essential that we provide some basis of comparison for Christopher's progress, even if the nature of his abilities meant that a traditional 'control' group was not feasible. Accordingly, we taught the same curriculum to a group of hearing, talented second language learners, who all spoke English as their first language. Recruitment was through an advertisement on the University language departments' notice boards for a free BSL course. Fortunately we were inundated with volunteers. We measured their abilities by using the University language assessment test for Spanish, French and German. This is a written multiple choice test which assesses grammatical knowledge. We narrowed down volunteers by selecting only those who scored in the 90 per cent range on the test. We were left with forty volunteers aged between 21 and 50 years old, with a majority (34) being female. All were enrolled on an undergraduate language degree with twenty-two studying French, seven Spanish and eleven German. That is, all of the comparator group were students who had progressed to post A-level[4] in one of these languages but were not native speakers of them.

Exposure to BSL lasted twelve weeks with a one-hour class once a week. Thus, they were exposed to comparable BSL input to that used for Christopher's teaching, albeit over a shorter time span. As our subjects were busy university undergraduates and our classes were in the evening we did not always have

100 per cent attendance at classes. As a result we cannot guarantee that all forty subjects received the same amount of input in BSL. A more serious limitation is that because testing often took place during evening classes there were sometimes not as many learners present as we would have liked. This means that in some of the assessments we present data from a smaller group of learners. When this is the case we give the relevant numbers.

3.4   Rationale for the selection of BSL phenomena

As documented in section 2.1, Christopher's superior performance in vocabulary and morphology vis-à-vis syntax in his non-native languages partly determined the choice of BSL phenomena to investigate in detail.

We opted for syntactic structures such as *questions* and *negatives*, which involve lexical signs (Wh- or negative), morpho-phonological marking (e.g. facial features) and syntactic marking (e.g. word-order). Further, to test whether Christopher's enhanced ability to learn inflectional morphology in his spoken languages generalised to sign language, we chose a class of BSL verbs, referred to as *agreeing verbs* (see ch. 2.3.3 above), which encode both subject and object agreement. These three topics of agreeing verbs, questions and negatives differ in the type of linguistic meaning they encode: questions and negatives involve sentence operators (Q and Neg respectively) whereas subject and object agreement are morphological processes whose relevance to semantics is restricted to the procedural meaning encoding the ability to refer (a property that all pronominals share and whose function is primarily discoursal or pragmatic). Although all of the above topics occur in the other languages Christopher speaks, we expected that, despite his morphological prowess, his comprehension of questions and negatives would be better than that of agreeing verbs. The reason is that agreeing verbs – and anaphoric devices more generally in BSL – involve using physical locations in sign space to mark the subject or object associated with the verb. In spoken languages, the use of pronominals (except some deictics) does not involve spatial cognition.

Agreeing verbs encode a type of anaphoric reference which is found in several other languages that Christopher speaks and which is regulated by language-specific properties of the inflectional system. As we have seen earlier, however, signed languages also use another class of anaphoric expressions, namely *classifiers* (Emmorey, 2003; Morgan & Woll, 2007). Although they serve a variety of functions and fall into different subclasses (see ch. 2.4), their shared property is that they encode physical features (shape, size and texture) of the antecedent. Entity classifiers (also known as person and object classifiers) form a subclass which is distinguished from other BSL classifiers in that they primarily encode relational, motion and location features. We included classifiers in our investigation as they allow us to compare Christopher's performance on anaphoric elements that draw heavily on the visuo-spatial component – puta-tively somewhat impaired in his case – with agreeing verbs, which are also anaphoric but which are less dependent on spatial cognition.[5] Moreover, none of the spoken languages Christopher knows has classifiers, whereas all of them have pronominals. Accordingly, a comparison of the two anaphoric devices is also relevant to the issue of transfer effects in the subjects' learning of BSL: there could be such transfer from the first or second languages in the case of pronominals but not in the case of classifiers.

In investigating the sign lexicon, we chose common nouns and verbs which were repeated in all stages of BSL teaching. Comprehension and production of individual lexical signs were compared with sign sequences (phrases or sentences) on the one hand, and with morphological signs on the other. This selection was motivated by the fact that Christopher's fast and apparently effortless language learning abilities are primarily related to vocabulary and morphology, and we wanted to see if these dissociated in BSL. We expected to see evidence of such dissociation in his performance for two reasons: first, the rote-learning involved in mastering the vocabulary of BSL is not supported by written feedback and, second, repeated exposure to the inflectional morphology found in agreeing verbs should encourage rule-formation and consequent over-generalisation errors.

As indicated above, the syllabus included other BSL material which was not systematically tested, either because it turned out to be too demanding or because not all the members of the comparator group were examined on it. As a result, the BSL phenomena we concentrated on for testing purposes were: vocabulary, Wh- and Yes–No questions, negation markers in different syntactic constructions, verb agreement and classifiers.

3.5   Specific predictions about BSL learning in the two groups

We made detailed predictions about Christopher's learning of BSL in section 1.7. Here our predictions are explicitly related to the comparison between Christopher and the comparator group with regard to the three areas that were our focus in the study: the production and comprehension of lexical signs, of grammatical devices, and of non-manual elements in BSL commu-nication. In fact, because of Christopher's apraxia our investigation of his production abilities for lexical signs and grammatical devices was necessarily more circumscribed than that of the comparator group.

As far as comprehension was concerned, we predicted that due to his autism, which underlies his overall lack of expressiveness and the impoverished into-nation of his spoken languages, Christopher would be good at learning lexical signs and grammatical devices and worse with facial action and expression. The comparator group by contrast was not expected to show such a difference. Our prediction about lexical signs being easy for Christopher was not unproblematic because of the fact that iconicity plays an important role in the formation of many signs in BSL. Given that the exploitation of iconicity requires using the meta-cognitive skill of visual abstraction, Christopher was expected to be worse in his learning and storage of lexical signs than of words in his spoken second languages. He was also expected to be worse on lexical signs than on grammatical devices and, within the latter category, we predicted that the members of the comparator group would find the learning of negation, questions, agreement and classifiers equally challenging, whereas Christopher would most probably have greater difficulty with classifiers. Finally, although we expected individual variation among the learners in the comparator group, as some might have weaker memory and storage abilities for signs than others, we anticipated that Christopher would be worse than the comparator group overall.

4   The results

4.1   Introduction

We have reported elsewhere (Morgan *et al.*, 2002a, 2002b) on Christopher's proficient development, both in production and comprehension, of single signs, and we observed that, despite deficits in motor coordination, he acquired the basic parameters of sign formation sufficiently well to underpin a good working vocabulary. This supports our prediction that he would be able to overcome his difficulties in motor coordination and develop mastery of the lexicon. Nevertheless, he showed certain modality effects in that his comprehension of signs was always better than his production and his signing was appreciably slower than his (L2) speaking. Further, despite his vocabulary learning being within normal limits, some interesting differences between Christopher and the controls with regard to sign formation and iconicity were found.

In this chapter we provide an overview of the learning of BSL by Christopher and the members of the comparator group (4.2), we continue with a discussion of the results of our tests of iconicity and gesture (4.3), and then look in turn at his lexical development (4.4) and different aspects of his mastery of syntax (4.5–4.7), especially classifiers (4.6).

It is important to note that the data we present represent language used in a classroom situation. It is common in signing classes for students to repeat teacher-led language, as well as engage in topic-led conversation between learners or between the teacher and the students. The data from Christopher and the comparator group are not therefore truly spontaneous signing but they have approximately the same content and, most importantly, they are comparable between the subjects.

4.2   Overview of Christopher's BSL learning

In view of his performance in his other non-native languages, Christopher had been predicted to show a dissociation between his mastery of morphology and syntax in BSL. Specifically, his ability in BSL should mirror his mixed abilities in spoken languages: he should make extremely rapid initial progress and his mastery of BSL morphology and vocabulary should be radically better than that of BSL syntax. He should find the coordination of manual and non-manual signs and the necessity of looking at the addressee during sign reception difficult, but this should not significantly impair his learning in general, as comprehension of BSL should be unaffected by his apraxia and he should overcome his autistic reticence to make eye-contact when he realised that looking provided him with linguistic information. Although we made no specific predictions, we were also concerned that some aspects of BSL might prove difficult even at the level of comprehension, due to Christopher's deficits in visuo-spatial cognition. In contrast, the controls should show no asymmetry in their learning of different aspects of the language.

In period 1, the overall performance of Christopher and the average learner of the comparator group was not radically different. However, in specific areas of the language, Christopher's comprehension and production showed systematic asymmetries not found in the controls. In particular, his BSL comprehension was considerably better than his BSL production, but he also showed asymmetries in the acquisition of the lexical and the syntactic phenomena tested. For example, BSL classifiers presented him with considerable difficulty in both comprehension and production compared to negation, question or agreement. This asymmetric pattern was not found in the performance of the comparator group.

The asymmetry between comprehension and production is partly attributable to Christopher's autism and apraxia which had not appeared to interfere with his development of spoken languages. For example, his avoidance of direct eye-contact did not impede his development of spoken languages either aurally or from print, but was a significant hindrance at the start of his learning of a sign language. Interestingly, he soon overcame his reluctance to look at his conversational partner during interaction, supporting our prediction that the linguistic nature of BSL would lead to such reduction in autistic behaviour. This positive development was in contrast with other aspects of his learning, such as his failure to recognize iconic links in his acquisition of signs.

We had expected that his apraxia would have two effects: in production it would slow down his articulation, and his poor coordination of manual and non-manual articulators would hamper his learning of negation and questions compared with the controls. Although he had difficulty in combining the use of non-manual and manual signs, by the end of the first learning period Christopher was able with some effort to use non-manual negation. On the other hand, he consistently failed to produce the correct facial question markers. This contrasts with his results on comprehension tests involving negation and questions, where he performed at a level comparable with that of the comparator group.

As mentioned above, one area of BSL syntax that presented Christopher, but not the comparator group, with considerable difficulty was the comprehension and production of classifiers. This is of interest on two counts: the contrast between him and the controls and, more importantly, the asymmetry between different phenomena of BSL in Christopher himself. In section 4.6 below, we explore why BSL classifiers proved to be beyond Christopher's linguistic abilities, elaborating on theoretical and empirical arguments in the sign linguistics literature regarding the interface properties of classifiers.

We had expected him to acquire BSL morphology with considerable speed and ease, so we tested him and the comparator group on the inflectional complexities found in subject and object verb agreement. As was expected given his autism, Christopher used inflections involving the movement of a sign towards the location of present referents more easily and productively than towards abstract locations in sign space. That is, he showed greater facility in using deictic than anaphoric reference. Although he was able to mark some simple predicates through the use of locations, e.g. YOU-TELEPHONE-ME, there were several gaps in this aspect of his grammar. However, by the end of his exposure to BSL, his mastery of verb agreement was within normal learner limits, though his performance was closer to that of the lower-scoring learners in the comparator group (see section 4.5 below). The implication of this finding is that there is no evidence to support our prediction that his BSL verb morphology would be significantly better than his BSL syntax.

As his syntactic performance in his spoken second languages is primarily English-based we further expected Christopher to experience difficulty with BSL syntax where it differs from English. The results were in fact mixed. In simple BSL sentences he coped well with non-English-like BSL syntax, not showing much evidence for transfer, unlike many of the learners in the comparator group; but his ability appeared to be somewhat limited in more demanding linguistic tests. Our syntax tests concentrated on negation and question marking, enabling us to look at the combination of syntactic structure and its interaction with non-manual markers carried on the face and head. In section 4.5 we present these results and compare them with the overwhelming transfer effect found in spoken non-native languages that Christopher knows.

4.3   Non-verbal communication, gesture and iconicity

At the beginning of the study, Christopher had reported that he knew some signing, but when questioned further, this turned out to refer merely to the letters of the manual alphabet, which he claimed to have learnt from deaf people. On his first exposure to BSL proper, Christopher already manifested characteristics in his production and reception of sign which marked him out as an atypical learner. The most striking of these were his echopraxia (repetition of signs without understanding them) and his avoidance of direct eye-contact with the signers around him. It is relevant to point out that echopraxia, perhaps surprisingly, may not be a good predictor of high imitation abilities, because many children with autism (who show echolalia) are not good at non-word repetition tasks (Kjelgaard & Tager-Flusberg, 2001). Initially Christopher avoided gazing at his tutor's eyes, contenting himself with rapid glances at her face. For instance, in a narrative story-telling task, Christopher took one glance at the addressee at the beginning and then averted his eye-gaze for the thirty seconds of the story, with the result that he had great difficulty in understanding what was being reported, especially the roles of, and switches between, characters. This behaviour is presumably a function of his mild autism, though as studies of native autistic signers (e.g. Bonvillian *et al.*, 1981) had revealed that they can learn to produce, understand and combine signs, we predicted that Christopher should be able to learn BSL to a reasonable level.

By contrast, after the same amount of exposure, the members of the comparator group all looked at the addressee's face throughout the narrative. They too had periodic problems of comprehension, but these were easily accommodated, as the conversation partner could infer their lack of understanding from their expressions. A further indication of Christopher's atypicality is that, if something else attracted his attention (e.g. if he saw a foreign-language newspaper on the table while being taught), he would often look away when his interlocutor was in mid-sentence. When he did pay attention, he appeared to fixate on one topic, and attempts by the teacher to open up the conversation to more general areas were met by Christopher insisting on bringing it back to this earlier topic. This may be a further manifestation of the obsession associated with his autism.

In the discussion of iconicity in ch. 2 we referred to tests we had used on Christopher and the members of the comparator group. We report on these tests and their results here. Fifteen members of the comparator group[1] watched a video of a person signing twenty single signs, ten iconic and ten non-iconic. After each sign there was a pause in the video (a blank screen). The learners were instructed to wait till each pause and then to tick with a pen the picture that corresponded to the sign they had just seen. Each trial was recorded on a separate piece of paper in a stapled booklet with four possible alternatives to choose from. This format meant that the participants were not asked to make guesses entirely at random, as the test offered only four possible meanings for each sign. The results for this test are given in fig. 12 in which Christopher appears as the rightmost participant, designated 'CHRIS'.

One subject (CP) behaved like Christopher, but a group comparison contrasting the averaged scores of the fifteen members of the comparator group with Christopher's results shows a striking difference, as indicated in the graph in fig. 13.

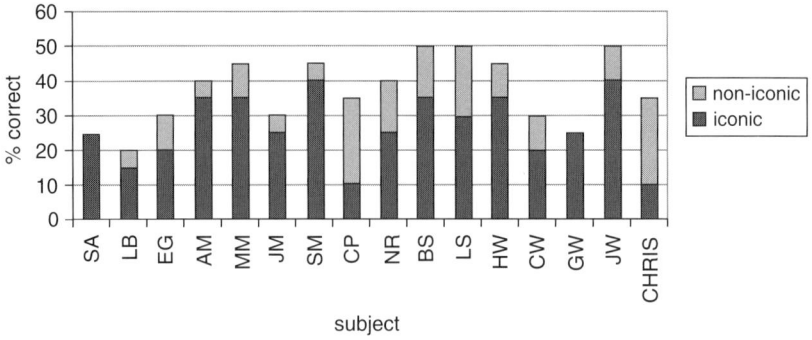

Figure 12 Identification of iconic and non-iconic signs

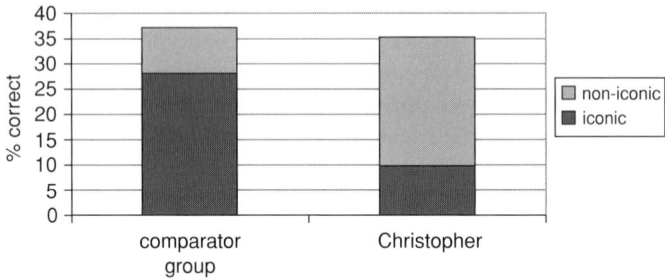

Figure 13 Identification of iconic and non-iconic signs: group comparison

The results of this initial test of sign comprehension were interesting. Christopher scored within the range defined by the comparator group but his judgements differed from theirs in two respects. First, he made abnormally quick responses as compared with the comparator group; second, the pattern of his results was idiosyncratic, as he guessed correctly more non-iconic than iconic signs. Of the twenty signs he was asked to judge, Christopher guessed two iconic signs and five non-iconic signs correctly for a total of seven (35%; chance was 25%). This compared with scores of between 20 per cent and 50 per cent correct on the same items by the comparator group. It is striking that, without any knowledge of BSL, some of the controls guessed half of the signs correctly and that Christopher scored above chance. This suggests that iconicity coupled with some knowledge of possible meaning is a powerful cue to understanding. However, Christopher's pattern of responses, with more non-iconic than iconic signs correct, may indicate that he approached this task in a somewhat different way to the majority of the comparator group.

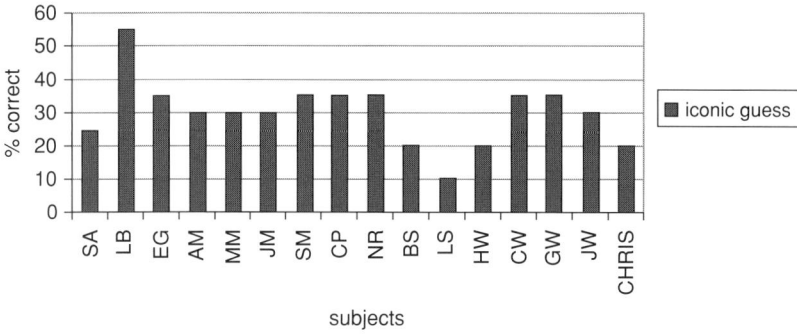

Figure 14 Percentage of wrong guesses that were guided by an iconic similarity between the sign and the picture foil

The decision as to whether judgements were determined by iconicity was based on the incorrect guesses made by the learners. If they were being guided by iconicity there should be some visually salient property of the sign which cued some aspect of the selected picture. For instance, the sign for SHARE might prompt learners to pick a picture of a door because the sign uses a gesture that could be interpreted as an image of a door opening. This type of selection was labelled 'iconic guess', and the percentage of iconic guesses made across all the learners is shown in fig. 14.

Figure 14 shows that Christopher appeared to have no preference for the iconic signs, but he did not ignore iconicity altogether. He selected pictures that had some iconic link in four of the twenty trials (20%) compared with iconic guesses in the comparator group of between 10 per cent and 55 per cent. Most of the comparator group (11/15, including the atypical subject CP) guessed iconically on six (30%) or more of the twenty trials. That is, Christopher made relatively fewer iconic guesses than the majority of the comparator group.

We also tested Christopher and the comparator group on their ability to describe different objects and actions through gesture. Performance on this test provides information about the production side of iconicity: the ability of learners to represent objects or actions by non-linguistic, gestural, means. This test was devised to reveal how expressive learners were in using mime before they had learned any signs or rules of BSL. It was expected that this task would show a difference between Christopher's typically non-communicative use of language and the more polished communicative skills of ordinary language learners.

In the test we showed all the learners forty pictures of entities and actions (e.g. a knife, a cow, an exhausted lady, a man fixing a bike) and we asked them to

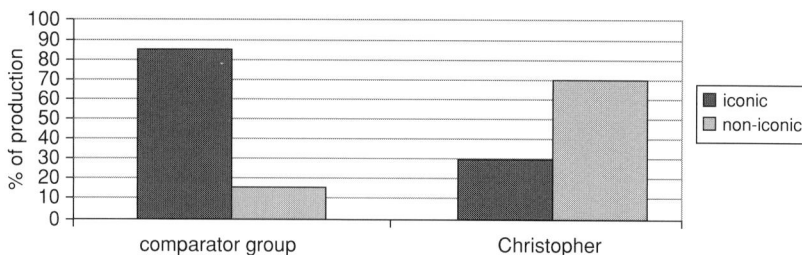

Figure 15 Production of iconic or non-iconic signs

come up with a gesture to describe what they saw in each picture. We coded the gestures as either a recognisably iconic representation (ICONIC), or as a non-recognisable non-iconic one (NON-ICONIC). These ratings simply reflected the transparency of the iconic representation. For example, if the picture was of a 'bus', gesturing the use of a steering wheel would be coded ICONIC and clapping your hands together would be coded as NON-ICONIC. The results are shown in fig. 15.

Christopher approached this test with no hesitations and immediately supplied gestures for each picture. This was in contrast with the controls who paused and considered their gestures and how to use them after each picture was presented. Moreover, his output was very different to that of the comparator group. The vast majority of their gestures (85%; range 80% to 90%) were plausibly interpretable as iconic representation of the entity or action depicted, in marked contrast with Christopher's score of 30 per cent. Thus there was a striking difference between the controls and Christopher in the number of non-iconic gestures produced in the test, the controls producing 15 per cent non-iconic gestures (range 10%–20%) versus Christopher's production of 70 per cent non-iconic gestures. Two caveats need to be entered when evaluating this performance. First, it is not possible to calculate a chance score because there was no restricted set of answers given in advance; second, Christopher's limb apraxia may have made some of his gestures look less iconic than he intended. Nonetheless, the contrast between Christopher and the comparator group is interesting.

As in the test of sign comprehension, Christopher seemed not to be exploiting the possibility of generating signs on the basis of their putative iconic relation to gestures. He was able to gesture some actions consistently, for example 'painting' (pretending to use a brush), 'typewriting' (imitating the hand movements), 'fork' (simulating eating) and 'smoke' (moving his hands up), but even these were often unusually formed. For example, when gesturing a picture of a cow he moved his flat hands onto the top of his head rather than indicating the horns by the more canonical movement of his hands away from his head.

The majority of his gestures were strange combinations of limb movements: for example, he gestured 'key' by drawing a large circle with a connected line in the air, 'dog' by licking his lips, 'knife' by rubbing his hands together and 'microphone' by pointing to the ground. All of these gestures could be thought of as having some connection with the referent but the link was too tenuous to be transparent.

By contrast, some examples of obviously iconic gestures from the comparator group were 'two hands open out' for 'window', 'hands make a flat surface then gesture the action of writing' for 'desk', 'flat hands move side to side' for 'skateboarding' and 'punch palm then turn hand over' for 'crashed car'. When the controls gave non-iconic responses it was because they were struggling to find an appropriate gesture.

It is of course possible that his non-iconic gestures were iconic for Christopher, with their iconicity based on some esoteric and private visual association, but compared with the controls' guesses they appeared markedly atypical. His performance on the production of iconicity paralleled his understanding of iconicity: when asked to guess the meaning of an unfamiliar sign he was unable to use the iconic route to come up with a sensible interpretation, even though in this case he was constrained to look for possible meanings in the picture stimuli he was presented with, rather than having to invent something on his own responsibility as he was in sign production.

As noted earlier, while Christopher's gestures were opaque and unlike those of the controls, this did not seem to inhibit him from gesturing. Indeed, he was very expressive and produced many gestures on request. Perhaps he thought his gesturing ability was high, as he did not hesitate to gesture when asked how one might sign a particular concept, but his enthusiasm for producing gestures was not matched by ability to understand them. The comparator group learners were able to offer many mimetic gestures for concepts, but reported that they found identifying the correct meaning for a novel sign more difficult. Despite this reported difficulty they were fairly successful at sign comprehension when given picture alternatives as cues.

The difference between Christopher and the controls lies in the extent to which the controls' presumably normal gestural and sign comprehension abilities were used. Although he was willing to gesture, Christopher's gestures were unrecognisable and, in comprehension, he appeared to be less successful in using an iconic link to a sign's meaning, even with pictures which guided this process. Nevertheless, his spontaneous attempt at gesture is surprising, as it contrasts markedly with the absence of gesturing when he is speaking. His willingness to gesture may be linked to the fact that he is aware of the arbitrariness of language units, whether these are signs or words. Knowing that BSL is a language like the spoken languages he is familiar with, he may not consider iconicity a useful guide to BSL production. A related observation is that during the entire twelve-month learning period Christopher (unlike all the controls) never exploited the opportunity to produce signs and spoken words at the same time.[2] For Christopher, English and BSL were separate and disjoint languages.

It is possible that the comprehension task would be equally demanding for children or those of limited intellect: that is, Christopher's performance may simply be a reflection of his reduced general intelligence. Yet learning and remembering vocabulary in many spoken languages is a particular strength of his. It is clearly the case that in order to identify the possible interpretation of an unfamiliar sign or gesture one needs to build on the intended meaning based on a chosen salient visual property. As discussed above, iconic signs pick out visual properties of referents (the whiskers for CAT, holding and turning a small object for KEY, crying for ONION) rather than attempting to describe every aspect of the action or object. Thus learners of signs have to be sensitive to possible links between visual properties inherent in concepts. In the comprehension task, subjects were required to compare these visual properties with the four candidate pictures presented. The problem for Christopher may have been that the task was too demanding in terms of keeping in mind the visual properties for long enough to compare them with the pictures and select the appropriate one. The task's complexity together with the predicted reduced role of iconicity in his use of language may be responsible for his poor performance. The production task, although relatively less complex, corroborates our initial suggestion that iconicity would facilitate performance in the comparator group due to its role in communication. Given Christopher's primarily non-communicative uses of language, the role of iconicity in gesture production was expected to be minimal.

4.4   Lexical development

Christopher's superb ability in learning and remembering vocabulary in his different spoken languages had led us to predict that he would be a good sign learner. Accordingly, we tested his lexical learning as reflected both in the comprehension and production of signs throughout the investigation. At the end of each period (see page 78) we selected two groups of twenty signs which he had seen in his classes during the relevant session (see app. 2, p. 190). For the measurement of sign comprehension he had to match a sign to an appropriate picture: his tutor signed each vocabulary item from one group of selected signs and Christopher had to point to the matching picture from a choice of four. For sign production we used the other group of signs and tested both whether he remembered them and the accuracy of his production of them. The tutor showed Christopher a picture, asked for the corresponding sign and scored the result accordingly. As with the tests where the subjects had to guess

tests of lexical signs

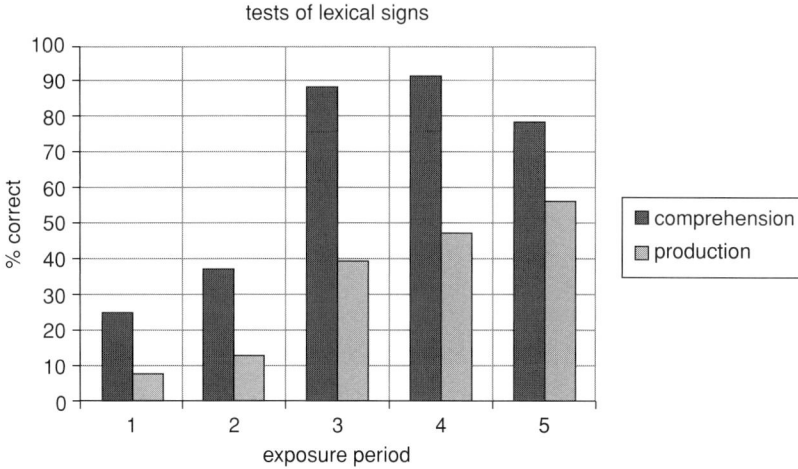

Figure 16 Tests of Christopher's comprehension of lexical signs

novel signs we checked his tutor's scoring by asking an independent native signer to identify Christopher's signs to show that they were recognisable out of context. We allowed two attempts at identifying the signs, as Christopher often looked away before he had seen a sign.

In each period, we focused on new vocabulary items that Christopher had been exposed to, so the vocabulary was different across the various periods of testing. Test scores for single sign comprehension and production are presented in fig. 16. As can be seen, Christopher made significant progress throughout the investigation, but his performance on comprehension eventually reached a plateau, whereas his productive ability continued to improve throughout (although it did not reach the level of his comprehension). Much of his core productive vocabulary was made up of signs he was able to produce easily despite his coordination problems: for example, signs such as BOOK, SIGN and DRIVE. His ability to produce recognisable signs increased steadily, and by period 5, he was producing over half (56%) of the signs in vocabulary tests correctly.

We were not able to test the comparator group on their comprehension and production of signs at all exposure periods. But we did test them at the start and end of the investigation. In period 1 we tested twenty participants on the comprehension and production of signs they had seen previously. We scored comprehension by their correct choice of a picture that corresponded to the sign when compared with alternatives. We scored production by rating the articulation of the sign, with all parameters correct scoring 1, with one parameter incorrect scoring 0.5, and with more than one parameter incorrect scoring zero.

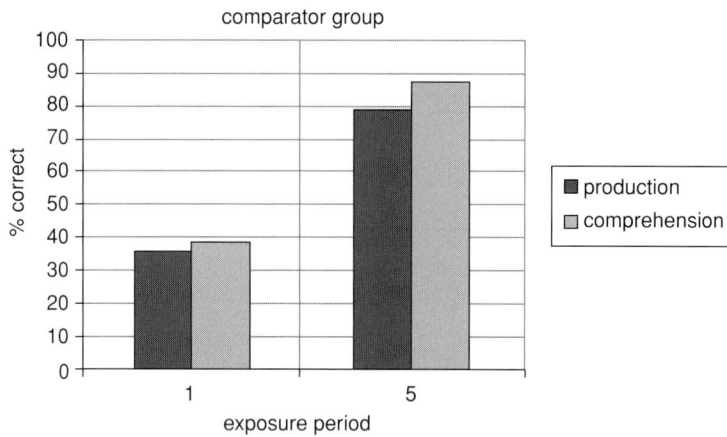

Figure 17 Comprehension and production of signs by the comparator group

In period 1 the mean correct score for sign comprehension was 38 per cent for twenty items (range 20%–55%), and for production the mean score was 36 per cent (range 30%–40%). Looking at fig. 16, we see that Christopher's initial score for sign comprehension was within the (lower end of the) comparator group range but his sign production was significantly impaired in comparison with the other learners. By period 5 the comparator group had made marked progress in their sign learning. In comprehension their mean score was 87.5 per cent correct (range 70%–100%) and production 79 per cent (range 65%–90%). Again, Christopher's sign production was weaker than the comparators' (56%) but his comprehension of single signs was again in the (lower end of the) range produced by the control subjects (78%) – see fig. 17.

One qualitative difference between Christopher's learning of BSL and that of the members of the comparator group was that he frequently gave evidence of having noticed all the formational parameters of a sign but, in production, failed to integrate them appropriately. Often one parameter was produced incorrectly, although in a subsequent attempt at producing the same sign this parameter might be correctly used, while another parameter previously selected correctly was incorrectly articulated. For example, the sign DOG in BSL is signed with both hands making small up and down movements in front of the signer at waist level. The handshape used is an H hand (the index and middle fingers are extended and they are touching each other). Christopher once signed DOG with his arms outstretched to the side but using the correct movement while on another occasion he used the correct location but moved his hands in circles rather than up and down. Another example was observed with the sign SISTER, articulated with the side of a bent index finger repeatedly tapping the bridge of the nose. Christopher used a flat handshape in the right location, but in subsequent conversation moved the location to his cheek while producing the right handshape. He showed similar behaviour in comprehension. Although he usually understood the signs correctly he once mistook the sign BEST for the sign GREEK (the signs have the same location), WAIT for DOG (the signs have similar movement), and the verb FISH for the verb COOK (the signs have a similar handshape). Strikingly, he once translated SISTER as 'rub your nose' despite having previously used and understood this sign some thirty times. This behaviour was radically different from the reaction of individuals in the comparator group when faced with novel signs. The default strategy by members of this group was to look for a plausible symbolic link between the form and its meaning. For example the sign SISTER might mean 'nosey' or 'curious' but not 'tap your nose'. The most common error in the comparator group was in articulating handshapes, while location and movements were mostly correct from the start of the learning period.

It is not clear whether Christopher had difficulty with the representation of sign parameters in his lexicon or was adopting some idiosyncratic and inconsistent way of accessing and producing signs. Both considerations may be relevant, though the latter is likely to be more important as his atypical signing is plausibly linked to his apraxia and his autism. However, this conclusion is not unproblematic, as Christopher's apparent failure to have recourse to sign iconicity when attempting to produce a sign suggests that his mental representation for the sign differed from that of the comparator group. For example, the sign DOG has a visual link to the movement of the paws of a dog. We know from other examples that Christopher had considerable difficulty in using the iconic properties of signs, so each time he attempted to sign DOG he had to remember the bare phonological form of the sign, while the comparator group could use some mnemonic strategies associated with the iconic features of the sign. Indeed, the members of the comparator group quickly learned to produce the sign accurately and often verbalised their memorisation strategy, such as 'it looks like the movement of a dog'.

This difficulty with integrating visually presented linguistic information either within a sign or at the level of the sentence was reinforced by the absence of a written form of BSL. It is clear that Christopher's exceptional ability in learning the vocabulary of spoken languages is partly dependent on the availability of such a written form. As all the information to be processed in BSL occurs fast and with rapid signal decay he had great difficulty in retrieving it *in toto* after its presentation. Despite this, the fact that some parameters of a sign's formation were retrievable, even if different ones on different occasions, implies that Christopher could store the sign essentially correctly. Individual sign production was presumably compromised by his apraxia and a lack of sufficient exposure to signs.

The relatively better performance in sign production by most of the members of the comparator group can be accounted for by the fact that their motor abilities, both gross and fine, are intact, and also in part by their ability to exploit the iconicity of some signs as a memorisation strategy. Even with non-iconic signs, or signs with reduced iconicity, the comparator group could memorise and imitate the movements in a sign better than Christopher, whose autism compromised his abilities. Since iconicity seemed to be largely irrelevant to his perception of signs, we can surmise that the representation of signs, both iconic and non-iconic, in his BSL was somewhat different from that of the average control.

Finally, the contrast between Christopher's inability to produce stretches of signed utterances and his relative ability to decode such sequences is common in language development, both native and non-native. Overall, his comprehension demonstrated knowledge of many more sign meanings than was evident from his production, and in some domains his comprehension was within normal levels for sign learners of his experience.

4.5   Morpho-syntax

In the following sections, we document Christopher's and some of the comparator group's comprehension in each area of BSL that we tested. The comparator group subjects took the same tests as Christopher, and their results are presented as group data. In addition, we give samples of the production data from each area of BSL in order to provide a comparison between Christopher and the comparator group's semi-spontaneous signing (guided interaction between control subjects, or between the teacher and a control subject). As the various BSL constructions were taught in different learning periods, the sample production data are drawn from the period during which the phenomenon was taught. Thus, there are data from the first two periods on questions and negation, but no data on classifiers from the same time, as classifiers were the last subject taught in the BSL syllabus.

4.5.1   Word-order

In his acquisition of various spoken 'second' languages, Christopher had shown a systematic tendency to transfer English syntax onto the syntax of the languages he was learning (see Smith & Tsimpli, 1995: 157–64). Although we had anticipated similar transfer effects in his learning of BSL, this expectation was surprisingly not fulfilled in general, as can be seen in the following examples of his spontaneous signing from the earliest stages, in which he successfully

produced a variety of orders impossible in English. Examples (1–4) were from
period 1, examples (5–8) from period 2, examples (9–12) from period 3. We
have used italics for all examples signed by Christopher and normal capitals
for BSL examples produced by anyone else.

(1)	*ME BUTTER EAT*	– 'I eat butter'
(2)	*ORANGE LIKE*	– 'I like oranges'
(3)	*BRUSH-TEETH LIKE*	– 'I like brushing my teeth'
(4)	*SANDWICH MAKE LIKE*	– 'I like making sandwiches'
(5)	*SWIM CAN ME*	– 'I can swim'
(6)	*BELIEVE HE ME*	– 'He believes me'
(7)	*UNDERSTAND HE ME*	– 'He understands me'
(8)	*FRUIT LIKE ME*	– 'I like fruit'
(9)	*LIKE ME MOW-LAWN*	– 'I like mowing the lawn'
(10)	*SIGNING WORK YOU*	– 'Your job is signing' [addressed to his teacher]
(11)	*ME TWO BROTHER*	– 'I have two brothers'
(12)	*MALTON LIVE ME*	– 'I live in Malton'

This apparent facility with a new word-order extended to negative sentences
including (O)V(S) order as in (13–17):

(13)   __hs
TELEVISION WATCH   – 'I don't watch TV'

(14)   ____hs
CHEESE   EAT   ME   – 'I don't eat cheese'

(15)   _____hs
ME SIGN   – 'I don't sign'

(16)   __hs
BEER (DRINK)   ME   – 'I don't (drink) beer'

(17)   __hs
FRENCH SPEAK   HE   – 'He doesn't speak French'

The transcription of non-manual actions in these examples is to be interpreted
as follows. In (13) the line spreading from the end of the sign WATCH indicates
the scope of the head-shake, which was produced after the manual signing had
finished. In contrast, in (14) the head-shake extended over the manual sign EAT
and into the transition between EAT and ME; and in (16) the head-shake was
produced between the signs BEER and ME.

Table 2 *Performance on BSL word-order in declarative and interrogative sentences by the comparator group*

Period and number of participants	Interrogatives		Declaratives	
	Target	Non-target (English)	Target	Non-target (English)
I (N=6)	58	2 (3%)	54	9 (14%)
II (N=6)	45	9 (16.6%)	40	17 (30%)

It is significant that when prompted to comment on BSL sign order, Christopher's (signed) responses revealed correct metalinguistic knowledge of the language, as illustrated in (18):

(18) a   NS: 'What order did you do the signs in?'
          C: *NAME ME CHRIS*   –   'My name is "Chris"'
     b   BW: 'Can you remember the order for questions?'
          C: *YOU NAME WHAT*   –   'What is your name?'
          C: *YOU HOW-OLD YOU*   –   'How old are you?'

Although his sign-order was more target-like than English-like, throughout the learning period he very rarely used any facial expression.

There was a tendency among members of the comparator group for English word-order to be transferred more frequently than was the case with Christopher and, as shown in table 2, more frequently in declarative clauses than in interrogative clauses. We suggest that this rather surprising result could be due to two factors: the presence of the syntactic Q feature in interrogatives – a property which triggers word-order changes in many languages, and the interpretive differences associated with interrogative clauses in general. That is, L2 learners are more likely to notice and learn a new word-order in interrogatives than in declaratives, so the higher percentage of English word-order used in declarative BSL sentences may not be fortuitous.

Typical conversational examples of their production of interrogatives and declaratives are given in (19) and (20) from periods 1 and 2 respectively:[3]

(19)   A: COME BRITAIN BIKE YOU   – 'Did you come to Britain by bike?'
        B: NO COME BRITAIN   – 'No, I came to Britain by plane'
           (says 'aeroplane' in English)
        A: gestures plane flying
        B: PLANE-FLY   – 'I came by plane'

(20)   B: YOU CAN MOTORBIKE   – 'Can you ride a motorbike?'
        A: *I CAN-NOT MOTORBIKE   – 'I cannot ride a motorbike'

Table 3 *Negative markers used by Christopher per learning period*

Negative markers	P1	P2	P3	P4	P5
Neg-incorporation (including overuse)	4	11			
Incorrect omission of neg-incorporation	1	8	3	1	2
Negation sign	5	2		8	
Head-shake across sign	2	14	4	11	5
Final head-shake	1	2	2		2

In (20) B's question should have had the order in (21):

(21)   YOU RIDE-MOTORBIKE CAN

and A's response (ungrammatical in BSL) shows a direct transfer of English word-order to BSL.

4.5.2   The face: negation and questions

We have mentioned more than once that Christopher found the use of facial action, especially its coordination with manual signing, difficult. This had a particularly adverse effect on his mastery of negation and questions, both of which make crucial use of such facial action.

4.5.2.1   Negation   As documented in ch. 2, BSL expresses negation in three ways: internal to the sign (incorporation), e.g. KNOW-NOT, HAVE-NOT; through a supra-segmental negation marker (head-shake); and by means of a separate manual negation sign, e.g. NOTHING. Combinations of the three are also possible.

Across the five periods of learning, Christopher used all these three negation devices in his spontaneous signing, and the incidence of each is presented in table 3. To avoid skewing the results, we have excluded from this table the large number of Christopher's uses of the head-shake alone, including only its use in conjunction with other manifestations of negation. As is described in more detail later, once Christopher had mastered the head-shake, he used it in contexts which normally require some additional manual element, as in (22). Note that a head-shake alone would be an acceptable response in informal use of BSL.

(22) a
```
                     _____bf
     teacher:        COOK YOU    –   'Can you cook?'
     Christopher:    head-shake  –   'No'
```

Rather than:

b   _____hs
           COOK I   –   'No, I can't'

All the judgements were, as usual, based on native signers' evaluation of Christopher's BSL utterances.

In period 1, Christopher used a combination of negation devices, as illustrated in (23). He used the manual negation signs NO and NOT-YET, as well as some verbs with negation incorporated into the sign, e.g. KNOW-NOT, WANT-NOT, AGREE-NOT. Occasionally, he overused this option, forming verbs with incorporated negation which disallow it in BSL, as in example (23a); and in one session (after three hours of exposure), he produced an ungrammatical as well as a grammatical use of negation for the same verb, as shown in (23 a and b):

(23) a   * *ME WATCH-NOT*   –   'I don't watch TV'
    b   _hs
    [= (13)]   *TELEVISION WATCH*   –   'I don't watch TV'

Although the use of the head-shake in (23b) is grammatical, it is unusual for it to follow rather than to be produced simultaneously with the verb. Throughout the first period, Christopher tended to separate the sign and the negation, producing head-shake-final sentences as well as head-shakes without signs. On occasion, however, he was able to combine the head-shake with other signs, as in (14) and (15) above, repeated as (24):

(24) a   ____hs
       CHEESE   EAT   ME   –   'I don't eat cheese'
    b   ____hs
       ME SIGN   –   'I don't sign'

This use of head-shakes may appear relatively simple, but his mastery of it is impressive when considered in comparison with his general lack of head-movement gestures in his use of spoken languages. It is also impressive when one considers his results on the Kimura movement copy test of non-representational gesture mentioned above (section 1.3.2), which show that he had major difficulties in controlling the movement of his head and face. For example, to show the action of sneezing he merely moved his hand to his face, and to show a kiss, he kissed his own hand. In another trial on this test he could not move his eyes up without simultaneously moving his whole head. These results suggest that his apraxia was severe but eventually overcome to some degree in his use of negation in BSL. Nevertheless, there was little use of facial expression in his production of negative BSL sentences.

During period 2, there was rapid development of Christopher's use of negation markers, and he produced twenty-nine negated sentences. He used appropriately verbs with incorporated negation, including HAVE-NOT and CAN-NOT, but at the same time he continued to over-generalise this strategy to verbs which are subject to a language-particular morphological constraint which disallows negative-incorporation, e.g. *DRINK-NOT, *WATCH-NOT and *EAT-NOT. Further, his previous use of the supra-segmental head-shake marker was typically replaced by a preference for using a head-shake between the object and the verb, as in (25):

(25) a   __hs
         *BEER (DRINK)   ME   –   'I don't (drink) beer'
                                   __hs
      b   FRENCH SPEAK   HE   –   'He doesn't speak French'

Although not fully acceptable in BSL, Christopher's production of such sentences indicates that, at the relevant stage of his BSL development, he was attributing morphological status to the head-shake marker of negation. This replacement of the supra-segmental head-shake by the purely morphological is consistent with his general difficulty in perceiving and producing supra-segmental features both in spoken languages and in BSL. Christopher also produced ungrammatical utterances with verbs which require incorporated negation. These signs can be accompanied by a head-shake but in his errors of this type he typically omitted the (incorporated) negation on the verb and used only the head-shake. There were five examples of this error, including those in (26):

(26) a   _____hs
         *WANT ME   –   'I don't want'
      b   _____hs
         *BELIEVE ME   –   'I don't believe'

Christopher's use of the head-shake with different types of verbs provides further evidence that it has morphological status in his sign language. Thus, in period 2, Christopher uses both incorporated negation (a bound morpheme) and the head-shake (a free morpheme) to encode negation. That mastering negation caused him some problems – presumably a reflection of the inherent complexity of negative sentences – is shown by the fact that there were several examples where he dropped verbs or other signs in his production of negative sentences, as in (25a), where he omitted the parenthesised DRINK. This dropping of signs suggests that he is not simply using English syntax translated into sign; rather, the source of the omission may be due to difficulty in signing caused by general production demands exacerbated by his apraxia.

The first two examples showing multiple negation markers appeared in this period after 6–8 hours of sign exposure, when Christopher combined head-shakes with the negation signs NO and NOTHING. The correct form he was aiming at is shown in (27a); Christopher's production can be seen in (27b) where the form 'NO' is the same as the sign used in yes-no questions. This was the most complex negation produced up to this point.

(27) a
                   _____hs

      CHEESE LIKE-NOT   YOU   –   'You don't like cheese'

   b
                       ___hs

      *CHEESE NO LIKE   YOU   –   'You don't like cheese'

In Christopher's production of (27b), negation is not incorporated into the verb 'LIKE' (i.e. LIKE-NOT), and the head-shake appears between the verb and the pronoun rather than simultaneously with the verb, just as with the V NEG (Subject) pattern in (25). In the target sentence (27a), the simultaneous production of the negated verb with the head-shake requires an analysis of the head-shake not as a morphological but as a supra-segmental marker of negation, something which was probably not part of Christopher's BSL grammar at this period.

In period 3 (10–15 hours of sign exposure), Christopher's signing was generally reduced, and he used fewer negation markers than in any other stage. He used only head-shake markers, with one example combining two negation markers: a head-shake both before and after the verb: *hs *LIKE* hs. Throughout this period, he continued to use citation forms of verbs with a head-shake, rather than modifying the sign to incorporate negation.

At the end of the programme we gave both Christopher and the comparator group two tests on the comprehension of negation. In the first test (referred to as 'NEG' below) we tested them on video-taped signed utterances with and without negative elements. The task was to pick the appropriate picture, e.g. 'the dog without the bone' from a set of four possible alternatives after having looked at a signed sentence. In the second negation test ('NEG*') we constructed a grammaticality judgement task involving signed sentences with negation on the verb, where half of the sentences involved ungrammatical combinations of the negative marker and the manual sign: e.g. *EAT-NOT. Christopher's performance in comparison with the mean score of the members of the comparator group is indicated in fig. 18.

As is clear from fig. 18, Christopher scored within normal limits on both tests. In the NEG task, he correctly identified thirteen out of fourteen negation

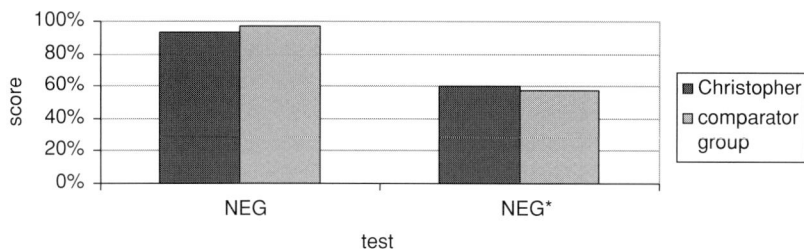

Figure 18 Relative scores of Christopher and the comparator group on two tests of negation

markers (93%). As chance was 50 per cent, his scores are comparable to the range of scores from the comparator group (between 86% and 100%; SD 4.8). In the NEG* task he scored six out of ten correct (chance again was 50%), compared with scores of 30 per cent to 80 per cent by the comparator group (SD 15.3).

Although in this final period his production of negatives was reduced, Christopher's performance on tests of comprehension was comparable to that of other learners. Moreover, although his production still included ungrammatical uses of negation markers, his grammaticality judgements suggest that his BSL development is within the range of the comparator group. In period 4, after 15–20 hours of exposure, Christopher produced nineteen negated utterances, eleven of which were marked appropriately by means of a head-shake simultaneous with the manual sign. He also seemed to be experimenting with the positioning of the head-shake when this was combined with other signs. We observed variation in his use of this marker, placing it before the sign, as in (28a), between the verb and the object, as in (28b), or correctly articulated over the signs, as in (28c):

(28) a   __hs
            ME LIKE   –   'I don't like'
      b   __hs
            RUGBY (LIKE)   *YOU*   –   'You don't (like) rugby'
      c   _____hs
            HAT NOTHING   –   'There's no hat'

Although the number of tokens of negation markers Christopher produced was relatively small, it would seem that by period 4 the head-shake was being correctly grammaticalised as the marker of negation in his BSL. Even though there was still some evidence (in the variation of its order with respect to the verb) for the morphological, rather than supra-segmental, status of the head-shake, he now used it not just as an independent segmental morpheme but as a supra-segmental feature, produced simultaneously with a manual sign. The scope of the head-shake was almost exclusively limited to single signs, rather than extended across multi-sign combinations, as would be common in fluent users of BSL. As this simultaneous pattern was also attested in period 5, we may tentatively conclude that the use of negatives from periods 4 and 5 marks a transition from the morphological to the target status of the head-shake in Christopher's BSL. An alternative possibility is that the head-shake had a dual status in Christopher's grammar at this stage, being optionally either a morphological marker or a supra-segmental feature.

Although it would be odd in a spoken language, this dual status could be related to the gestural nature of the head-shake in his developing BSL grammar. In the final period, five of his seven negations were expressed through a head-shake across the sign, but he continued to make errors in using head-shakes where a verb should have been modified by incorporated negation. Two examples of this from his spontaneous signing are shown in (29), where he appears to have adopted the strategy of using just a head-shake without negative incorporation. As with other aspects of his signing (e.g. questions), this reduced production relied for its successful interpretation on rich exploitation of context.

(29) a   _____hs
      *WANT   –   'I don't want'
    b   _____hs
      (b) *LIKE   –   'I don't like'

As we suspected that Christopher might be more competent with negation than was observable in his spontaneous signing, towards the latter stage of his BSL learning we tested his ability to repeat some thirty negated sentences more complex than those he had previously produced himself. His tutor (A) signed the sentence, and Christopher had to repeat it 'sign-for-sign' including all the non-manual elements. The same patterns observed in his spontaneous signing appeared across the thirty negated sentences. He often delayed the negating head-shake to the end of his signed sentence, as in (30), and in several sentences he omitted parts of the target sentence in his repetitions, as in (31) where he failed to reproduce the inflection for subject and object agreement on the verb HELP:

(30)   _____hs
      A: CINEMA   ME CAN-NOT GO – 'I can't go to the cinema'
                              __hs
      C: CINEMA ME CAN-NOT GO   – 'I can't go to the cinema'

(31) a   A: HOME-WORK TEACHER   –   'The teacher didn't help
          _____hs   me with my homework'
          ₃HELP-ME₁   –
                    __hs
          C: *ME TEACHER*   –   'The teacher didn't (help
                                            with my homework) me'

     b   _____hs
          A: CAR FATHER₃ ₃HELP-MEᵦ ME₁ –   'My father didn't help
                                            me with my car'
                         __hs
          C: *CAR FATHER ME*   –   'My father didn't (help)
                                            me (with my car)'

Even when his tutor attempted explicitly to correct his omissions, Christopher
persisted in producing the reduced sentence, as shown in (32):

(32)   _____hs
          A: ₃HELP-ME₁   –   '(he) didn't help me'
                      __hs
          C: *CAR FATHER ME*   –   'My father didn't (help) me (with
                                            my car)'

We return now to a discussion of how best to interpret Christopher's changing
use of negation. In more complex negative sentences he seemed to be unable
to process the sign semantically to retain the correct scope. We suggested
above that he was progressing in his use of the head-shake from treating it
as a purely morphological feature to treating it as a supra-segmental feature.
However, the fact that he failed to use the head-shake as a supra-segmental
feature in the imitation task indicates that its linguistic status for him was
different from its status in the target language. In other words, his inability to
produce the head-shake as a supra-segmental feature forces an analysis of it as
a morphological element equivalent to 'not' or the anaphoric negator 'no', as is
in fact characteristic of cases in BSL where the head-shake is used on its own
without any accompanying manual sign.

If the head-shake across signs is indeed a morphological negative, rather than
a supra-segmental scope marker, it suggests that Christopher has identified
the head-shake as a productive affix in the syntax, while the incorporated
negative in KNOW-NOT is lexical only. In other words, he uses only one
productive, syntactic affix in his BSL, the head-shake. In turn, this suggests
that he has over-generalised this form of affixal negation, thereby giving rise
to a more consistent grammar in his mind, in that KNOW-NOT type verbs,
with incorporated negation, are subject to a lexical rule rather than a general
morphological rule. This lexical analysis of incorporated negation is reinforced

Table 4 *Negative markers used by the comparator group*

Period & number of learners	Total number of negatives	Negative sign (manual)	V+Neg	Head-shake on BSL sentence	Head-shake without BSL sentence, mouthing or gesturing negation
Period 1 (N=6)	30	23	10	3	10
Period 2 (N=6)	23	9	8	15	12

by the input where some, but not all, BSL verbs have an incorporated negative form. Because of the unpredictable nature of the input, Christopher attributed lexical status to the incorporated negated verbs, treating them as comparable to 'refuse' and 'deny' which have an inherently negative meaning in English. Assuming that target BSL includes incorporated negation as a morphological process, the implication is that Christopher has not as yet figured out the semantic class of verbs which are negated in this way. The examples which he over-generalised to show incorporated negation on verbs which disallow it in BSL were restricted and included verbs which occasionally appear negated with a head-shake (e.g. WATCH). It is perhaps significant that there is a semantic link between WATCH and verbs which use incorporated negation. These verbs encode the semantic function of agent or experiencer, and WATCH can be interpreted as AGENT + EXPERIENCE.

The pattern in Christopher's development of negation was not characteristic of the members of the comparator group. Their performance on negative sentences shows that they produced verbs with incorporated negation right from period 1, as can be seen in table 4.

Many of these negative utterances included more than one expression of negation, as is typical in BSL; hence the total number of negative sentences is smaller than the sum of the individual expressions of negation. For instance, a verb with incorporated negation could include a negative gesture or a head-shake at the same time. It is important to note that throughout this period negative signs were used for verbs both with and without incorporated negation, and that Christopher's common error of using incorporated negation on verbs that did not allow it was not found in the members of the comparator group. They used only a very restricted number of negative verbs, namely LIKE-NOT and WANT-NOT, indicating that they had learned them as separate items rather than as the output of a productive rule. The head-shake was used either independently or together with gesturing or mouthing of negation. This was markedly different from Christopher's production of the head-shake, which had become the main marker of negation in his BSL grammar. A negation form like NOT (which can be signed with a side to side movement of the head) is likely to have been linguisticised in BSL from a gesture (just like the head tilt in Greek SL). Learners using such forms may either be inserting gestural material into the sentence or they may not have recognised the difference between linguistic and gestural forms in such cases. As the difference between the comparator group and Christopher is consistent with his reduced use of gestures in both his native and non-native (spoken) languages, we think that he was treating the head-shake in BSL as a linguistic element from the start, whereas the comparator group fluctuated between ascribing it linguistic and non-linguistic status.

Some examples from the production of negatives by the comparator group in periods 1 and 2 are presented below. It should be noted that most examples showed negation as marked by shaking the hand or a finger, i.e. gesturing rather than signing. In (33) both examples show incorporated negation:

(33) a   E: WANT-NOT DRIVE   –   'I don't want to drive'
     b   D: YOU m-i-s-s u-s-a   –   'Do you miss the USA?'
         E: NO LIKE-NOT LIKE   –   'No, I don't like (USA), I like
            ENGLAND   England'

(34) a   E: CAN YOU MOTORBIKE   –   'Can you ride a motorbike?'
         D: MOTORBIKE gestures 'no'   –   'No, but I can ride a bicycle'
            shakes hand and mouths 'but'
            CAN CYCLE
     b   B: I WANT-NOT HOUSE   –   'I don't want (to go to) the
                                                            house'

                           _____hs
         I: waves hand WANT-NOT   –   gestures 'no, don't want (to
             HOME HOUSE   go) home, the house'
     c   E: YOU (pl) DRIVE HOME   –   'you all drive home, the
            HOUSE   house?'
         D: I NEVER HOME HOUSE   –   'I never (go) home, the house'
         D: I NEVER DRIVE   –   'I don't drive'
                            _____bf
         D: I HAVE (mouths 'no') CAR   –   'I have no car'
         ___hs
         D: ME HAVE-NOT BLUE   –   'No, I haven't a blue pen'
                PEN

Further evidence for Christopher's problems with negation is provided by a translation task which was administered to him and the comparator group at the end of the programme. We tested his ability to translate BSL sentences into written English, and we compared these translations with translations into English from some of his other second languages, specifically Greek and Spanish. Examples are provided in (35). Although his understanding and production of negation markers in BSL was comparable to that of the other learners, he experienced more difficulty where sentences involved additional components of BSL grammar (such as agreement in (35b)):

(35) a   _____t

                              _____hs

        Teacher: PLAY-PIANO SISTER KNOW-HOW
        'As for playing the piano, my sister doesn't know how to'
        C: Sister did not play any piano.

     b   _____t

                         _____hs

        Teacher: MY BIRTHDAY HUSBAND IX COOK   NO
        'As for my birthday, my husband didn't cook anything'
        C: Her husband hates his birthdays

     c   _____t

                    _____hs

        Teacher: NEW PUB m-a-r-y GO   NO
        'Mary didn't go to the new pub'
        C: Mary hates a pub

These examples show that Christopher's translations were unlike those he produced from written input in his spoken languages (see Smith & Tsimpli, 1995: 156ff.). In particular, his translations from BSL to English are not word-for-sign or literal. It is also interesting that, although he failed to translate the negative sign in (35b, c), his choice of the verb 'hate', with its inherently negative meaning, suggests that he may have perceived the negation sign in the original BSL sentence, but for phonological reasons had misidentified the signs for the verbs COOK and GO. This is further evidence suggesting that Christopher assigns lexical status to manual negation adjacent to the verb. That is, he seems to have taken the 'NO' sign as negating the verb lexically rather than syntactically and hence translates it with a semantically negative verb.

In these translation tasks, there seem to have been two factors which affected Christopher's processing of BSL negation. First, he often mis-analysed signs, either because of their phonological similarity to other signs or his inability to analyse the sign according to all its formational parameters (see section 4.4 above). Second, as a special case of this mis-analysis he sometimes based his translation on a literal (visual) representation of the sign: for instance, mistaking the sign SISTER for 'rub your nose' and MIRROR for 'wave your hand'.

Although Christopher was able to identify negation markers, his general problem with processing longer stretches of sign compromised his ability to translate negated elements correctly. An example of translation involving the sign CAN, which he had used several times and which was clearly part of his productive vocabulary, will serve to illustrate this tension. In a sentence including this sign *and* a negation marker, Christopher translated CAN as 'nose', making a visual error caused by the fact that the location of the sign for CAN is close to the nose.[4] Such errors highlight the difficulties he experienced with the non-written form of linguistic input, which he seemed unable to retain in his processing system for an adequate length of time. As he does not have this processing problem with spoken languages it must be caused by constraints on his visuo-spatial processor or by visual memory problems.

That a processing capacity problem may be relevant is also suggested by the fact that Christopher had difficulty in retaining signs from the beginning of a sentence long enough to let him see the whole sentence, process it and then translate it. It was apparent that the first signs produced by the tutor were often omitted in the translations, with BSL signs proving more of a burden on his visual memory than comparable examples from Greek and Spanish presented in a more permanent written form. That is, having to deal with complex signed sentences had an adverse effect on his ability to process and retain negation. A perennial problem for Christopher with BSL input was that it is not written, imposing time and complexity restrictions on its perception and analysis. If learners have difficulties perceiving and analysing all the information in a sign, it is obviously difficult for them to store and repeat it. This processing overload may also contribute to the misperceptions arising from phonological similarity between the sign presented and other signs known to him, making his translations intermittently far from target or pragmatically odd.

In such cases, Christopher sometimes resorted to a word-for-sign translation strategy, ignoring plausibility effects at the sentence level. This mirrors his performance in other languages, where misperception and incorrect translation are due to a variety of factors: for instance, his weak central coherence prevents him from inhibiting an inappropriate response, and he may be misled by a spelling similarity between the word to be translated and another word in English (see Smith & Tsimpli, 1995: 157ff. for examples). We can thus conclude that the translation data, although interesting for a number of reasons, do not give an unambiguous indication of Christopher's underlying knowledge of the grammatical or lexical properties of negation. They do, however, offer important converging evidence – with that from all of his 'second' languages – to the effect that his language processor appears to suffer from deficiencies in capacity.

4.5.2.2 Questions As with negation, Christopher's mastery of BSL questions was undermined by his failure to use appropriate facial action. Across the five learning periods he used the question signs WHAT, WHERE and

WHEN regularly but, apart from one example, he used no accompanying facial action. The incidence of his use of questions in his spontaneous signing is shown in table 5, which includes the total number of utterances used with a question function, as expressed either through the use of a question sign (Wh-interrogatives) or through sign-order (Yes-No interrogatives).

In the first class of period 1, Christopher had to repeat short sentences offered to him by a deaf signer (EF), as illustrated in (36). As these were Wh-questions, EF used a furrowed brow (bf) simultaneously with the signs. As before, the horizontal line shows the scope of the Wh-marker across the manual signs. However, Christopher's response in (36b) shows no appropriate brow furrow.

(36) a   _____bf
         EF: HELLO NAME YOU WHAT   – 'Hello, what's your name?'
   b   C: *HELLO NAME ME WHAT*   – 'Hello, what's my name?'

It is important to note that Christopher was not asked to answer the question, but was supposed to repeat the sentence verbatim. It is characteristic of BSL classes at this level to be taught like this, with attempts made to shape the students' signing. Interestingly, Christopher did not point away from himself to indicate 'YOU', but pointed at himself, 'ME', copying the direction rather than the meaning of the personal pronoun. We cannot, of course, be certain that he had properly understood the instruction 'Now you do the same'. Nevertheless, all of the comparator subjects carried out the instruction without difficulty, and none of them reproduced the kind of anomalous result shown in (36b).

The total absence of facial action accompanying the sign sequence is parallel to the general absence of paralinguistic and facial expression from Christopher's spoken languages. However, it is important to note that, just as he is sensitive to intonational differences in his reception of spoken input, he does pick up on some facial grammar in his comprehension of questions and negation markers. Although Christopher made no use of the facial action needed to signal questions he did place the Wh-sign correctly at the end of the sentence. This might have been purely imitative in the first example (36b), as his response a few minutes later to the suggestion that he 'maybe ask [EF] now' was the ungrammatical *WHAT NAME YOU NAME – 'What's your name, name?' However, as we saw in the section on word-order above, when asked in English about the order of the signs he had used, he replied correctly in sign, as shown in (18), repeated here as (37), and generalised the pattern to new question types, as in the correct (38):

(37) a   NS: 'What order did you do the signs in?'
          C: *NAME ME CHRIS*
   b   BW: 'Can you remember the order for questions?'
          C: *YOU NAME WHAT*

(38)   C: *YOU HOW-OLD YOU*   – 'How old are you?'

Table 5 *Interrogative utterances produced by Christopher per learning period*

Interrogative utterances	P1	P2	P3	P4	P5
Total Wh-questions (with or without a Wh-sign)	25	5		24	29
Wh-sign used	13	4		9	13
Wh-final	5	2		7	7
Wh-sign not used	12	1		15	16
With facial action				1 (the *bald* example)	
Yes-No questions	2	3		9	1

Looking in more detail at the questions used in period 1, it seems that although Christopher used Wh-signs appropriately in the copying tasks, many examples of questions produced in spontaneous signing were articulated without a Wh-sign. As with negation, he relied – consciously or unconsciously – on the context to make himself understood. For example, after being asked his age he attempted to ask the same question, but only managed to sign: AGE YOU, a sequence which, in an appropriate context, is an acceptable and interpretable question in BSL. In fact, most of his putative Wh-questions produced without Wh-signs were correctly interpreted by the person he was signing to. Other examples are given in (39), where (39c) was his attempt to respond to a question about which languages he knew with the same question to his interlocutor:

(39) a   *AGE YOU WIFE YOU*   –   '(What is) your wife's age?'
     b   *YOU SPORT YOU*   –   'Do you (play) sports?'
     c   *LANGUAGES YOU*   –   '(Which) languages do you (know)?'

We have not included such sentences in the numbers in table 5 and there were not enough occurrences of spontaneous production of Wh-questions in the early periods for us to conclude that Christopher had mastered Wh-final before period 4.

In period 2 there were few examples of spontaneously produced questions, and in general he used question syntax inconsistently. He often appeared to ask questions omitting the relevant signs, such as: *BROTHER YOU*. He had previously been asked if he had brothers or sisters, and his signed sequence here was therefore plausibly interpreted as 'Do you have a brother?' In none of these examples did he make any recognisable use of facial action to signal the question function.

In period 4, after fifteen hours of sign exposure, we observed considerably more signed sentences involving question forms (24 tokens). Of the nine examples of Wh-questions, seven showed correct BSL order: i.e. a question-final

Wh-sign. The remaining two examples were produced with the Wh-sign in the middle of the sentence, as in *AGE WHAT YOU*. Even this may be due in part to the fact that YOU often occurs in sentence-final position as an indication that the signer is relinquishing his or her turn.

It is significant that in this period none of the nine Wh-questions had a Wh-sign in initial position: that is, none had the word-order characteristic of English questions. This is despite the fact that there had been some occurrences of initial Wh- in his spontaneous signing, and Wh-signs can occur initially in BSL, though when they do there is usually another Wh-marker at the end of the sentence.

The complexity of his question forms also became gradually more sophisticated in this period. After sixteen hours of BSL, Christopher asked his sign tutor: *YOU MOTHER FATHER LIVE* '(Where) do your mother and father live?' and after nineteen hours, he asked: *MAN BEARD NAME WHAT* 'What's the man with the beard's name?' It was also in this period that we observed Christopher's single use of facial action for asking a question. After his tutor had spoken about her father, Christopher signed:

(40)   _____br
         BALD   –   'Is (he) bald?'

In period 5, Christopher continued to use the correct sign-order in most utterances containing Wh-signs, but he persisted in asking the majority of his questions without any question signs. This reliance on the pragmatic context is illustrated in (41)–(43):

(41) a   Teacher: LIVE YOU WHERE   –   'Where do you live?'

Christopher replied to the question then asked:

     b   C: *YOU LIVE*   –   '(Where) do you live?'

His 'question' received an appropriate answer, indicating that it had been correctly interpreted.

(42) a   Teacher: WORK YOU WHAT   –   'What work do you do?'
     b   C: *WORK YOU*   –   '(What) work do *you* do?'

(43) a   Teacher: MOTHER YOUR   –   'When was your mother born?'
         BORN WHEN
     b   C: *FATHER YOUR BORN*   –   '(When) was your father born?'

Although Christopher produced some multi-sign questions, he was typically repetitious, asking the same question again and again (as he does in his general conversations in English and other spoken languages). Overall, however, his development of sign-order in questions was quite good. In the majority of cases where he used a Wh-sign he used it appropriately in sentence-final position – in contrast with his inconsistent usage in period 1. This implies that transfer effects from English syntax, especially in periods 4 and 5, were not found. On the other hand, his frequent omission of the Wh-sign is interesting and problematic at the same time. It might be that it was just difficult for him to encode all the relevant information in the signed sequence, but equally it may be that he was relying on his interlocutor to exploit the context to interpret the sentence as a Wh-question. It is also of interest that nothing similar to this omission of Wh-words is found in his other 'second' languages (though it is found in other populations – see e.g. Tsimpli & Stavrakaki, 1999, for Greek SLI). It is problematic in that it is not clear how successful this strategy would be with another deaf signer in normal conversation.

This tacit reliance on pragmatics (if this is what it was) resulted in his producing elliptical utterances which would often be acceptable in an appropriate context, just as the omission of Wh-phrases in spoken languages is acceptable in specific registers and contexts. Christopher's failure to use Wh-signs consistently is not evidence of his lack of the relevant linguistic knowledge, since he did produce them appropriately during the same periods that he produced questions without them. Thus, omission cannot be unambiguously the result of either lack of lexical knowledge of the Wh-sign or of its syntactic distribution. Furthermore, what was omitted was usually the Wh-sign alone rather than other lexical signs in the sentence, making it difficult to motivate an explanation in terms of processing load. However, an additional requirement of target Wh-questions is a particular facial expression: specifically, a furrowed brow. This facial expression has its starting point preceding the Wh-sign but must obligatorily coincide with the Wh-sign in sentence-final position. We therefore suggest that, by omitting the Wh-sign with its required facial action, Christopher made the task of producing Wh-questions easier. Since using facial expressions is clearly difficult for him, and since there is evidence throughout the learning period of his inability to use them to mark Yes-No questions too, it is plausible that his omission of the Wh-sign is a function of its necessary association with a facial expression. This would be consistent with our previous claim about Christopher's mis-analysis of the head-shake in negatives as being a morphological rather than a supra-segmental feature. That is, in both negatives and questions we find a tendency to simplify double marking of the same feature. Given his comprehension abilities, we suggest that Christopher's omission of the Wh-sign with its associated facial expression, parallel to his treatment of the head-shake in negatives, indicates that he realised from early on that facial expressions are linguistically important in both domains.

This suggestion is somewhat problematic as Christopher was less successful in translating BSL questions into English: out of thirteen BSL interrogatives he had not been presented with before, he translated only one accurately: 'How

Table 6 *Interrogative utterances produced by the comparator group*

Period and number of learners	Interrogatives	Wh-questions	Yes-No questions	Preverbal subject (out of total N of overt subjects in questions)	Question facial expression
Period 1 (N=6)	60	11 (10 Wh-initial & 1 Wh-only)	49	16/50 (4 with both initial and postverbal subject)	14/60 (23%)
Period 2 (N=6)	48	5 (4 Wh-final & 1 Wh-only)	43	16/37	10/48 (21%)

old are you?' He recognised a question function in four others and failed to recognise the interrogative function in five other sentences. The remaining examples he didn't attempt to translate at all. This drop in performance in translation tasks involving questions is consistent with his poor performance in the translation of negative sentences discussed in the previous section and in those involving verbs with agreement morphology discussed in the following section.

Turning to the use of questions by the comparator group, there were examples of Wh- and (mainly) Yes-No interrogatives from the beginning, but the use of facial expressions to mark questions was rare. Questions were typically either verb-initial or complement-initial and the subject pronoun YOU was typically produced postverbally (either sentence-finally or sentence-medially), although by the second period preverbal subjects were becoming more frequent – presumably as a result of transfer from English. Wh-signs were also few in number and started appearing in final position in period 2. Table 6 presents a summary of the data from the first two periods. There were no examples of questions in the subsequent periods, as the teacher had moved on to the next part of the curriculum.

Typical examples from period 1 are given in (44) and from period 2 in (45):

(44) a   F: LONDON LIKE YOU [no   –   'Do you like London?'
                 facial expression]

      b   D: THROAT SORE THROAT   –   'Do you have a sore
                 _____br   throat?'
                 HAVE YOU

      c   _____br
          D: YOU COME WALK   –   'Do you come (here) on
                                                      foot?'

(45) a B: YOU COME-HERE gestures   –   'Will you come here after
        'after' CHRISTMAS [no facial   Christmas?'
        expression]

  b   B: POSSIBLE YOU WALK-TO   –   'Is it possible for you to
        UNIVERSITY [no facial   walk to the university?'
        expression]

  c   _____br
        D: GREEN WATCH YOU YOURS   –   'Is that green watch
                                                yours?'

  d   A: YOU LEARN WHERE [no   –   'Where did you learn . . . '
        facial expression]

  e   B: YOU LEARN WHERE WHAT   –   'Where did you learn
        [no facial expression]   what?'

A significant difference between Christopher and the members of the comparator group is that he systematically omitted Wh-signs whereas they did
not. Both he and they tended to omit facial expressions in their production of
BSL questions, but while his omission was systematic, theirs was sporadic.
Moreover, it is important to note that the facial expressions in BSL questions
produced by the comparator group were categorically distinguished as br for
Yes-No questions and bf for Wh-questions: that is, largely the same contrast
as is made by deaf signers (see section 2.3.2.2). The implication is that the
comparator group realised from early on that facial expressions are (distinct)
linguistic markers of BSL questions. Their omission is then probably due to the
learners' difficulty in coordinating their facial expression with the manual sign
sequence, rather than being an indication of their having mis-analysed the facial
expression as an optional non-linguistic marker. In fact it is noteworthy that the
BSL learners in our study showed a more categorical distinction between the
facial actions used for Yes-No and Wh-questions than do native signers, who
may vary facial action depending on pragmatic factors (Reilly & Bellugi, 1996;
Campbell *et al.*, 1999; Anderson & Reilly, 2002). For example, a Wh-question
with a high degree of surprise may have raised eyebrows; a Yes-No question
expressing puzzlement may have lowered brows. Wh-questions with known
answers, such as those addressed by parents to children ('What's this?') have
raised brows. It would seem that the BSL learners were over-regularising a
distinction they had been explicitly taught.

4.5.3   *Sign space and verb agreement*

As described in ch. 2, verb agreement in BSL relies on indicating locations in sign space as well as marking inflections by movement. Bearing in
mind Christopher's general difficulty with visuo-spatial information in the

non-linguistic domain, we were interested to see the extent to which this aspect of BSL would be accessible to him.

When he was first taught how to use BSL verb morphology to indicate the verb's arguments, he had persistent problems in using the correct directional affix on the verb stem. For example, in trying to copy a sign such as HELP, produced by his tutor, which moved from Christopher's location towards his tutor's location to express 'you help me', Christopher instead moved the sign from himself towards his tutor's location, signifying 'I help you'. His difficulty in appreciating the visual dynamics of the sign and thus understanding the intended meaning appropriately persisted across several months of exposure to BSL. There was a similar problem in his first uses of pronominal points, where he also produced the mirror image of what he was seeing, rather than adapting the directional affix to reflect the point of view of the signer. Whether Christopher misunderstood the instruction to 'copy' the tutor's signed sentence and, as a result, copied the reverse subject and object pronominals is unclear.

This was not an error we observed in any of the comparator group, whereas in Christopher it was systematic rather than random, making the idea that he misunderstood the instruction more plausible. If this is the case, then his anomalous use of 1st and 2nd person pronouns is not a matter of his grammar, but a problem of comprehension. It is well known that learners have problems with 'shifters' (Jakobson, 1957; see Petitto, 1987) but Christopher had no difficulty with the labels for 'I' and 'you', as he used them appropriately in his spoken languages. It is also relevant to note that the use of pronominal points involves indicating the location of the referent in a way which is identical to a gesture. The use of a directional affix on the verb in BSL has no such relation to a gesture but is a fully grammaticalised sign.

Throughout period 1, Christopher's performance in using spatial locations to anchor signs was limited, and in spontaneous signing he used only five tokens with verb agreement morphology. These inflections were limited to present referent locations, and four of them involved the verb GIVE moving between himself and his teacher as 2nd person. At this stage, then, it appears that Christopher had not yet begun to use subject and object agreement morphology; rather, the restriction to present referents indicates that his use of different locations was regulated by the actual context rather than by sign space.

In period 2, Christopher began to produce verb predicates without directional affixes but with correct pronominal points. For example, in copying the sentence YOU-TELEPHONE-ME ('you telephone me'), in which the sign TELEPHONE moves from 2nd person to 1st person, Christopher signed the inscrutable *TELEPHONE YOU TELEPHONE*, rather than mirroring the signs as in earlier examples. It should be emphasised that signers repeating a sentence involving a directional affix on a verb modify that verb to show their own location rather than that of the original signer. Thus I-TELEPHONE-YOU meaning 'I telephone you' (where the sign moves from location A to location B) should be repeated back by another signer with the sign moving from location B to location A to conserve the same meaning: i.e. 'I telephone you'. This is also true if the signer is repeating a sentence where end points were in the right and left of sign space. In the repetition the signer would reverse the start and end points.

However, in more complex sentences involving 3rd person locations, Christopher produced two examples where he persisted in copying sign direction, rather than adapting the sign movement to encode the same meaning that he had been asked to repeat, so YOU-TELEPHONE-HIM ('you telephone him'), for instance, was repeated as *HIM ME TELEPHONE HIM* ('Him, I telephone him'). He used four other examples of verb signs with a directional affix to encode agreement, where these were also tied to present referents. He did not use locations for referents not present in the sign space until period 3.

In his spontaneous signing during this second period, Christopher attempted to encode agreement with eight different verbs: ASK, TELEPHONE, LOOK, HELP, TEACH, GIVE, PAY and SEE. Although he was now using agreement more widely, he produced mostly ungrammatical sentences. Of eight tokens, three involved omission of the subject affix: *ASK-HE ME* ('I ask him'), *GIVE-HE ME* ('I give him'), *PAY-HE ME* ('I pay him'), where the canonical target would have been: ME-ASK-HIM) ('I ask him') and so on. That is, Christopher moved his sign from neutral space forwards (only encoding the object). By not moving the sign from his own chest he failed to encode the subject. It thus seems that the data from copying, as well as the data from spontaneous production, show that agreement morphology was not yet part of his BSL grammar. To be more precise, agreement morphology was produced but the pronominal choices (the value of the pronominal element used) were in many cases wrong. Further, in his ungrammatical uses of agreement morphology, Christopher usually signed the subject as a free pronoun at the end of the sentence, whereas object agreement morphology appeared easier for him. As subject agreement marking is frequently optional, it is the placing of the pronoun at the end of the sentence which is ungrammatical, rather than the omission of subject agreement. The fact that he mastered object agreement more easily may reflect its obligatory nature. The simultaneous marking of subject and object agreement was anyway clearly problematic for him. This finding contrasts with Christopher's productive use of subject agreement in Berber, but partially echoes his use of subject and object agreement in Epun (Smith & Tsimpli, 1995). Epun had overt subject–verb agreement which Christopher usually handled correctly, but, on occasion, he imposed object agreement on the verb instead of subject agreement, despite the fact that there was no object agreement in the input. On balance it seems that his performance in BSL is a result of the difficulties he has with the signed modality and the increased load associated with double-agreement marking in sign morphology.

In period 3, Christopher gave evidence of having grasped the notion of sign space in both his comprehension and production of agreement morphology. After thirteen hours of exposure, he began to use a location to either side of himself to refer to a non-present referent, as in: *I-GIVE-HER* and *I-HIT-HER*; and after fifteen hours, he attempted to inflect signs between two abstract grammatical locations in sign space. This was first seen in the use of lexical items, as in: *BOY GIVE GIRL* 'The boy gave the girl (something)'; then through the use of his own location, as in (the ill-formed): *GIRL I-POINT-AT-HIM BOY* 'The girl points at the boy'; and finally through the use of two non-present 3rd person locations, as in: *SHE-HIT-HIM* '(The girl) hit (the boy)'. The problem with this use of syntactic sign space was that referents had not been previously established before moving a verb towards or from them, giving rise to contextually uninterpretable sequences such as the examples cited above: *I-GIVE-HER, I-HIT-HER*. Nevertheless, at this period, we think that agreement morphology was gradually becoming part of Christopher's grammar.

While the establishment of a referent in discourse is not, strictly speaking, a matter of the syntax, this claim is supported by two kinds of evidence. First, he produced examples which involved the use of non-present referents, indicating that sign space, rather than the actual context, was responsible for establishing pronominal points; second, he produced data which included both a lexical sign, establishing the subject or object referent, and a pronominal agreement affix on the verb, co-indexed with the established referent. Thus, he was obeying the requirement for arguments to be realised in the sign sequence and his development in this period shows that he was moving from a lexical (pronominal) representation of subjects and objects to a grammatical one, i.e. subject and object agreement. In this respect, his BSL grammar was developing in the right direction but reference-assignment was problematic for reasons outside the grammatical system, most plausibly his difficulty in accessing the syntax–discourse interface, an area that he has problems with anyway (see Smith & Tsimpli, 1995: 169). Despite this progress, the optionality of either the referents or the agreement morphology in Christopher's production, which made it difficult to interpret his sentence production, shows that we cannot yet speak of mastery.

In tests of his comprehension of verb agreement morphology during this period, Christopher performed at a level comparable to that of the other learners, although still at the poor end of the scale. We administered two tests of verb agreement comprehension: in the first (labelled AGR1 in fig. 19) subjects were shown signed sentences on video. All the sentences had an agreeing verb which moved to show agreement with the subject and direct object, (see ch. 2 for discussion). Each signed sentence contained two referents (e.g. 'John' and 'Alison'). After each signed utterance, subjects had to pick that written English sentence which constituted the more appropriate translation. There

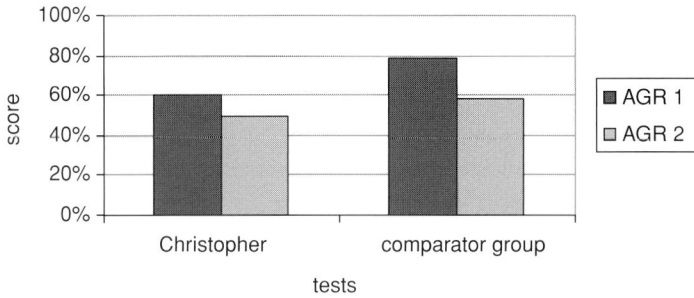

Figure 19 Relative scores on two tests of agreement in period 3

were two sentences to choose from, which varied the role the referents took as subject or direct object: e.g. John did the teasing or Alison did the teasing. The second test (labelled AGR2 in the figure) measured subjects' ability to judge whether verbs in different sentences were appropriately used to encode person agreement through movement between indexed locations. Agreeing verbs such as ASK, GIVE or TEASE, can move between spatial syntactic locations to encode person agreement, but other verbs such as LIKE, KNOW or WANT cannot (Padden, 1988). Subjects viewed a signed sentence with a grammatical or ungrammatical use of verb agreement along with an English translation, and were asked to judge whether the BSL sentence 'was well-formed or not'. The performance of Christopher and the comparator group on both tests is shown in fig. 19.

On AGR1 the comparator group scores were between 60 per cent and 100 per cent (SD 13.3), Christopher scored 60 per cent correct (chance was 50%). On AGR2 he answered by simply alternating his response between A and B, scoring at chance (50%), whereas the scores of the comparator group ranged from 40 per cent to 100 per cent (SD 16.6).

In period 4, Christopher was using non-topographic space more consistently, but it was difficult to interpret his agreement marking, as previous reference was again not made clear. Interestingly, he did not resort to the omission of all morphological marking, as he tended to do with Wh-signs and negatives.

By the fifth period of exposure, Christopher was spontaneously producing simple directional affixes on verbs correctly, indicating that he could reverse the direction of verb movements to preserve the desired meaning, though this ability was limited to simple sentences. Of the total tokens from this period, nineteen out of twenty-six sentences (73%) involved verb inflections to non-present 3rd person locations, with little or no other syntactic information in the sentence. However, even at the end of the period of instruction, he characteristically still made the error of mirroring a verb's directional affix in some of his attempts at copying sentences, signing the utterance *ME-HELP-YOU* 'I help you' with the opposite intended meaning of 'You help me'.

Christopher's persisting problem reversing first and second pronouns is presumably attributable to the way reference is established in BSL, i.e. by indexing. Hearing children who reverse pronouns in the early stages of first language acquisition reverse 1st and 2nd person pronouns, not 3rd person (see Chiat, 1986), and Christopher too soon overcame his tendency to reverse 3rd person pronouns. That is, the restriction of pronoun reversal to 1st and 2nd persons is driven by the pragmatics of language, not just the morpho-syntax of BSL.

With the onset of pointing to 3rd person referents not present in the sign space, it is clear that the originally deictic use of pointing to establish reference has been grammaticalised. In this case, there is no confusion between a gesture and a grammatical function, since the actual space does not include a point that corresponds directly to a referent. On the other hand, in the case of 1st and 2nd person referents, the deictic function of a pointing gesture to the signer and the interlocutor may be difficult for an adult second language learner to separate from the grammatical use of sign space (see Poizner *et al.*, 1987, for discussion). In these cases, Christopher failed to distinguish reference established via gestures from the grammatical use of 1st and 2nd person, and hence the reversal required in copying tasks proved difficult for him. By the end of the learning period, he had used sign space correctly with the following agreeing verbs: GIVE, ASK, LOOK, HELP, TEACH, PAY, SEE, HIT, BLAME, THROW, PAINT, FEED, TELEPHONE and INVITE.

As with the use of negation markers, we assessed the limits of Christopher's understanding of agreement morphology by getting him to translate into English BSL sentences which involved more complex verb morphology. As with negation, his intermittently incorrect processing of signs and his limited short-term memory for long sentences made this task difficult for him, and he correctly identified only one out of six sentences (46d). The examples of his mistranslations in (46) illustrate the difficulty occasioned by sentential complexity. For instance, he was well aware of the form of the sign TELEPHONE, and also that it could be moved around sign space to indicate the relevant arguments – see (46d), yet in (46f) he mistranslated it, with devastating effect on the overall meaning.

(46) a T: STUDENT++ CL-MANY-PERSON$_a$ TEACHER TEACH$_a$
            'The teacher teaches the students'
        C: Students sit at the teacher's desk

     b   _____t
        T: RED CAR$_a$ CL-CAR-DRIVE-PAST LOOK$_a$
            'I watched the red car drive past'
        C: The red car is in the road

c T: b-i-l-l IX$_a$ j-o-h-n IX$_b$ $_a$TEACH$_b$ GREEK SATURDAY
       'Bill teaches John Greek on Saturday'
   C: Bill and John eat Greek food on Saturday
d T: MORNING s-a-l-l-y$_a$ $_a$SHE-TELEPHONE-US$_b$
       'Sally telephoned us this morning'
   C: Sally rang in the morning
e T: CAT IX$_a$ CHILDREN$_b$ $_b$THEY-LOOK-DOWN$_a$
       'The children look at the cat'
   C: The cat pushed children away
f T: LAST-NIGHT FATHER HE-TELEPHONE-ME
       'My father telephoned me last night'
   C: Father had a cup of tea last night

The errors in (46c) and (46f) can be explained on the basis of the phonological similarity between the pairs of signs EAT and TEACH, and TELEPHONE and TEA. For instance, the sign TELEPHONE shares its place of articulation and part of its handshape with the sign TEA. As discussed in the previous section, translation data impose additional problems on Christopher's processing of the BSL input, and cannot be assumed adequately to reflect his competence in his developing grammar.

The use of agreeing verbs by the comparator group can best be illustrated on the basis of examples from elicited narratives. They were asked to describe a wordless picture book ('the Paint story', Karmiloff-Smith, 1979) with two participants and an action event of painting with an agent-affected theme. The agreeing verbs used were PAINT, THROW-ON and GIVE, all of which provide obligatory contexts for subject and object agreement. Twenty subjects from the comparator group participated in this production task, of whom eleven did not use sign space at all. Table 7 details the overall performance.

Example (47) illustrates appropriate target use (47a), as well as subject (47b) and object (47c) agreement:

(47) a   BOY IX-RIGHT PAINT GIRL IX-LEFT HE-PAINTS-HER
         'The boy paints the girl'
     b   BOY GIVE-HER GIRL PAINT
         'The boy gives the girl paint'
     c   IX-RIGHT THROW-ON-LEFT
         'He throws (water) on (her)'

In all, it seems that the participants from the comparator group had some problems with using agreeing verbs to provide both subject and object agreement. This is clear in the different rates of subject and object omission of agreement marking shown in table 7. Nevertheless, the structure as such did

Table 7 *Use and omission of agreement marking on agreeing verbs by the comparator group*

Oblig. contexts for subj. & obj. agreement	Agreement use		Omissions		No use of sign space
	Subj.	Obj.	Subj.	Obj.	
70 (35 sentences)	23/24 (96%)	17/24 (71%)	1/24	7/24	22 (11 sentences)

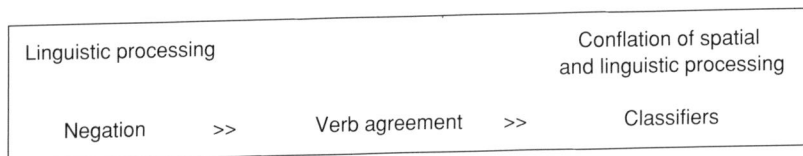

Linguistic processing	Conflation of spatial and linguistic processing
Negation >> Verb agreement >>	Classifiers

Figure 20 The visuo-spatial mapping continuum for BSL

not present them with much difficulty. Considering that in 'the Paint story' both subject and object referents are 3rd person, the comparator group performed considerably better than Christopher, who showed restricted use of 3rd person referents in his production of agreeing verbs.

4.6   Classifiers

As is clear from the preceding discussion, BSL has systematic recourse to linguistic structures with greater or less involvement of visuo-spatial mapping. This can be represented by the hierarchy in fig. 20, which shows how classifiers are at the extreme end of a continuum involving both purely syntactic and visuo-spatial mapping: they are at the interface between syntax and space.

We suggest that this extreme position on the hierarchy goes some way to explaining Christopher's poor performance on this characteristic sign language phenomenon (see section 2.4.2 above). Throughout his exposure to BSL, Christopher was not observed to use entity classifiers spontaneously, preferring to act out an action such as WALK, SIT or JUMP rather than exploit a classifier form such as CL-PERSON-V-WALK ('person walk') for 'someone is walking'. Using his own body rather than a classifier was a common strategy for him to describe the movement of a person. For example, when describing someone walking or running he often moved his feet as well as swinging his arms backward and forward. This is reminiscent of the behaviour of young children acquiring ASL as a first language who have been reported as showing involvement of their lower as well as upper limbs in comparable situations (Meier, 2000).

Christopher's readiness to act out an action in this way accords with his use of gestures in his own production despite his having difficulty understanding equivalent signs. Because classifiers rely on specific handshapes and intricate movement of the articulators, his clumsiness made his use of them in spontaneous signing difficult to assess. Similarly, when we tried to elicit classifiers, his apraxia made parts of the response uninterpretable. For example, after fifteen hours of BSL exposure, Christopher attempted to copy his tutor (T) signing classifiers describing people involved in different activities (running, walking, kneeling, etc.), but it was unclear from his signing if he was aware of the classifiers' internal structure. In two-handed signs where, for instance, one hand represented a tall flat object and the other a moving person, Christopher produced identical handshapes (see (48) below). In this example, the model offered by his tutor includes noun class information in the handshape, while movement and the manner in which it is carried out are provided by the verb stem. Both hands are used in this sentence, with the contrast between the person and the wall marked by two different handshapes V and B. The non-manual marker (pursed lips), produced across the whole predicate, encodes the meaning 'with difficulty'.

(48)   pursed lips_____
         T: dominant hand: BOY CL-V-PERSON-JUMP-WITH-EFFORT
            Non-dominant hand: CL-B-WALL
            'The boy just managed to clear the top of the high wall'

Christopher's attempt at copying this sentence (49) included very little information:

(49)   C: *BOY hands-cross-in-space*[5]   –   'The boy moved'

During the same period we attempted to elicit signs from Christopher by asking him to describe drawings which depicted objects and people in different locations and with different types of movement (e.g. a man doing the high jump, a car moving over bumpy ground) as in figs. 21 a and b.

As a basis for comparing the target sign and Christopher's elicited production, the signs were coded in terms of three parameters (handshape, movement and palm orientation). In (50)–(55) the boxes show the intended meaning of the classifier in the top left cell. 'Target' indicates the well-formed version of the classifier sign that his teacher used, and 'Christopher' shows the handshape that Christopher used in his attempt at describing the pictures. In

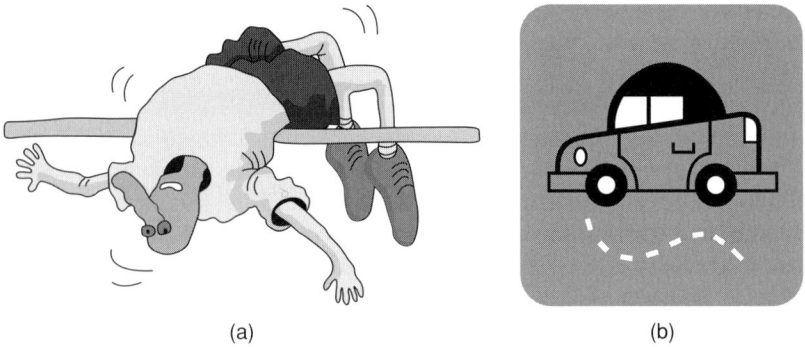

(a)   (b)

Figure 21 Picture stimuli used to elicit classifiers

many examples, his signing accurately captured some but not all of the three parameters.

(50)   A person standing

A person standing	Handshape	Movement	Palm orientation
Target	V	No movement	Towards self
Christopher	5	Up and down	Towards self

(51)   A person approaching

A person approaching	Handshape	Movement	Palm orientation
Target	G	Straight horizontal path towards self	Towards self
Christopher	G	Straight horizontal path towards self	Down

(52)   Five people moving along

Five people moving along	Handshape	Movement	Palm orientation
Target	5	Straight horizontal path	Left
Christopher	G	Straight horizontal path	Down

(53)   A sailboat sailing along (classifier picks out sail of boat)

A sailboat sailing along	Handshape	Movement	Palm orientation
Target	B	Zigzag horizontal path away from self	Left
Christopher	B	Up and down	Towards self

(54)   A nodding head

A nodding head	Handshape	Movement	Palm orientation
Target	S	Up and down	Down
Christopher	S	Side to side	Down

(55)   A solid round object (e.g. a boulder)

A solid round object	Handshape	Movement	Palm orientation
Target	S	No movement	Down
Christopher	S	No movement	Down

Christopher often omitted parts of the information encoded in the classifier sign, as in (53) where he omitted the crucial movement of the classifier as well as using the wrong palm orientation. The putative iconicity of a classifier handshape, as in examples (50) and (52), appeared not to be helpful, but where signs were phonologically simpler, as in (55), he was more successful, and he was generally better at producing static classifiers as used to describe a tree, or a person kneeling, than classifiers involving movement.

A separate problem in Christopher's use of classifiers was that when they were elicited, he often produced them without any preceding signs. Classifiers normally work anaphorically: a single handshape may refer to any of many potential objects, so without an antecedent, comprehension of his signs was difficult. This suggests that he may not perceive the classifier as including a proform but as being a synonym of the antecedent itself. Interestingly, both of these features of Christopher's use of classifiers (incomplete structure and ambiguous use) are characteristic of first language acquisition (see e.g. Schick, 1990; Morgan et al., 2008).

Although Christopher's apraxia meant that he had difficulty in the production of classifier signs, he did show some understanding of them in that he was able to select the correct pictures on the basis of seeing the classifiers for items

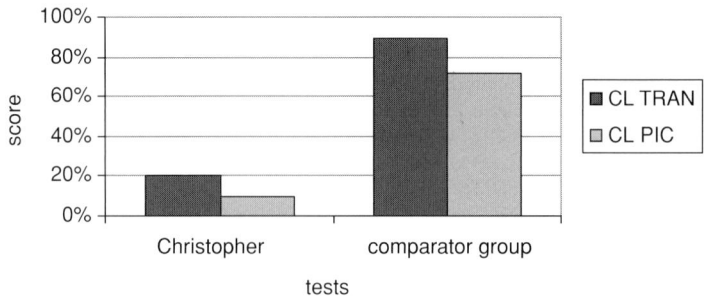

Figure 22 Comparative scores on two tests of classifiers

such as 'a flying person', 'a person walking', or 'a small animal jumping', even though these were pictures he had been unable to describe appropriately himself. Accordingly, we devised further tests involving the comprehension of sentences containing classifiers. The first of these (CL TRAN) required subjects to watch ten signed sentences involving a classifier and then for each to choose one of three written English sentences. For example, in one item the BSL target was 'a line of telephones' produced with a Y hand shape articulated several times in a straight line in sign space, and the choices were a line of horses, a line of cars and a line of telephones. In the second test (CL PIC) subjects watched ten signed sentences and for each then picked a corresponding picture from four alternatives. The results of these two tests for Christopher and the comparator group are given in fig. 22.

In the CL TRAN test Christopher scored 20 per cent correct (worse than chance which was 33%), whereas the scores of the comparator group were between 80 per cent and 100 per cent (mean 89%, SD = 9.9%). In the CL PIC test Christopher scored 10 per cent correct (chance was 25%), whereas the controls scored between 50 per cent and 100 per cent (mean 72%, SD = 13.8%).

These results highlight the fact that the comparator group had few problems learning classifiers and using them appropriately in describing the position of objects in space. This is in sharp contrast with Christopher, who not only showed very poor performance in the production of classifiers but also had only very limited ability in their correct interpretation.

For the members of the comparator group, producing classifiers, which had been taught in period 3, seemed relatively straightforward. Examples of their production data are given in (56) and (57) below, where they had been asked to use classifiers in BSL sentences to describe a picture from memory. Specifically, after looking at an arrangement of objects on three shelves and practising the correct classifiers the students were instructed to ask each other questions. They were drilled on this for thirty minutes before being asked to repeat the relevant sentence verbatim. It was clear from their first productions that in many of these utterances they were exploiting their ability to use gestures. Example (56) is an unsuccessful attempt to use a classifier; the handshape is wrong and there is a vague pointing gesture to a space in front of the student. In contrast, (57) is well-formed and involves the use of a two-handed classifier:

(56)   A: WHERE PLANTS (no question face expression)
             'Where are the plants?'
         B: *PLANTS object-placed up-and-left (gestures this)
             'They're up on the left'

(57)   A: WHERE TWO BOOK-THICK
             'Where are the two big books?'
         B: TWO-OBJECTS-THICK
             CL-2-FLAT-UPRIGHT-OBJECTS-LEFT
             'They're up on the left'

In one transcript from period 3, four students from the comparator group signed in total sixteen exchanges of the kind seen in (56) and (57). Of these, only three were signed incorrectly. Two included errors in the orientation of the handshape as in (58) below, where the student signed with the palm upwards rather than downwards:

(58)   E: WHERE LETTER
             'Where is the letter?'
         F: *LETTER CL-FLAT-HAND-TOP-RIGHT
             'The letter's up on the right'

Finally, in example (59) below, subject D used a classifier which describes handling an object, rather than using a whole entity classifier handshape. Since the use of a handling classifier in this context was one of the options given by the teacher, this was considered appropriate. We include the sentence in the three errors, however, since he used the handling classifier together with a predicate indicating movement rather than with a static locative:

(59)   E: WHERE BOX
             'Where's the box?'
         D: ?BOX CL-HANDLING (HOLDING OBJECT WITH
             TWO-FLAT-SIDES)-MOVE-OBJECT-TO-MIDDLE-RIGHT
             'The box is in the middle on the right'

By contrast, Christopher was at a loss in this kind of situation: he did not use representational space or classifiers to stand for objects at all. His poor overall performance with classifiers contrasts sharply both with the performance of the members of the comparator group, and his own better performance on agreement, negation and the lexicon. He performed markedly worse on the tests of comprehension of classifiers than did the controls.

This systematic asymmetry between Christopher's performance on classifiers and other aspects of BSL is striking, especially when viewed in contrast with that of the comparators, whose performance was consistent across these different domains. Christopher's pattern suggests a dissociation between the cognitive components – linguistic and spatial – involved in the representation of classifiers; in particular it suggests that he has problems with features that draw on or interface with spatial cognition, an area in which he is known to have a deficit. This deficit is seen at its most severe where there is no explicit morphological expression of such features: for example, in the case of incorporated prepositions (see section 2.4 above) or classifier constructions more generally. These are interpretable only on the basis of the grammaticalisation of spatial features, and Christopher's problems in this area led to his below-chance performance.

It is important to underline the fact that Christopher's chance performance on agreement indicates a different state of knowledge from his below-chance performance on classifiers. Whereas the latter is linked to a deficit in spatial cognition, the former seems to be associated with his (and the comparators') level of competence in BSL at the time of testing. It is also relevant that Christopher's performance on agreement is significantly worse than his excellent mastery of morphological agreement in his spoken 'second' languages. That is, it seems that in some respects the signed modality inhibited Christopher's otherwise enhanced language learning abilities. Moreover, the comparator group's performance was similar to Christopher's in this domain, suggesting that his superiority to ordinary L2 learners is limited to spoken (especially written) languages. As mentioned above, there were also important asymmetries in Christopher's mastery of BSL, as seen in his differing performance on negation, agreement and classifiers. Table 8 shows that he performed radically worse on classifier tests than on tests of negation or agreement. Agreement also involves the use of sign space (through indexing and movement incorporated into the predicate) but to a lesser extent than classifiers do in their description of object placement in sign space.

Christopher's poor performance on classifiers contrasted sharply with the performance of all the seven subjects from the comparator group who took the test. For all these subjects, performance on test 1 for each phenomenon was better than performance on test 2: that is, matching signs to pictures systematically caused them fewer problems. Moreover, the comparators' performance on negation was better than their performance on agreement and classifiers. In fact, both Christopher and the comparator group found negation to be relatively straightforward. However, whereas for the comparators, Ag2 seemed to elicit the poorest performance, and classifiers appeared to be easiest, for Christopher

Table 8 *Comparison of Christopher's performance with that of a subset of the comparator group on different tests*

Code	CL1 (range 80–100% Chance = 33%	CL2 (range 50–100%) Chance = 25%	Neg1 (range 86–100%) Chance = 50%	Neg2 (range 30–80%) Chance = 50%	Ag1 (range 86–100%) Chance = 50%	Ag2 (range 30–84%) Chance = 50%
1	90	50	93	60	70	33
2	100	60	93	80	100	58
3	90	60	86	40	70	50
4	80	60	100	50	100	75
5	90	60	100	60	90	42
6	90	60	100	60	100	42
7	100	60	100	60	90	60
CHRIS	20	10	93	60	60	50 (random)

'Code' identifies the subject; 'CL1' was a signed sentence to picture match test (from four alternatives); 'CL2' was a signed sentence to written English sentence match (from three alternatives); 'Neg1' was a signed sentence to picture match test (from four alternatives); 'Neg2' was a signed sentence grammaticality judgement test; 'Ag1' was a signed sentence to picture match test (from four alternatives); 'Ag2' was a signed sentence grammaticality judgement test.

performance on Ag2 was at chance level and his performance on classifiers was below chance in both tests. Table 8 shows that three subjects performed below chance on Ag2 and one performed at chance level. However, these same subjects were above chance on classifiers and negation, indicating that it was subject–object agreement which was particularly difficult for them. This could be due to the increased load of grammatical information carried by an agreeing verb, since Ag2 generally seemed to be harder for controls than either negation or classifiers. We do not have comparable production data from the controls on agreeing verbs, but in all the sessions where the teacher went through agreement the comparator group were very good at copying the constructions. However, there were no opportunities for the students to practise these in more complex situations or to attempt more ambitious language. We see more errors with Christopher, as he was trying to use these verbs much more in conversation with his teacher.

In general, the more information that was encoded within the classifier sign the more difficult it was for Christopher to extract the full meaning, but there was again an interesting asymmetry. In choosing pictures which corresponded to sentences with classifiers, he typically made errors which showed that he had correctly identified the main lexical category but was making mistakes with the location of the objects recognised. For instance, after seeing the sign sequence BED BOOK CL-Bent-B-BOOK-ON-CL-B-BED which translated as 'a book on a bed', Christopher correctly identified the lexical information expressed in the sign for a 'flat object' (a book) as opposed to a 'round object' (a ball), and chose the picture of 'a book under a bed', rather than either of the other pictures which showed 'a ball under a chair' and 'a comb on a bed'. Thus it seems that his poor performance was, at least in part, due to difficulty in identifying the spatial relations between the objects depicted when there was no overt morphological realisation of this relation.

To summarise: Christopher did not use classifiers in his spontaneous signing at all. His understanding of them was limited to simple morphological forms and he had particular difficulty in decoding the spatial relations between objects whose positions were represented across two handshapes. However, he did understand the lexical component of the classifiers and thus could pick out the correct referent from the range of possible choices. That is, his problem with classifiers was with the agreement features, spatial or locative, that they encoded, rather than with the entities they described.

Christopher's poor performance in using classifiers is probably a specific reflection of a more general problem with abstract referential sign space. On one occasion when he saw a signer using index points to set up abstract referential locations, he reacted as if he expected the referent to be present. When his interlocutor signed MAN and pointed to an area in sign space, Christopher interpreted this as meaning something like 'there is a man there'. His apparent presumption that an actual physical interpretation rather than a symbolic one was appropriate was even seen in his copying of simple signs. The sign for YESTERDAY in BSL is articulated by a point to a location over the signer's shoulder. When he first learnt this sign, Christopher pointed towards the same location in space as his sign tutor had, pointing not over his own shoulder, but to a location beyond the tutor's shoulder in front of him. This suggests that Christopher was unable to use the partial iconicity of BSL as an aid to learning, either because he failed to recognise the symbolic nature of space in BSL – a matter of competence, or because the sensory and motor impairments arising from his apraxia and autism meant he was simply unable to – a matter of performance.

4.7   Further tests

In our earlier discussion of the source of Christopher's difficulty with classifiers, we suggested two possibilities, which are not mutually exclusive. The first has to do with his spatial deficit, the second with his lack of experience of languages with a classifier system. In order to tease apart these alternatives we devised a number of further tests. The results of these tests are suggestive rather than conclusive, because it proved difficult to exclude interference from a variety of other factors, in particular because Christopher's understanding of sentences containing classifiers was negatively correlated with the amount of information embedded within them. However, our impression is that the processing of topographic information about where objects are positioned relative to each other in space consistently raised more difficulties for him than purely syntactic information.

For the first test ('Syntactic versus topographic space') we devised fifty-two signed sentences, half of which (twenty-six) involved classifiers encoding a syntactic contrast in sign space (plurality, aspect, movement and manner distinctions, etc.) but with no topographic information. An example is shown in (60), in which the classifier encodes the path of the person's movement, but does not specify any location. The other twenty-six sentences involved classifiers which did encode topographic information in sign space; an example is shown in (61).

(60)   MAN RAIN UMBRELLA CL-G-PERSON-WALK
         'The man walked through the rain with his umbrella'

(61)   HOUSE CL-5-CLAW-HOUSE-LOCATED-AT-FAR-RIGHT
         'The house was over on the far right'

Each of the fifty-two sentences corresponded to a picture stimulus, and the 'topographic' and 'syntactic' examples were randomly ordered. Christopher was asked to watch the signed sentence and select the corresponding picture from a choice of four alternatives. Somewhat surprisingly, given his previous poor performance on the comprehension of classifiers, he identified thirty-one of the fifty-two classifiers correctly (59.6%; chance = 25%). But there was an interesting, and expected, asymmetry: he selected the correct picture for eleven (42%) of the twenty-six topographic sentences, and for twenty (77%) of the twenty-six sentences with classifiers encoding just syntactic functions.

These results are not as conclusive as we would wish, for several reasons. First, we do not have scores from the comparator group on this test, so we cannot compare Christopher's performance with that of other learners. Second, the lack of standardised scores more generally means that we do not know whether the two sets of sentences are equally easy to process and understand. Third, the distinction between 'syntactic' and 'topographic' sign space in these sentences is not entirely clear-cut, as all the sentences involve some features of both, albeit to different degrees.

Nevertheless, we suggest that Christopher's differential comprehension of classifiers relates to properties that make the 'topographic' sentences representationally distinct from 'syntactic' ones. Specifically, the 'topographic' sentence in (61) indicates the static location of the single argument (the house), whereas the 'syntactic' example in (60) includes appreciably more information: about a man, an umbrella, the rain, and movement (walking). To arrive at an appropriate interpretation of (61) one needs to decode both the lexical representation of the concept 'house' and the spatio-syntactic mapping of its topographic location. To arrive at an appropriate interpretation of (60), on the other hand, involves decoding more lexical information but, crucially, no topographic signs. A learner with only partial knowledge of BSL syntax but good mastery of the lexicon could assign an interpretation to both (60) and (61) by mapping purely lexical information onto a predicate–argument structure. However, a learner with only partial knowledge of BSL syntax and with a spatial deficit would be expected to show differential performance on these two types of sentence. For such a learner the 'topographic' predicate (LOCATED-AT THE FAR RIGHT) would render (61) uninterpretable. On the other hand, in (60) the classifier encodes the path of the person's movement, but is simpler in not requiring any mapping of physical location.

Some corroboration for this suggestion comes from Christopher's differential performance in other areas of BSL which involve 'topographic' information. Specifically, he performed worse on the verb agreement tests than on the negation and question tests, although the comparators showed no such difference. This can perhaps be accounted for in terms of the spatial (topographic) information which is present in verb agreement markers but absent from negative markers. Such a conclusion is also consistent with the findings from the study by Atkinson *et al.* (2002), whose participant Heather (see ch. 5.5) also had specific problems with agreement markers incorporating a topographic element.

If it was decoding topographic relations that Christopher found difficult, we needed to identify what aspect of the topographic encoding lay at the heart of the problem. To explore his ability in manipulating topographic maps using BSL we designed a further series of experiments. The first study ('Giving directions') focused on the analysis and articulation of spatial relations using sentences with classifiers.

This task involved the use of sign space for following and giving directions about how to get from one place to another. Signers specify a route, using relational terms such as 'right' and 'left', where the path taken is described from the perspective of the signer (Emmorey & Falgier, 1999; Morgan, 1999). Landmarks important for understanding the route (traffic lights, buildings, trees, etc.) are articulated using classifier predicates. Importantly, in order to understand the directions given, the addressee must mentally rotate the description 180 degrees so that it matches their own perspective.

In the first part of this task Christopher's sign tutor gave directions between landmarks in the town where both of them live, e.g. from the post-office to the church, and Christopher drew the route described on paper as the signer gave directions. Ten routes were devised between five familiar landmarks. These varied in complexity from 'simple', involving a straight line, to more complex routes travelling between three landmarks, which involved several right or left turns. In the comprehension part of the task, Christopher successfully identified four simple routes, but when attempting to follow the more complex paths he asked for several repetitions of each segment of the route which he mapped onto the paper in the form of a line drawing. Thus he was able to hold simple sign space representations in working memory long enough to transfer them to paper and build up a succession of paths between locations. In this first task, then, Christopher had both to comprehend BSL classifiers and to use his visuo-spatial working memory.

In the second, production, part of the test, we gauged Christopher's ability to use sign space and classifiers to give directions. He was successful in communicating the desired route on only one of the ten trials, and he never used classifiers to mark landmark locations. Instead of using a succession of path descriptions, Christopher repeated directions without giving reference or orientation points, with the result that it was impossible for the viewer to follow the description. It appeared that he could follow simple sign directions only when a real-world map was available (on paper) to capture the spatial relations in a static form. When the sign directions involved more information even this strategy was unsuccessful.

The absence of classifier signs in Christopher's production might be attributed to his failure to understand the task. However, as he had reacted appropriately to his tutor's signing in the comprehension part of the task, it should have been clear what was required of him. Although the sign tutor had clearly used locations and classifiers articulated in sign space, Christopher traced out directions and paths on the table rather than using sign space himself. To summarise: in this initial test of the use of classifiers to mark spatial routes, Christopher was able to follow simple descriptions but was unable to use a spatial map in his own production. As with other aspects of his signing, he relied on real-world anchor points rather than using representations in sign space.

When tested on a comparable task in spoken English, Christopher was able to comprehend a series of directions and arrive at the target destination on all of the ten trials given. We can therefore conclude that it is the representation of spatial relations in the signed input which causes him problems. We are confident that this is not just a contrast between ability in his first language English and a second language, as he often requested that the directions be given in one of his spoken second languages. Thus 'right', 'left', 'under' or 'across' in spoken languages seemingly carry little iconic topographic spatial information (hence their phonological forms differ across spoken languages in a way that the signs in signed languages do not). We take it that in Christopher's BSL, and possibly in that of any hearing person for whom BSL is a second language, signed directions involve starting from spatial information, decoding the sign, translating it into the spoken L1 format, and re-translating it into a

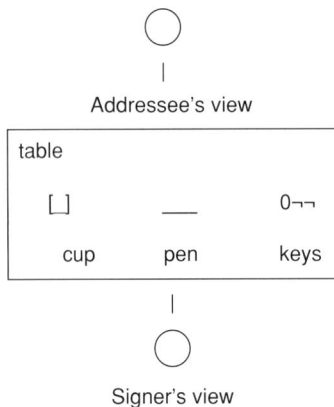

Figure 23 The format for 'Setting the table'

non-linguistic representation including spatial information to produce the map. With a spoken second language, one goes from language (L2) to language (L1) to space, which seems to be simpler, in that it does not involve the language–space interface required to perform the task in a sign language. However, even in spoken language we observed the same production problem in giving directions as in the signed equivalent of the test. Christopher had difficulty explaining to an uninformed addressee how to traverse a route that he knew himself, often neglecting to describe intermediate steps between locations necessary for the full realisation of the task. We assume that the reason for his poor performance on this spoken production task is not linguistic but cognitive. His failure to take adequate account of the other person's viewpoint – whatever the modality – is presumably due to an impairment in his theory of mind.

The second set of studies we devised ('Setting the table') focused on the spatial relations between classifiers in sign space and the effect of rotation on Christopher's ability to interpret them. Specifically, we assessed his understanding and use of classifiers to describe different arrangements of two, three or four objects on a table. It required a more complex use of classifiers than the previous task as it involved not only the mental reversal of perspective but also the holding in memory of the correct locations of an array of classifiers. The set-up for the test is illustrated in fig. 23 above and the configurations for the various sub-tests are shown in table 9.

The first column of table 9 gives a schematic representation of the participants' position relative to the table. This was either side-by-side, e.g. sub-test (i), or face-to-face, e.g. sub-test (ii). The second column shows in what mode the instructions to set the table were given: either through the placement of real-world objects (OBJECT) or through the use of a classifier for that object

Table 9 *The various sub-tests of 'Setting the table'*

Sub task-position of participants	Instruction mode	Response mode
(i)	OBJECT	OBJECT
(ii)	OBJECT	OBJECT
(iii)	CL	OBJECT
(iv)	CL	OBJECT
(v)	CL	CL
(vi)	CL	CL

(CL). The final column indicates the mode required for the response: either placing a real-world object where it had previously been placed during the instructions (OBJECT), or using a classifier to represent that object where it had been placed during the instructions (CL).

Each of the sub-tests involved fifteen trials with Christopher sitting variously beside or opposite the experimenter in the task. The experimenter either placed two, three or four objects in a specific spatial configuration in front of her or, using the appropriate classifiers, described in BSL an array of the same objects in front of her in sign space. The objects were a book, a cup, a bunch of keys and a pen (represented by B, C, 5-claw, and G handshapes respectively). Christopher had identical objects in front of him. Once the experimenter had finished arranging the objects or describing the spatial layout through classifiers (instruction mode), Christopher was asked to copy the arrangement using either objects or classifiers (response mode). That is, we manipulated the level of complexity across these tasks in two ways, either using no-reversal (participants

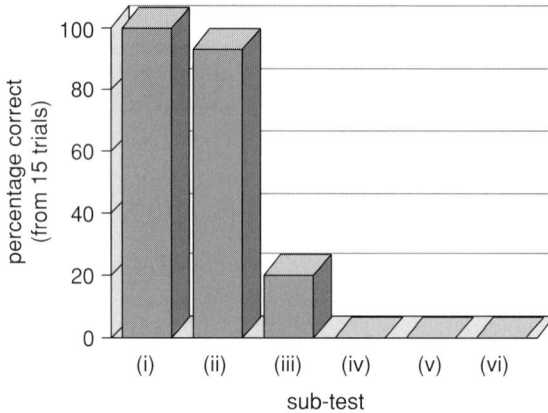

Figure 24 Christopher's performance on the sub-tests of 'Setting the table'

side-by-side) or reversal (participants face-to-face); and using either real objects or combinations of classifiers in both instruction and response modes.

At first sight it appeared that Christopher performed much better in the sub-tests involving instructions or responses in the object mode than in the classifier mode. The caveat is because when he was arranging objects on the table, he appeared to have worked out a reversal algorithm which, although it produced the right result in all but one of the trials, seems to have been based on a simple rigid transformation, as he also reversed 'on-top-of' to 'underneath'. Be that as it may, in all the sub-tests that involved using classifiers in sign space, whether in the instruction or response mode, Christopher performed systematically worse, failing on all trials in sub-tests (iv)–(vi). Moreover, whenever the experimenter used a classifier sign, Christopher would reach out to grasp and place the appropriate object before the instructions were finished, despite being instructed not to do so.

His difficulties increased in the face-to-face position. Rather than constructing a sign space, Christopher relied on deictic reference, using real objects rather than classifiers, and available real-world surfaces for both objects and signs. He failed to maintain the relative locations of signs required to keep the configurations of objects consistent in relation to himself. Instead he produced the mirror image of what he was looking at or what he had just seen. This was comparable to his errors in the use of signs involving directions, pronouns, and examples such as YESTERDAY, where he also often produced a mirror image of what he had just observed. His performance on the six sub-tests is given in fig. 24.

In a variant on the same test we decreased the task demands by using picture-matching rather than sign-copying. After seeing a signed 'setting the table' description, Christopher had to pick the corresponding picture from a choice of alternatives. The correct choice maintained the relative relations between the objects and so relied on the subject's ability to remember the locations of the classifiers and match them with the corresponding picture. Even without the difficulty of mental rotation Christopher had severe difficulty: once the experimenter had signed the first classifier, he chose any picture that contained the relevant object; and after the second classifier sign he chose a different picture which contained the second object. As a result his performance was random, though at least it suggested that his problems were not in sign recognition.

To provide a basis for comparison we tested him on the same 'setting the table' task using some of his various spoken languages (English, Spanish and Greek). As with his performance on the task of giving and following directions, Christopher did better on comprehension, scoring 13/15 (87%), than on production, where he scored 10/15 (67%). His main difficulty was with using unambiguous spatial language, as he sometimes used a description that omitted any indication of overall relations (for instance, he talked about one object in relation to another but not both in relation to a third), or he failed to provide any information about precisely how to position objects in real space (for instance, he used topographically vague terms like 'next to' or 'first', 'second' and 'third'). When questioned further he always provided a more informative description, suggesting that his initial failure represented a reduced awareness of his conversational partner's mental point of view rather than a spatial deficit.

4.8   Summary and conclusions

We can draw a number of conclusions from the results presented in this chapter. At the most general level, Christopher clearly treated BSL as a natural language; he expressed his enjoyment at learning it and was able to communicate with his sign tutor on a range of topics. However, it seems that the signed modality had some inhibiting effect on his ability to demonstrate his enhanced language learning abilities. The comparator group's performance was similar to Christopher's, suggesting that his superiority to ordinary second language learners is limited to spoken (especially written) languages. One obvious manifestation of this was the complete absence of facial action from his signing. Christopher found the use of facial action, especially its coordination with manual signing difficult. This had a particularly adverse effect on his mastery of negation and questions, which make crucial use of such action.

More interestingly, the results showed a number of asymmetries, both as between Christopher and the comparator group and between different aspects of Christopher's own developing mastery of the language. His vocabulary development was within normal limits but, because of his autism and apraxia, he emerged at the lower end of the normal spectrum, and showed the expected asymmetry as between comprehension and production. His vocabulary development was different from that of the comparator group in that there was no facilitatory effect of iconicity despite his readiness to use (uninterpretable) gestures.

There was a further expected asymmetry as between his lexical learning and some aspects of his syntactic learning, though this did not manifest itself entirely in the way we had anticipated. Most strikingly, there were fewer transfer effects from English than in his spoken languages. There was a tendency among members of the comparator group for English word-order to be transferred more frequently than was the case with Christopher and more frequently in declarative clauses than in interrogative clauses. Christopher also seemed to place a greater tacit reliance on pragmatics than did the members of the comparator group. His translations were partially unlike those he produced from written input in his spoken languages (see Smith & Tsimpli, 1995: 156ff.). In particular, his translations from BSL to English were generally not 'literal', except occasionally when the absence of any written form for BSL led him to have recourse to a word-for-sign translation strategy, ignoring plausibility effects at the sentence level. This effect of the translation task, then, did mirror his performance in other languages.

For most of the constructions tested, in particular negation and questions, Christopher performed within the range shown by the comparator group. For instance, despite his failure to use facial action, his partial mastery of the head-shake for negation was impressive, especially when considered in comparison with his general lack of any bodily gestures to accompany his use of spoken languages. Although his production of appropriately constructed negatives was reduced, Christopher's performance on tests of comprehension was comparable to that of other learners. Moreover, although his production included ungrammatical uses of negation markers, his grammaticality judgements suggested that his BSL development was within the range defined by the members of the comparator group.

As with negation, Christopher's mastery of BSL questions was undermined by his failure to use appropriate facial action. Although he produced some multi-sign questions, he was typically repetitious, asking the same question again and again (as he does in his general conversations in English and other spoken languages). Overall, however, his development of sign-order in questions was quite good. An important difference between Christopher and the comparator group was that Christopher systematically omitted Wh-signs whereas the comparators did not. This is again probably a reflection of his reliance on the pragmatics of discourse to effect reasonable communication.

When we turn to agreement phenomena the situation is a little murkier because it was not always clear that Christopher understood the relevant instructions. On the one hand there is evidence that the rules controlling agreement morphology had become part of his grammar, as in tests of his comprehension of verb agreement morphology he performed at a level comparable to that of the other learners, although still at the poor end of the scale. On the other hand, the simultaneous marking of subject and object agreement was clearly problematic for him, a finding which contrasts with his productive use of subject agreement in Berber, but partially echoes his use of subject and object agreement in Epun.

The area which was most revealing, in that it showed an asymmetry both in Christopher's own performance and between him and the members of the comparator group, was the use of classifiers. The comparator group had no problems learning classifiers and using them appropriately in the description from memory of object placement in space. This was in sharp contrast with Christopher, who not only showed very poor performance in the production of classifiers, due in part to his apraxia, but also had only minimal ability in their correct interpretation. He did not use representational space or classifiers to stand for objects at all. His poor overall performance in this domain contrasted sharply with the performance of the comparators on the one hand, and his own better performance on agreement, negation and the lexicon, on the other.

Christopher's pattern of performance, showing a systematic asymmetry between classifiers and other aspects of BSL (whilst that of the comparators was consistent across these different domains) suggests a dissociation between the various cognitive components – linguistic and spatial – involved in the representation of classifiers. As he had greater difficulty with the topographic use of classifiers than with their syntactic use, it seems that his problems were with features that draw on or interface with spatial cognition. That is, his poor performance in using classifiers probably reflected a more general problem with abstract referential sign space. As with other aspects of his signing, he relied on real-world anchor points rather than using a representation in sign space. This suggests that his differential comprehension of classifiers derived from properties that make the 'topographic' sentences representationally distinct from 'syntactic' ones. It is important to note that when tested in spoken English on tasks whose BSL equivalents caused him such problems, Christopher had no comparable difficulty. For instance, he was easily able to comprehend a series of directions and arrive at a target destination. Thus we have here what appears to be a genuine modality difference between his mastery of signed and spoken language.

5   Christopher in the wider context

5.1   Introduction: dissociations revisited

In this chapter we look at Christopher in comparison with other subjects who are atypical signers in order to see if the dissociations manifest in his case are *sui generis* or reflect deeper generalisations. The hope, of course, is that such generalisations will emerge and will also serve to corroborate the details of the model of the mind we sketch in the next chapter.

By way of background to the present discussion it is worth briefly summarising the dissociations Christopher showed. Most obviously, there is an asymmetry between his striking linguistic ability and his impaired general intelligence, as seen in his performance on tests of theory of mind and on visuo-motor tasks. He showed a further asymmetry between his near-perfect first language ability and his flawed second language learning prowess. This was most obvious in the contrast between his mastery of the lexical properties of his 'second' languages and his more limited abilities in coming to grips with the computational system: specifically, his remarkable skill in morphology vis-à-vis the plateau effects seen in his learning of the syntax. His apraxia and mild autism led us to expect a dissociation between his sign and his speech, and between his abilities in language and in gesture. Within BSL this translates into a contrast between his use of syntactic space versus his relatively poor use of topographic space, especially when these come together in the use of classifiers.

We look at both developmental and acquired cases, beginning with signers who are aphasic following a stroke.

5.2   Aphasic signers

5.2.1   *Background: unimpaired signers*

Underpinning analyses of impairments in sign language following stroke are a number of neuro-imaging studies of unimpaired signers (see MacSweeney *et al.*, 2008b, for a review). Two neuro-imaging studies have specifically explored the use of space in sign language. MacSweeney *et al.* (2002) asked deaf native signers to view topographic and non-topographic BSL sentences. Topographic sentences elicited greater activation than non-topographic sentences in posterior middle temporal cortices bilaterally and in the left inferior and superior parietal lobules. Hearing non-signers viewing audiovisual English translations of these sentences did not show such differences. In a PET study, Emmorey *et al.* (2002) showed deaf signers of ASL pictures of, for example, 'a paintbrush in a cup'. Participants were then asked to produce the appropriate classifiers or the preposition sign IN. Greater activation was found for classifiers than prepositions in the parietal lobes bilaterally. Thus, it seems that the processing of topographic space requires intact left hemisphere skills. When further spatial processing is required, such as mapping between real-world spatial relationships and an internal representation of sign space during production, right parietal mechanisms are further engaged. Right parietal activation can also be observed when hearing non-signers describe spatial arrays of novel shapes (Damasio *et al.*, 2001).

5.2.2   Signers with stroke

There is a reasonably large body of studies of signers with stroke, exploring language impairments in right- and left-lesioned signers. This research provides somewhat conflicting results. It is well established that the use of topographic space and classifiers can be affected by right (Poizner *et al.*, 1987; Atkinson *et al.*, 2005; Hickok *et al.*, 1999, 2009) as well as left hemisphere lesions (Atkinson *et al.*, 2005). Additionally, deficits in the use of agreeing verbs have been identified in some signers with right hemisphere lesions (Poizner *et al.*, 1987), but not in others (Atkinson *et al.*, 2005).

Turning to the left hemisphere group, these individuals coped better with classifiers than prepositions in a test of locative sentences in BSL (Atkinson *et al.*, 2005). The right hemisphere group generally performed poorly on non-language visuo-spatial tasks, such as drawing, block design, and line judgement. Some also showed evidence of unilateral spatial neglect: for instance, failing to detect the left-most items in a line cancellation task.

These difficulties may have underpinned their topographic impairments. In line with this, those who were impaired on the non-language tests were also impaired in locative and classifier comprehension, while those who showed no generalised visuo-spatial impairments, were not.

The visuo-spatial difficulties of the right hemisphere group did not impair all aspects of comprehension. For example, these individuals could still understand the reversible items in the verb and sentence comprehension test (Atkinson *et al.*, 2005).[1] It seems, therefore, that they could process non-topographic but not topographic uses of space. We would therefore argue, in line with the functional imaging studies described above, that some people with right hemisphere damage can no longer map non-arbitrary sign locations on to real-world spatial positions because this mapping calls upon their impaired visuo-spatial skills, including their visuo-spatial memory.

The difficulties of the right hemisphere group, with their visuo-spatial processing impairments (although these have very different origins) show the same sorts of dissociations between topographic and non-topographic processing as Christopher, and confirm the hypothesis that such dissociations arise from impairments external to language.

5.2.3   Sign versus gesture: Charles

One of the most striking dissociations reported in the literature is that between sign and gesture. The clearest example is provided by 'Charles' (Marshall *et al.*, 2004), an aphasic signer whose gesture production was markedly superior to his sign production even when the forms of the sign and the gesture were similar. Charles was a strongly right-handed man who was born deaf to hearing parents and had used BSL as his preferred means of communication from the age of 5 and throughout his life. At age 54 he had a stroke involving 'the left posterior frontal and parietal lobes in a wedge-shaped fashion, extending into the corona radiata and possibly just involving the temporal lobe' (Marshall *et al.*, 2004: 540). He performed well on visuo-spatial tasks but had significant sign anomia. In a picture-pointing (comprehension) task his performance was excellent, indicating that he knew the signs involved and could use them appropriately, but in naming tasks he had considerable sign-finding difficulties which were exacerbated in accessing low-frequency items and which were not attributable to motoric difficulty. There was moreover no effect of iconicity on his ability to produce or comprehend signs. But, significantly, he often substituted gestures for signs that he was unable to produce.

Most strikingly, Charles was significantly better at gesturing than at signing a wide range of activities (e.g. holding and using a toothbrush). This (partial) dissociation is significant because of the light it throws on current debate on the relation between sign and gesture. It confirms that sign and gesture are processed differently, have different internal structure (phonological, in the case of signs), and are not 'integrated' (certainly not for lexical signs) in the way suggested by, for example, Schembri (2002) and Liddell (2003), but are similar simply because of constraints of the medium. Charles can access the common semantics underlying sign and gesture; he cannot access the phonological code for signs, but can access the action schemata underlying gestures (Marshall *et al.*, 2004: 552). Such dissociation would be unexpected on the kind of integrated analysis suggested by Liddell (2003).

A comparison with Christopher is revealing. Recall (see p. 7 above) that Christopher had scored extremely poorly on the Kimura test of non-representational gesture (Kimura, 1982), but had shown considerable willingness to use gestures even when these were implausible and arbitrary. In comparison with the controls and with Charles, Christopher was poor at identifying gestures, weak at reproducing them and, despite his willingness to experiment, showed no real differentiation of signs and gestures. Perhaps more accurately, one could say that he had no mastery of gestures at all and substituted signs for them where possible. The parallel irrelevance of iconicity in the two cases is presumably for slightly different reasons: with Christopher it is because his enhanced but encapsulated language faculty seems to be impervious to external influence, as is characteristic of first rather than second language acquisition; with Charles, it is because the source of his difficulties with language – the inability to access phonological structure – cannot be helped by his intact abilities to gesture.

5.3   Robert

In this section we report on a case of a signer with acquired cerebellar damage (Tyrone *et al.*, in press) in order to provide a comparison with Christopher, who has been diagnosed as having a degree of cerebellar atrophy (O'Connor *et al.*, 1994; see section 1.3 above). Robert is a 36-year-old male who was born deaf into a hearing family. He began acquiring BSL at age 5 when he attended a non-residential school for deaf children. Robert suffered a cerebellar infarct at age 33 following surgery to correct an arteriovenous malformation, when the surgery caused extensive haemorrhaging, which was most severe in the right hemisphere of the neocerebellum (equivalent to the left hemisphere of the cerebrum), but extended into the medial cerebellum as well.

Although cerebellar damage in humans is rare, there is nonetheless a reasonable body of experimental research suggesting that the cerebellum is important for processing sensory information as it pertains to movement (Jueptner *et al.*, 1996; Ohyama *et al.*, 2003), helping maintain a sense of where the limbs are located relative to each other and relative to movement targets. The cerebellum coordinates components of such movements, possibly by comparing motor output against both motor plans and sensory feedback and adjusting the output accordingly (Blakemore *et al.*, 2001).

The overall pattern of disrupted movement typically resulting from cerebellar damage is referred to as ataxia. Given that Christopher is apraxic, it is important to note that the symptoms of ataxia and apraxia overlap considerably, with the main difference residing in the neurological aetiology of the conditions. Ataxia is generally associated with damage to the cerebellum, apraxia with damage to the frontal and/or parietal areas of the brain. It may well be that Christopher has diffuse damage affecting both/all areas.

Clinical research suggests that in patients with cerebellar ataxia, voluntary movements are slow, large and jerky, and often disrupted by tremors (Duffy, 1995). The tremors occur during voluntary movements of the limbs (as distinct from tremors associated with Parkinson's disease that occur when the limb is still) and are consequently referred to as intention tremors. The practical effects of the physiological and psychophysical aspects of ataxia are dysmetria (or spatial inaccuracy), dysrhythmia and dysdiadochokinesia (or disruption to the control of rapidly alternating movements). A further manifestation of the condition is ataxic dysarthria – articulatory disability arising from the uncoordinated movements and hypotonia of the speech muscles. Such speech is generally perceived as slow and imprecise, with irregular variations in pitch and loudness, and a 'scanning' rhythm (Duffy, 1995).

Although the cerebellum is best known for its role in movement, recent research suggests cerebellar damage may cause disturbances to language as well as speech (Fabbro et al., 2000; Marien et al., 2000) and disturbances to neuropsychological functions such as learning and memory (Lalonde & Botez-Marquard, 2000). Because the right cerebellar hemisphere connects (indirectly) to the left cerebral hemisphere, it has been suggested that it has a more important role in both language and articulatory function (Marien et al., 2000). However, Fabbro et al. (2000) claim that both the left and right cerebellar hemispheres as well as the cerebellar vermis are important to language function. This seems to be at variance with the condition of Christopher, whose cerebellar vermis is hypoplastic.

Purely linguistic deficits in Robert's signing were not obvious on casual observation, though it is possible that they were masked by his more severe movement deficits. He showed no difficulty understanding ordinary conversation, and his production deficits were largely motoric. On explicit testing, he exhibited a mild impairment on comprehension of negatives, both manual and non-manual. On all other linguistic tests, he performed within the normal range.

Informal observation of his spontaneous non-linguistic movement reveals unsteady posture and head position, and difficulty coordinating the two hands and reaching intended targets in day-to-day movement tasks (e.g. picking up a cup, adjusting his glasses). Additionally, his limb control is typical of ataxia, with big, irregular movements and frequent intention tremor.

Broadly speaking, Robert's signing is oversized and uncoordinated. Additionally, his signing is slow and often disrupted by intention tremor. His movements are proximalised on some signs, in other words, he produces the sign using articulators proximal to those normally used for its production (e.g. the wrist instead of the base of the fingers). Similarly, he also produces some signs in locations high and far away from the body, relative to the sign's citation form. Robert has an overall pattern of enlarged signing, but it can take a variety of forms: large movements, distant sign locations, and overextended articulators. He has difficulty coordinating his hands to produce two-handed signs. He is not always able to make his hands begin moving together, come to the same place, or produce the same movement, when required to do so. He also has difficulty coordinating the movements of independent articulators on just one limb: correctly timing separate movements relative to each other and suppressing involuntary movements that emerge during voluntary movement.

Robert was asked to perform a series of non-linguistic motor tasks (pointing and grasping) and a signing task, in which he copied individual signs after they were produced by the experimenter. Robert produced a large total number of errors, a large number of errors per sign, and a broad variety of errors. The most frequent was involuntary movement, which was probably a manifestation of intention tremor. The next most frequent errors in his signing were handshape errors and errors in the coordination of the movements of proximal and distal articulators, for example, the elbow and the wrist. Robert had great difficulty moving articulators on the same arm in a coordinated manner in the signs that required it; furthermore, he added articulator movements in signs that did not require them. Similarly, he had difficulty coordinating movements of the two limbs on two-handed signs, and in some cases, produced one-handed signs with both hands. On the whole, Robert was more likely to add handshape or orientation changes than to omit them. Additionally, he produced several errors in the static components of signs, including errors in orientation and location. Though Robert produces a range of sign errors, in general, he has more trouble with dynamic components of signs than with static components: involuntary movement, coordination (proximal/distal and bimanual), handshape change and orientation change.

Comparison with Christopher is not straightforward, but given the common cerebellar damage it is noteworthy that Christopher has a slight speech impediment, his posture and gait are awkward and clumsy, he has some degree of dysdiadochokinesia, and his signing is oversize and uncoordinated in a way reminiscent of Robert. It is nevertheless important to stress the differences: despite the partial parallelism of pathology, Christopher has a general linguistic talent that remains inexplicable in terms of cerebellar function or malfunction, and the details of his problems with signing are only broadly comparable.

5.4   Autistic signers

The literature on those on the autistic spectrum who have acquired sign language is extremely sparse. Most of the apparently relevant research in fact pertains to hearing autistic people who have been taught signs to compensate for their difficulties with speech. There are, however, some reports in the literature, of which the best-known is that of Poizner *et al.* (1987: 70) who write of a deaf autistic signer: 'Judith M. is echolalic and avoids eye contact or any other contact with people. She rarely signs spontaneously except for the minimum necessary to satisfy basic needs; she appears to have little or no cognitive communicative intent.' Some of these characteristics are reminiscent of Christopher: the avoidance of eye-contact and the infrequent initiation of conversation, for instance. But, as is obvious, his linguistic expertise is strikingly superior.

5.5   Heather

Heather is a young Deaf woman with specific visuo-spatial impairments reminiscent of Williams Syndrome (Atkinson *et al.*, 2002). Despite this disability her fluency and command of British Sign Language are relatively good in comparison with those of her learning-disabled peers. Like Christopher, she shows a dissociation between language and general cognitive abilities and, again like Christopher, it transpires on closer examination that there are subtle spatial errors in her signing, with clear dissociations between linguistic structures that rely on space and those that do not.

Heather shows some but not all of the classic features of Williams Syndrome, including a number of dysmorphic facial features, and an exuberant personality, with sometimes excessive social friendliness. She also displays anxiety and behavioural difficulties around maintaining friendships. She does not, however, have classic Williams Syndrome, as a fluorescence *in situ* hybridisation (FISH) test revealed no deletion of elastin on chromosome 7.

Heather uses British Sign Language as her preferred method of communication, though she has some limited ability to lip-read and use spoken and written English. She was educated in a school for children with learning difficulties and first came into contact with adult Deaf native signers at aged 14 years. She lives independently in sheltered housing for Deaf people with additional disabilities and regularly attends local Deaf clubs and mixes in the Deaf community. In terms of its greater fluency and complexity her command of BSL is strikingly different from her Deaf intellectual peers living in the same sheltered accommodation.

Heather shows atypical patterns of hemispheric dominance. She is ambidextrous for writing and tool use, and continually switches hand dominance during signed discourse, showing no clear hand preference, suggesting a lack of hemispheric dominance for sign language. Her cognitive abilities are very similar to the cognitive profile typical of people with Williams Syndrome, with language abilities well in advance of her visuo-spatial abilities and well-preserved face recognition.

On testing, her sign language vocabulary showed that she was well beyond a mental age of 11 years. On two tests of comprehension of BSL vocabulary she scored 64/68 items correct on each of two trials. Interestingly, the lexical items on which she made errors seem to be related to spatial concepts, e.g. PARALLEL, SHAPE and UNEQUAL. She has difficulties with these items despite the fact that clues about spatial relations are explicit in the BSL signs (fig. 25), suggesting that her problems with visuo-spatial cognition affect her

'PARALLEL'

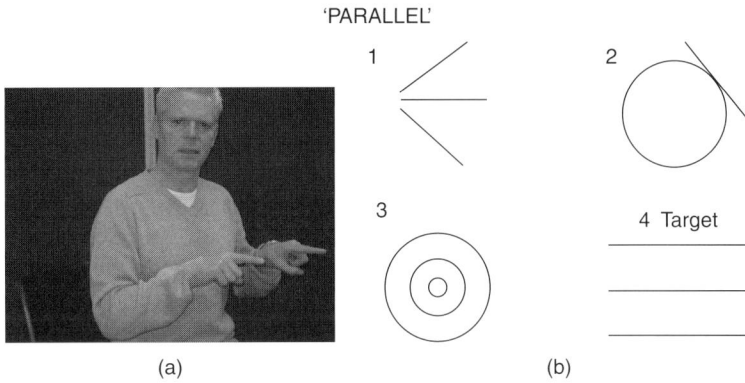

(a)   (b)

Figure 25 Item from the British Sign Language vocabulary assessment. The target sign is shown in (a). The subject must choose the correct picture (the one on the lower right) from the four shown in (b)

comprehension of real-world and conceptual space in BSL. It also suggests an insensitivity to the iconic properties of signs.

Additionally, Heather showed near-perfect performance on the Atkinson *et al.* (2005) noun comprehension test, scoring 39/40, where a score of 38 and above is within the normal range.

Her syntactic ability in BSL likewise falls within normal limits. She was tested for her production and comprehension of BSL grammar, and for her production of BSL narrative. The comprehension test, designed to be similar to the English test for reception of grammar (TROG) (Bishop, 1983/2003), contains eleven sections focusing on different grammatical devices, crucially including items assessing knowledge of topographic and non-topographic use of space.

Heather's pattern of results suggests a dissociation between abilities in the topographic use of space and other areas of grammar in both comprehension and production. She has a solid command of plurals, noun–verb distinctions, negation, embedded clauses and agreeing verbs. These structures, with the partial exception of agreeing verbs, do not exploit spatial relations to convey meaning. Heather performs well on comprehension of simple locatives but makes errors on other structures that incorporate classifiers, for example, spatial verbs, complex locatives, size and shape specifiers and body-part classifiers. In summary, Heather shows marked impairment on constructions that use classifiers and directly exploit space for grammatical purposes.

Her production errors are more obvious than her comprehension errors. Heather has unimpaired production of negatives and noun–verb distinctions, and was able correctly to inflect the single example of an agreeing verb included in the test. However, her production of spatial verbs shows consistent impairment in spatial representations. She appears to try to deal with her dif-ficulties by choosing English-like structures and a fixed sign-order resem-bling English. For example, she uses the prepositions UNDER, ON and IN rather than classifiers to incorporate information about referents and the spatial relations between them. Static locatives using topographic space are rarely used. It seems that Heather is able to understand the use of simple placement classifiers when used by others and has some knowledge of how to produce these structures individually. However, she has severe problems in integrating these structures to show the spatial relationships between referents in topographic space.

This asymmetric pattern of errors was repeated in tests of her ability in pro-ducing BSL narrative. This was seen in her failure to maintain correct verb agreement with location and person, in the absence of pronominal referencing, and in her problems in using classifiers correctly. Taken together, these obser-vations suggest a general impairment in using BSL structures that require the joint mapping of linguistic and spatial representations, while linguistic devices which do not incorporate spatial relations such as noun–verb distinctions and negation, are preserved. This conclusion was supported by the results of the Atkinson *et al.* (2005) test of verb comprehension (see note 1), which indicated that the more spatial aspects of non-topographic syntax may also not be wholly intact: that is, her command of agreeing verbs is incomplete.

Like Christopher, Heather was a late learner of BSL, but whereas he had learned English as a first language normally, she came to BSL in a rela-tively language-less state and can be considered a late learner of BSL as an L1. Early acquisition of competence in either spoken or signed language is a prerequisite for left hemisphere specialisation for language. Heather's lack of clear hemispheric dominance for sign language might be accounted for by her late acquisition of BSL, since Deaf subjects who acquire sign language late do not show conventional patterns of left hemisphere dominance (Neville, 1991). However, late learners show the same ability as natives in overtly correcting errors in simple unembedded grammatical constructions (i.e. verb agreement, Emmorey *et al.*, 1995). It is possible that the grammatical errors that Heather makes are partly attributable to her late age of acquisition and atypical language experience. However, late learners do not usually have problems with simple grammatical constructions and have no problems at all with spatial mapping, so any errors Heather makes in these areas are more likely to be attributable to her pattern of learning difficulties.

Jarrold *et al.* (1999) suggest that visuo-spatial memory is selectively impaired in hearing individuals with Williams Syndrome, accounting for the pattern of preserved language and impaired visuo-spatial cognition. The island of preserved functioning within the language domain relates to structures that do not involve the processing of spatial relations. These structures might be processed by a language-specific memory mechanism. Since the structures that Heather has most difficulty with are those that directly exploit spatial relations, it may be that these structures are reliant on intact visuo-spatial memory. This explanation is plausible because the processing of spatialised linguistic structures relies on the maintenance in memory of multiple spatial loci and the relations between them. This would explain the finding that Heather's language abilities appear to be in advance of her visuo-spatial abilities except where language functions exploit spatial relations, and that increasing spatial complexity (for example, in narratives) interferes progressively with her BSL.

We need at least three stages of information processing for sign language comprehension. First, the input characteristics of the visual display need to be analysed at a level suitable for delivery to cognitive systems. The language system can then effect a linguistic-level analysis of the structure of the message. Finally, a conceptual-level representation is delivered by the linguistic analysis, which forms the basis for understanding the message. If topographic and non-topographic sentences are processed by a single language processor, Heather's difficulties with the processing of only spatial structures in BSL must be due to logically antecedent processes – within the language processor itself and/or in visual input/output processors.

The pattern of Heather's BSL abilities is reminiscent of Christopher, with language in general well in advance of her visuo-spatial abilities and a dissociation within BSL grammar between devices that depend on grammatical processes involving space and those that do not.

5.6   Bilingual twins with Down Syndrome

Ruthie and Sally are hearing twins with Down Syndrome, who are functionally bilingual in speech and sign, and whose language development was studied over a period of some fourteen years, though test results are limited to the period from age 10 to age 16. They are identical twins with Mosaic Down Syndrome. Both parents are deaf, and members of the Deaf community. The twins were educated at their local primary school, and transferred to a residential school for children with learning disabilities at the age of 11. They then came home to attend a Further Education college at the age of 16. They had no contact with deaf children at school, although they had occasional contact with signing children at the local Deaf club. Their hearing and sight were within normal limits; Sally is predominantly left-handed, with some cross-over, and Ruthie is right-handed. The twins were tested at ages 10 and 16 on a battery of tests, including auditory memory span, visual memory span, the British picture vocabulary scales (BPVS), the test of reception of grammar (TROG), and various measures of BSL vocabulary and grammar.

Results showed a consistent advantage for the visual over the auditory modality, in memory, semantics and morpho-syntax. Despite this advantage it is noteworthy that the twins showed a clear preference for speech, which was used for all relevant conversational functions of language. Sign was only used when communicating with deaf people (family and researcher), with some words mouthed but not spoken, and the order following BSL not English. By contrast, speech was used to communicate with hearing people and speech was always used in communication with each other, unless they were involved in a three-way conversation with a deaf person.

In both modalities, lexical aspects were stronger than morpho-syntactic ones. Least progress was made in the area of receptive spoken grammar. At age 10, Ruthie's scores on comprehension of BSL grammar were consistently below Sally's, but at age 16 she had caught up so that their profiles were very similar. At age 10, Sally showed a small but clear superiority over her twin in all aspects assessed, and came over as the more confident and communicative child. Like Ruthie, she made significant gains over the time period, except in the areas of morpho-syntax, where she seemed to have reached a plateau in both sign and speech – receptively at least.

By age 10 Sally was able to use classifiers to show spatial relationships grammatically: to sign *the cup is on the table* she showed the flat hand classifier for TABLE and placed CUP above it. Ruthie at the same age was unable to use these classifier structures. To sign *ball under table* at age 10, she signed UNDER and said *table* simultaneously. At age 16, despite her advanced competence in receptive sign grammar, Ruthie indicated these relationships lexically rather than using the appropriate spatial representation: *dog in box* was signed as BOX DOG IN. Both girls also experienced continuing problems in areas of greater morphological complexity such as distributive plurals. Unlike English, where simple affixation is used for plural forms, in BSL distributive plurals are formed in a similar way to spatial relationships. The lexical sign is articulated (e.g. CAR) and then followed by the appropriate classifier (flat object in this case), which is repeated, each repetition being along a horizontal line or arc. At age 10, neither twin was able to produce these correctly. Sally did produce one attempt: a pile of alphabet bricks was described as BRICK STACK (but without the correct classifier handshape for a three-dimensional object). Ruthie was unable to produce any plural forms: she responded to a picture of pairs of shoes in a row by silently mouthing *shoe*.

At 16, both twins were still having problems with distributive plurals. Sally described a picture of a crowd of people by signing MAN WOMAN CHILD STAND while mouthing *people stand*; Ruthie described rows of parked cars as ROW CAR while mouthing *cars*. It can be seen here that the semantics of plurals has been mastered by both, but only the English form, which is structurally much simpler, is produced correctly. The incomplete mastery of complex morphology by the twins is not surprising. Studies of classifier acquisition have reported that classifiers are not mastered until age 9 in Deaf children acquiring BSL as a native language (Woll, 1998; Morgan & Woll, 2003; Morgan *et al.*, 2006). What is apparent from the study is that a dissociation between lexical and grammatical acquisition was evident in both modalities, suggesting that the morphosyntactic difficulties for people with Down Syndrome are not specific to speech and the auditory-vocal modality. It seems that there is a common set of grammatical principles or mechanisms underlying morphosyntactic structures in all human language, regardless of language typology or modality.

Again, an explicit comparison with Christopher is illuminating: the twins showed a basic ability to master languages in both modalities; their mastery of sign progressed in a manner which was independent of their visuo-spatial ability; they had a greater mastery of lexical than of syntactic knowledge; their syntax seemed to reach a plateau beyond which they could not progress; and they manifested a comparable dissociation between syntactic and topographic uses of space.

5.7   Daniel Tammet

Up to now we have compared Christopher with straightforwardly 'patholog-ical' cases of the acquisition and use of sign language. The next example is somewhat different in nature. Daniel Tammet (see Tammet, 2006) is on the autistic spectrum – he has Asperger's Syndrome – and additionally he has remarkable abilities of memory, of arithmetic computation, of synaesthesia and, most relevantly in the current context, of language. Unlike Christopher, he is able to look after himself and makes his living by producing web-based language tutorials.

Daniel became widely known even before the publication of his autobi-ography because of his record-breaking memorisation of the value of π (to somewhat over 20,000 places), and his remarkable ability to see and manipu-late numbers in terms of colours and shapes, enabling him to carry out complex calculations with striking facility. Of relevance to us is that he also has a talent for learning languages. He is reasonably fluent in Lithuanian, Spanish, Roma-nian, Esperanto and Welsh; he has some knowledge of French and German; he has invented his own language (Mänti) based largely on Estonian; and he learnt Icelandic in a week.

When we met him, we tested him on a variety of spoken languages (including English and Icelandic) and we also exposed him for the first time to BSL (he refers to this meeting in his book: Tammet, 2006: 181, 237) to see how he fared in comparison to Christopher on the identification of iconic and non-iconic signs.

In preliminary data on his initial guessing of signs, we observed that Daniel was able to guess the meaning of some two-thirds of the signs shown to him. This was at the higher end of our comparator group scores and significantly better than Christopher. He also remembered the meaning of the signs he had got wrong and when retested on just those he was near 100 per cent. Although he had difficulty understanding metalinguistic negation of the kind exemplified by 'John isn't tall, he's a giant', the combination of his phenomenal memory, his intelligence and his imagination meant that he was able to represent, memorise and access the meanings of signs using some metalinguistic ability. In particular, the majority of the signs that he guessed correctly were iconic, in marked contrast with Christopher.

5.8   Conclusions

The series of case studies discussed above resemble and contrast with Christopher in different ways. Some of Christopher's difficulties with sign production may reflect cerebellar difficulties, such as those of Robert, but where closer parallels are found they seem to reside for the main in the contrast between topographic and non-topographic uses of space, and in the relationship of language to visuo-spatial cognition. Complex visuo-spatial skills are needed to acquire any aspect of a sign language which requires the integration of spatial information, and several subjects had difficulties in this area. The impact of developmental difficulties with visuo-spatial cognition can be seen in Heather, many of whose problems with BSL are strikingly similar to those of Christopher.

Once acquired, however, syntax becomes a dimension of language and is no longer processed by exclusively visual systems: the visual system functions simply as a transducer and the real analysis is carried out internally to the language module. As a result, when there is acquired visuo-spatial damage, some topographical as well as non-topographical syntax can continue to function, as in patients following stroke.

It is plausible that a third superordinate neural structure mediates functions in both domains. We assume that the spatial aspects of cognition and sign language are controlled by a higher-level representational system – some kind of 'executive', damage to which would cause other representational abilities such as gesture to be impaired as well. As was seen in section 5.1 above, while the use and comprehension of gesture is conveyed in the same visuo-spatial modality, it is organised differently from sign language at neural levels. As a result, the mastery of gesture may dissociate in pathology from the control of sign language. More generally, none of the specific dissociations shown by Christopher is unique to him, suggesting that we are well motivated in seeking to use his case as evidence for the nature of the human mind.

6   Modality and the mind

6.1   Introduction

In ch. 1 (section 1.4.4.2) we outlined the model of the mind we had previously argued for in an attempt to accommodate the abilities both of Christopher and the general population. In this chapter we return to the role of modality, sign versus speech, in the representation of language in the human mind. We begin by summarising the putative modality differences between signed and spoken languages, looking at 'articulatory' differences, at deixis and the use of space more generally, at iconicity and the special case of classifiers, and at the role of facial action (the other major area where signed and spoken languages look superficially most different). We then elaborate a revised model of the mind. It should be emphasised that we cannot hope to address the whole range of phenomena that have been treated under the heading 'modality' in sign language research and will restrict ourselves to dealing with issues pertinent to the construction of a model adequate to describe the abilities of Christopher and those we have compared him with. We end with a detailed exemplification of how the model allows for the description of the full range of Christopher's (and others') abilities, and finally draw our conclusions.

6.2   Modality effects

In this section we revisit and elaborate our earlier discussion of the differences between signed and spoken languages and include some discussion of the results of Christopher's learning of BSL.

6.2.1   Articulation

Obviously the articulators used in signed and spoken languages are radically different. However, as Petitto (2005) has convincingly argued, there is a good case for the neutrality of the neural substrate underlying both signed and spoken languages. She produces several kinds of evidence showing 'surprising similarities in the overall time course and structure of early signed and spoken language acquisition as well as in their neural representation' (2005: 89). The evidence comes first from 'milestone data', whereby babbling (both syllabic and jargon), and the first two-word stage of acquisition all came on stream at essentially the same time in deaf (signing) and hearing (speaking) infants. Second, the babbling of both populations showed comparable syllabic structure, on the hands or the tongue. Third, hearing and deaf infants showed categorial perception for manual configurations exploited in signed languages (specifically ASL in her studies). There is, however, an interesting asymmetry in the abilities of hearing and deaf subjects, with categorial perception for handshape being linguistically (and not just perceptually) determined, and hence found preferentially among the deaf (Baker *et al.*, 2005). Importantly, this categorial ability appears to be shared by hearing and deaf infants at 4 months but is retained only by deaf infants at 14 months (Baker *et al.*, 2006).

A fourth kind of evidence comes from 'structural data', whereby the role of babbling was shown to be linguistic – rather than just motoric – in both modalities. There has been a long debate in the literature discussing whether babbling was simply a result of infants exercising their motor abilities – Jakobson's (1941) 'purposeless egocentric soliloquy of the child... biologically oriented "tongue delirium"' (cited in Menn & Stoel-Gammon, 1995: 338; for discussion, see also Jusczyk, 1997: 171–2; and contrast Grégoire, 1937), or whether it was the first systematic product of the faculty of language – a precursor to language. Holowka & Petitto (2002) showed on the basis of meticulous measurements of the mouth opening of infants producing babble, smiles and non-babbling sounds, that it was unmistakeably linguistic. The argument was based on the well-known and widely accepted belief that the language faculty is lateralised. Because of this, there is a right asymmetry of mouth aperture in adults which correlates with the performance of linguistic as opposed to non-linguistic tasks, and is taken to indicate left hemisphere cerebral specialisation for language. If babbling is linguistic, then babies' mouth opening would show the same right asymmetry; if babbling is motoric, then babies' mouth opening would show no right asymmetry, but symmetrical mouth opening.

Fifth, there is evidence from research on short-term memory that 'whatever the structure of *phonological* STM (spoken or signed), the same processes are involved, and reflect a common mechanism' (Jacquemot & Scott, 2006: 482). Sixth, and finally, imaging data showed that linguistic processing in both modalities exhibited comparable increases in cerebral blood flow in identical brain regions (inferior prefrontal (Broca's) and superior temporal (Wernicke's) areas). Areas that in hearing people are involved in processing complex sounds are also involved in sign language phonology. Petitto *et al.* (2000) reported that the perception of discrete signs from two signed languages (ASL and Québecois Sign Language), as well as invented phonologically well-structured 'nonsense' signs, activated the superior temporal cortex bilaterally, including the planum temporale, in deaf native signers but not in hearing non-signers.

The authors concluded that superior temporal regions are specialised for the analysis of phonologically structured material, whatever its input modality (see also MacSweeney *et al.*, 2008b for a comprehensive review of the sign language imaging literature).

6.2.2   *Simultaneity (the non-concatenative nature of BSL)*

It is frequently emphasised that more than one part of the morpho-phonology of a sign, even more than one sign, can be produced simultaneously (Brentari, 2002; Aronoff *et al.*, 2005). That is, a morpheme may be distributed throughout the sign rather than constitute a segment in a fixed position. It is not clear (to us) that this is really very significant, in that the implied contrast with spoken languages is moot. Consider the spoken language phenomenon of morphological fusion whereby, for instance, the '*-o*' at the end of Latin '*amo*' ('I love') represents morpho-syntactically all of the five or six semantic categories 'first person', 'singular', 'present tense', 'indicative', and 'active'. In (relatively) agglutinating languages such as Turkish each of these semantic categories would be morphologically autonomous with a separate suffix for each one, but the 'simultaneity' of the Latin has no wider conceptual implications. That is, the situation where 'sign languages have a proliferation of monosyllabic, polymorphemic words' (Brentari, 2002: 56) is not as drastic a difference as she suggests, though it may be that sign languages represent a typological extreme.

Aronoff *et al.* (2005) claim that morphology in sign languages typically manifests two strongly contrasting characteristics: simultaneity for inflection, and sequentiality for derivation, where moreover, the simultaneity is typically iconically based. We are not convinced that the difference is as profound as they suggest: all aspects of morphology in signed languages also show up in spoken languages, even if the particular combination of characteristics is typologically unique.

To take the argument a little further, the similarities between the phonologies of signed and spoken languages seem overwhelmingly more important than the differences. As an example, consider the spoken language universality of consonants and vowels and the parallel sign language universality of elements described in terms of the more consonant-like IF (inherent features) and more vowel-like PF (prosodic features) in Brentari's (1998, 2002) work. A further striking example is the universal – i.e. cross-modal – role of sonority (Perlmutter, 1992; Brentari, 2002: 44). In both signed and spoken languages the distribution of elements is determined in part by a common 'sonority hierarchy'. In spoken languages this hierarchy proceeds from open vowels, e.g. [a], at the top, to close vowels, e.g. [i, u], to sonorants e.g. [n, l], to fricatives, e.g. [f, s], to obstruents, e.g. [p, t] at the bottom. In signed languages, the corresponding hierarchy is based on visual salience and proceeds from shoulder movements to elbow movements, and via wrist movements to hand-internal movements

(Brentari, 2002: 43). There are, of course, differences, especially with regard to the simultaneity of the articulation of 'consonants' and 'vowels' in signed languages, and Brentari specifies a major contrast between the distribution of vowel and consonant information in signed and spoken languages. However, as she suggests (2002: 45), coarticulation effects in spoken language are closely reminiscent of the simultaneity of C and V articulations in signed languages. We do not wish to deny the differences that Brentari identifies in her elegant work, nor that they are attributable to 'the advantage of the visual system for vertical processing' (2002: 61), but we do not think that they have radical implications for the nature of the human language faculty nor for the model of the mind we need to postulate. Rather, with Hohenberger *et al.* (2002) we would view this as mainly a function of language typology rather than modality.[1] It may well be that the idiosyncrasy apparently characteristic of non-concatenative[2] systems can anyway be done away with: see Gafos (1998); Ussishkin (2005).

6.2.3   Iconicity

Aronoff *et al.* (2005) emphasise that the role of iconicity is (potentially) different, in quantitative but also perhaps in qualitative terms, in the two modalities, with greater facility in encoding spatial relations in signed than in spoken languages. We have already discussed the role of iconicity in the lexicon (3.1.2 above) and we return to a discussion of iconicity and its dependence on encyclopaedic knowledge below. For the moment it is sufficient to note that Christopher, unlike most of the BSL learners in the comparator group, did not show any preference for iconic signs. This was manifest both in his performance in experiments in BSL and in his translation between signed and spoken languages. His failure to exploit iconicity the way other adult learners do in such translation tasks leaves him with the need to store meanings for signs as English words or their conceptual equivalents: i.e. he has to create a (phonological) form–meaning link without the facilitating intervention of iconic, gestural, representations in the visual modality. Because of this, he either needs more exposure to the sign in order to make the metalinguistic comparison between signed input and spoken form, or he has to memorise the sign on the basis of some other of its properties or of the context in which it was presented to him. These correspondences seem to be robust for him but without the ability to record them in print and review them frequently he loses access to them more quickly.

6.2.4   Orthography

The choice of modality correlates with the (non-)existence of a written script. As we have seen, Christopher's preoccupation with the written word was a strong contributory factor in his finding spoken languages easier than BSL. Although orthographies differ widely from language to language – alphabetic, syllabic, phonetic-semantic[3] – the absence, except for research purposes, of a written variety of any signed language has an obvious effect on accessibility and cultural transmission.[4] It is, however, not inherent to signed languages that they have no written form and, on the traditional view in linguistics that the 'spoken' rather than the 'written' form is basic, we do not see this contrast as being of direct relevance to the elaboration of a model of how the language faculty relates to the rest of cognition. The one caveat in this regard is that we need to take into account the fact that the written form of spoken languages and the basic form of signed languages both necessarily involve the operation of the visual system and both involve the activation of phonological representations.

6.3   Deixis in English and BSL: apraxia revisited

Deictic elements traditionally fall into three categories, i.e. person, place and time: such expressions as the personal pronouns *I* and *you*, locatives such as *here* and *there*, and past versus present tense, where these 'characterize the features of the speech context which help determine which proposition is expressed by a given sentence' (Stalnaker, 1972: 383). 'Deixis' in BSL seems, unlike in spoken languages, to be precisely what is suggested by the etymology – pointing. Deictic relations as expressed in signed languages are systematically iconic, whereas in spoken language deixis may be supplemented by pointing but the lexical encoding itself is not iconic. As a result of this difference, it has been claimed (McBurney, 2002: 350) that 'spatial marking within signed language pronoun systems is qualitatively different from what we see in spoken language pronoun systems'. We disagree: signed languages are again at one end of a continuum but are not different in kind from spoken languages. This is because the 'pointing', despite its apparently iconic status, is nonetheless arbitrary, as in the directional contrasts between past and future: a point leftwards indicates 'earlier' and rightwards indicates 'later'; a point backwards indicates past, forwards marks future. The arbitrariness of these signs is made abundantly clear by the fact that some sign languages use forward pointing for the past (the imagery being that things that have happened are visible), and BSL itself has forward movement for both TOMORROW and YESTERDAY – the distinction is that in YESTERDAY the palm faces forward and in TOMORROW it faces backward. Even where some iconicity can be perceived, the sign is so tightly integrated into the linguistic system that the deictic element is dissociated from the lexical content. This becomes clearest in pathology.

Consider again the standard effects of cerebral lateralisation, whereby the left side is controlled predominantly by the right hemisphere and the right side by the left hemisphere. Recall moreover that the language faculty is usually concentrated in the left hemisphere, so that damage to that hemisphere typically causes aphasia as well as right hemiparesis, whereas damage to the right hemisphere 'merely' causes paralysis on the left. Poizner *et al.* (1987) contrast the remarkable cases of aphasic patients who lost the ability to point (because of right hemisphere damage) versus those who lost their use of language because of left hemisphere damage. The former could still sign the form for 'you' but were unable to 'point at' someone, despite the identity of the movements involved, whilst the latter had precisely the inverse loss. A comparable dissociation is sometimes manifest in the normal population as well. In about 25 per cent of typically developing children there is a stage of 'pronoun reversal' in which they use 'I' to refer to their interlocutors and 'you' to refer to themselves. This is not as surprising as one might think: the child is simply using the pronouns as though they were proper nouns treating 'Give it to Daddy' and 'Give it to me' as equivalent. Remarkably, some deaf children go through the same developmental stage in which they point at someone else to refer to themselves, and at themselves to refer to their interlocutors (Petitto, 1987; for discussion, see Emmorey, 2002: 182–3). The implication is that the signs, while etymologically iconic and gestural, have been incorporated into the linguistic system with the same Saussurean arbitrariness as any other word. (For wider discussion of lateralisation effects see Corina, 1999 and Atkinson *et al.*, 2005.)

This difference between the linguistic and the gestural is reinforced by the observation that gestures are non-compositional whereas pronominal signs are compositional so that 'the component parts convey different grammatical distinctions' (Emmorey, 2002: 52). Emmorey (ibid.) goes on to discuss Meier's (1990) claim that signed languages, unlike all spoken languages, make no phonological distinction between 2nd and 3rd person referents: rather, the distinction is conveyed by an associated gesture. It is not clear if the claim is accurate, and we are sceptical. However, to substantiate our suspicions would require evidence that is currently unavailable: we would need data about bound variable usage, data from pathology to see if the 2nd person/3rd person distinction survived right hemisphere damage, and comparable data from pronoun reversal in first language acquisition.

The dissociation between language and gesture suggests that it would be unsurprising if Christopher's apraxia had no – or minimal – effect on his linguistic knowledge, even though it might impinge disadvantageously on his use of that knowledge. In spoken languages he coped well with deictic alternations between *this* and *that* to indicate proximate and distal entities, and in BSL he had no difficulty in associating appropriate signs with their English language deictic equivalents. That is, in translating both from BSL into English and from English into BSL he gave fully appropriate translations of *this, that* and the proximal/distal signs that convey the same content. There is, however, a problem with this interpretation of the evidence in that it was not always transparent whether his responses were really translations of a sign or interpretations of a gesture. Thus he had problems using points in sign space as 3rd person reference points with agreeing verbs, which might reflect a problem distinguishing between sign and gesture or a problem with using abstract locations in general: he found it difficult to sign object locations when the objects were in front of him, so it may be that his problems are with abstract space. Where deixis was grammatically formal in that it marked agreement, he had difficulty encoding it in production because his BSL was not sufficiently advanced to enable him to represent pointing gestures as agreement signs. However, in cases where there was overlap between English *this/that* and some gestural representation of them in spoken language, he could 'translate' them from and into BSL. Deixis is the domain where the grammar and pragmatics meet; we turn next to a more general discussion of Christopher's pragmatic ability in BSL.

6.4   Space, syntax and pragmatics

In section 1.4.5 we made the observation that Christopher's pragmatics is, given his other cognitive limitations, surprisingly good. In his spoken languages he is able to use modus ponens, discourse connectives like *anyway*, and he can even derive explicatures by enrichment. Moreover, in his BSL syntax he appeared fairly systematically to rely on context in his use of elliptical questions, omitting the question sign, signing *YOU LIVE* instead of YOU LIVE WHERE, for instance. This omission is significant because we had expected his articulation problems to lead him to produce signs but without appropriate movement: just holding the handshape in the location where the hand-internal movement should take place, for example. The implication is that the omission is the result of a pragmatic strategy and not just a function of articulatory difficulties.

In his use of both spoken and signed languages he is unable to use his metalinguistic ability to derive implicatures or to use sentences 'interpretively'. Apart from this, in the sign language domain he had pragmatic problems of three kinds: his failure to benefit from iconicity, presumably because of the concomitant demand for inferencing; his failure to use topicalisation in pragmatically appropriate fashion, despite his syntactic mastery of the relevant word-order; and his failure with examples which imposed some processing overload. We discuss each in turn.

As inferencing of the kind exemplified by the use of modus ponens is within Christopher's ability, at least in spoken (and written) language, we suspect that his problems with iconicity are due not only to the fact that BSL is a 'second' language for him, but more basically to his difficulty in exploiting non-linguistic representations at all. All adult learners of BSL should be helped by iconicity because, at least in the early stages, it facilitates the memorisation of the sign (or parts of the sign) needed to access meaning. With advancing knowledge and fluency, the representation may not activate iconic features anymore, but

Christopher found the initial use of a non-linguistic representation as a step towards a linguistic representation to be beyond him.

His failure to use topicalisation appropriately is partly expected, partly puzzling. He consistently failed to make correct acceptability judgements of sentences involving topicalisation in English or dislocation in Greek – so *a fortiori* one would expect him to have problems with BSL. However, he seemed to have minimal difficulty in internalising the non-English word-order of BSL, so his failure is somewhat unexpected. The asymmetry is presumably due to the fact that he represented the BSL word-order not as pragmatically derived but as a syntactic property (encoding the basic headedness) of the language.

Christopher's problems with examples that led to processing overload were of two kinds: garden-path structures in his first language and, in his 'second' languages, examples such as Greek dislocation, where he could not provide the right context to interpret the marked word-order. In garden-path structures we claimed that he could either not entertain two different representations, the garden-path and the correct one, at the same time (a capacity problem); or that, once garden-pathed, he could not inhibit the wrong analysis and construct the correct one (a problem of inhibition). On either interpretation, his failure with such examples is a special case of his limited intellectual ability. Sperber & Wilson (2002) (cf. Wilson & Sperber, 2002) argue that comprehension is a dedicated sub-module of the mind-reading (theory of mind) module, and one might expect of a (sub-)module that its activities be in principle independent of those of other components of the mind. This account is incomplete, however, because Christopher can comprehend sentences in terms of their argument and event structure, and he can also access their semantics, even if sometimes too literally, as in his reaction to contradiction in metalinguistic negation. What he fails to do is comprehend the enrichment of propositional content by making use of the current context or by entertaining alternative models of the world so that a particular utterance may have a relevant interpretation in a fictional context. Assuming that comprehension is the usual compromise between the costs of processing and the benefits of the cognitive effects achieved by that processing, this failure is a function of his inability to devote enough resources to the task in hand. It may also be that his problems with theory of mind prevent him from appreciating the benefits of the cognitive effects obtained. His putative problems with inhibiting an interpretation he has accessed are orthogonal to this.

6.5   Classifiers revisited

BSL is based on the encoding and decoding of the visuo-spatial into the linguistic and vice versa, and classifiers are the prototypical example of a category at the language/visuo-spatial interface. Correctly representing a BSL classifier involves not only accessing the grammatical features in its lexical entry but

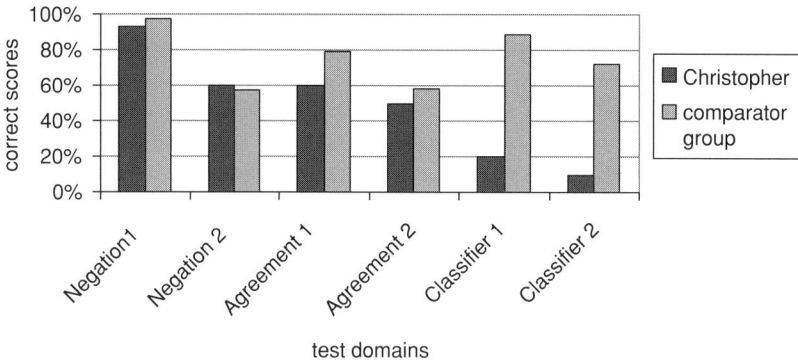

Figure 26 Comparison of different test results by Christopher and members of the comparator group

also encoding (and decoding) the visuo-spatial relation of the classifier and the rest of the clause. It is striking that classifiers were entirely absent from Christopher's signing, and fig. 26 shows the radical asymmetry between his performance and that of the members of the comparator group on a variety of tasks. While at the lower end of the spectrum, his performance on tests of negation and agreement was within the range of the comparator group, but on classifiers he was dramatically worse. Why should this be?

In his case, but not in that of the comparator group, it appears that the encoding and decoding of spatial relations was difficult because of his deficit in visuo-spatial processing. BSL sentences containing classifiers are defectively represented at the relevant interface because that representation depends on the accurate encoding and decoding of the classifier's inherent spatial relations and their integration with the rest of the sentence. All BSL signs involve visuo-spatial representations, but classifiers are an extreme case. When Christopher is presented with, for instance, a negative BSL sentence, he can comprehend each sign individually and then project this onto a linguistic structure which coordinates the individual meanings. With classifier sentences he cannot apply the same simple strategy, because successful comprehension of the classifier alone involves the simultaneous comprehension of its visuo-spatial properties and their relation to the predicate and the other participants or objects in the sentence. Christopher's linguistic prowess is unable to compensate in this area for his visuo-spatial deficit.

6.6   Facial action, intonation and morpho-phonology

As discussed in ch. 2, BSL, like all other sign languages, uses movements of the head and variations in facial expression to convey linguistic meaning.

There are both similarities to and dissimilarities from the corresponding use of intonation in spoken languages. Variations in pitch may be either 'affective' or grammatical, a paralinguistic part of the 'tone of voice' (see e.g. Crystal, 1975) or a linguistic means of conveying such grammatical information as the contrast between statement and question. The issue that concerns us in the present context is, then, whether the range of functions carried by facial action in signed languages is crucially different from the range of functions carried by intonation in spoken languages.

It is probably true that no spoken language distinguishes statements and conditionals by purely intonational means in the way that ASL, for instance, differentiates them by facial action (Emmorey, 2002: 46). The question is whether this difference is qualitative or (merely) quantitative: that is, to what extent is Emmorey's claim (2002: 48) that 'the use of facial expressions to mark grammatical contrasts is unique (and apparently universal) to signed languages' a 'phonetic' claim about realisation, and how far is it a more interesting 'phonological' (linguistic) claim about the language faculty. The quantitative aspect is striking: the range of semantic contrasts that are linguistically encoded in facial action is clearly dramatically greater than what is encoded intonationally or paralinguistically. This contrast leads to a further radical, and qualitative, difference. Failing to identify intonational differences may prevent you from getting the correct pragmatic construal of an utterance, so that irony or exaggeration, for instance, may be missed, but the basic propositional content will still be correctly retrieved. Failing to identify facial action, however, may lead you to construct a linguistically incorrect representation. Consider as an example the processing of those negative BSL sentences which do not include a manual negation sign at all, but only facial action and a head-shake. Failing to interpret the non-manual content would result in the construction of the wrong propositional content. Christopher's production and comprehension of spoken languages is not deficient in terms of content but only in terms of pragmatics. It follows that for him the difference between reading and listening to a spoken language is not of great importance. If anything, the written form is easier for him because it lacks these 'extras' (intonation, tone of voice, and so on) whose pragmatic implications make comprehension more complex. To the extent that BSL uses facial action to convey propositional content it is then qualitatively different from spoken languages, and Christopher's mild autism, with its concomitant inhibiting effect on his comprehension of such action, partly neutralises his linguistic talent.

6.7   A model of the mind

It is a truism that the human mind/brain is the most complex entity in the universe, and lies at the very limits of human understanding. Indeed, it may be that many aspects of cognitive functioning are 'mysteries' rather than 'problems' in Chomsky's (1980: 6–7) sense. Nonetheless, if we are to explain, and not merely describe, Christopher's talents and limitations it is essential that we suggest an explicit model of the mind sufficiently complex and detailed to accommodate both his and the typical adult population's behaviour, and to make falsifiable predictions. We accordingly modify and elaborate the model that we proposed in *The Mind of a Savant*.

6.7.1   The framework

The core of the proposal is an amalgamation of Anderson's (1992) theory of intelligence, Chomsky's theory of language, Fodor's (1983) modularity hypothesis, and our own earlier account of Christopher exploiting a contrast between modules and 'quasi-modules' (Tsimpli & Smith, 1998). We also appeal to Sperber & Wilson's (1986/1995) theory of relevance and Baddeley's (2007) theory of working memory which, following him, we take to be domain-specific (where a 'domain' is essentially a quasi-module), whereas short-term memory is domain-neutral. Our aim is to be able to provide for each of spoken and signed language (with a contrast between English and other languages) an account of all of the linguistic phenomena we have described above, including those in (1):

(1) a   comprehension (spoken/written/   (language as an input system)
        signed)
    b   spontaneous speech/writing/signing   (language as an output system)
    c   conversation (involving both (a) and (b) and how these are
        dependent on some element of mind-reading)
    d   translation (lexical, sentential; spoken/spoken; signed/spoken;
        spoken/signed)
    e   giving judgements of   (involving (a) and some
        well-/ill-formedness   element of introspection)

These will also involve some account of:

    f   the roles of iconicity and gesture, and their implications for the
        relations between natural language and the language of thought
    g   the role of facial action, and its putative parallels with prosody

In addition, we need to account for Christopher's (and others') abilities in:

    h   doing IQ tests (verbal and non-verbal, especially 'visual' tests such
        as the Rey-Osterrieth)
    i   doing theory of mind tests (of false belief) and their differential
        results
    j   memory anomalies

In section 1.4.2 we drew a contrast between the central system in Fodor's sense and the various input systems, which correspond to the senses. The central system is responsible for problem-solving, the 'fixation of belief' and, in the form of the supervisory attentional system, for the overall control of the rest of the mind/brain, including the control of inhibition. It is fed partly internally – from memory and inferencing from currently accessible stored information – and partly by the input systems: audition, vision, touch, olfaction and so on. The structure of the supervisory attentional system or executive is largely mysterious and is crucially not modular or quasi-modular (see Fodor, 2000, for discussion).

As language is also an output system, we followed Chomsky in dissociating ourselves from Fodor's position that the language faculty is exclusively an input system, and we further argued that it must lie partly inside and partly outside the central system. Also following Chomsky, we further assume that the internal structure of the language faculty is as hypothesised in current work in the Minimalist Program, comprising a lexicon and a computational component (C_{HL}), the 'computation for human language', where moreover, C_{HL} may itself be modular in the style of Government & Binding theory (Chomsky, 1981). As will become apparent, we deviate from both Chomsky and Fodor in our treatment of the language faculty, especially with regard to the lexicon, which we ascribe in part to the central system and in part to the non-central domain.

As suggested above, an important influence on our research has been Anderson's 'cognitive theory of intelligence'. Building on his work, we assumed that the central system was characterised by a knowledge base (including part of the language faculty), by a basic processing mechanism, whose speed of operation defines the elements of intelligence (in particular Spearman's g), and by a number of specific processors, most notably one (SP_1) dedicated to 'visuo-spatial' processing and one (SP_2) to 'verbal-propositional' processing. We have already indicated (pp. 28–9 above) that the basic processing mechanism is undesirable, and we return below to the issue of whether we need such specific processors and, in particular, what the status might be of some processor for other sensory inputs, including the kinaesthetic. These specific processors convert sensory representations into representations in the language of thought (LoT), as in Fodor, 1975. A schematic representation of Anderson's model was given as fig. 5 (p. 28 above).

In addition to the constructs provided by Anderson, we have assumed that the central system is partly defined by a set of 'quasi-modules': number, music,[5] moral judgement, folk physics and so on, with well-defined properties. As with Fodorian modules, the evidence for quasi-modules is largely drawn from the possibility of double dissociations (see Smith, 1998a, 2003). That is, the various functions attributed to the mind appear to be relatively autonomous: one can be impaired in respect of any sub-component independently of one's abilities in the other domains. For instance, intelligence and linguistic ability doubly dissociate, musical and mathematical abilities are not necessarily linked, and even moral judgement can be affected or impaired in isolation from other faculties, as witness the case of Phineas Gage (Damasio, 1994: 10–11). In the case of both language and other faculties, there may also be dissociations of the sub-modular structure. In language, the lexicon and the computational systems may be differentially impaired; in the number sense, patients with different kinds of cerebral lesion may doubly dissociate with regard to their ability to cope with small (subitised) numbers and approximations, whereas others may have difficulty only with exact large numbers.

We leave to one side a range of further complications: for instance, the status and role of the emotions (but see Smith *et al.*, 2003, for some discussion). We are assuming, perhaps counterfactually, that language and the emotional system(s) are related only via the central system, and that the interaction of the emotional system with the visual system (see e.g. Ekman, 2007) is independent of this. We return below to the role to be attributed to the 'executive', the putative controlling mechanism that oversees the operations of the remainder.

We have argued elsewhere that the language faculty is partly a module, partly central, where this distinction is fleshed out in terms of a contrast between the (central) conceptual lexicon and the (modular) functional lexicon, essentially the linguistic lexicon. This is reminiscent of Platzack's (2000) analysis of the language faculty where 'systems of thought' access the 'designated interfaces' THEMATIC FORM (basically, theta theory, couched in something like predicate logic or image schemata), GRAMMATICAL FORM (including voice, aspect, mood, etc.), and DISCOURSE FORM (including 'focus'), associated with the output of the three 'computational' domains. A further assumption, which is critical in the present context and which we will have reason to re-evaluate below, is that the language faculty is to a first approximation neutral as between vision and audition (Morgan *et al.*, 2002b; see Petitto, 2005). That is, following Chomsky (1995, etc.) we take the crucial levels of representation for both signed and spoken language to be semantic and phonetic/phonological, ('LF' and 'PF' in traditional terminology) with interface connections ensuring 'legibility' with the conceptual-intentional and sensori-motor systems respectively. We discuss the need for deviations from this assumption below, where we investigate whether the interfaces of Minimalism are adequate to the task of describing knowledge and use of language on this idealising assumption.

Further insight into the overall structure of the mind comes from the fact that the operation of its various sub-systems may be differentially accessible to introspection. This is most clearly apparent in the case of the visual system, where some processes can, but others cannot, be brought to consciousness. For instance, the Titchener illusion indicates that one visual sub-system is conscious, another unconscious.[6] In an experimental illustration of this illusion subjects are presented with two discs in an array where judgement of their relative size is problematic (one disc is surrounded by a circle of smaller discs, the other by a circle of larger discs), and are asked to grasp the left-hand disc if it is larger than the right hand one. Subjects are consistently wrong in their conscious visual judgement of how large the disc is, but measurements of their grasping hand as it reaches for the disc demonstrate that unconsciously they must know the correct size, because the configuration of their hands reflects the actual size of the disc with considerable accuracy (Carey, 2001).[7] That this distinction is not an isolated example is suggested by the contrast between prosopagnosia and Capgras' delusion. In prosopagnosia, the perceptual process of face recognition is defective, and sufferers exhibit bizarre behaviour of the kind documented in the title case study in *The Man Who Mistook His Wife for a Hat* (Sacks, 1985). Oliver Sacks's patient was unable to distinguish faces from similarly shaped entities, but as soon as he heard his wife's voice, he could recognise her for who she was; it was only one part of his visual system, in particular his processing of faces, that was defective, and his memory and emotional responses were otherwise fine. Crucially, he was all too conscious of the parlous situation he was in. The converse of this case is provided by Capgras' delusion, in which the face recognition process is perfect, but it evokes *no* emotional response and the identification of the person recognised is therefore 'disbelieved' by the central system. That is, the sufferer is convinced that the person whom he has recognised *looks like* his wife, but is simultaneously convinced that this person is an impostor, because there is no appropriate emotional response. In such cases subjects have no conscious awareness of their condition, suggesting that conscious/unconscious is orthogonal to the compartmentalisation that includes face recognition. That is, one sub-part of the visual system constitutes face recognition, but – perhaps like all modular systems – this is differentially accessible to consciousness. This phenomenon is reminiscent of the two steps involved in lexical access. In retrieving a word from memory, one first recognises the phonological properties of the word form, and only subsequently is the meaning accessed. It is at this second stage that one talks of lexical access. The parallel is not perfect because accessing meaning is not necessarily conscious, but the first, recognition, stage is entirely unconscious. The wider implication of this differential access to consciousness may be that all the (Fodorian) modules need to be fractionated in such a way that their properties may be either encapsulated, like input systems, or unencapsulated, like the central system. We do not equate 'central' with 'conscious': the operations of theory of mind are generally not conscious, for instance; but accessibility to consciousness generally correlates with being central. That is, we assume that some input modules have central counterparts – there is both a visual input module and a central visual quasi-module, an auditory input module and a central auditory quasi-module, for instance. Some input modules have no such central counterparts – olfaction, for instance; and some central quasi-modules have no Fodorian input counterparts – theory of mind or moral judgement, for example (see fig. 30 on page 175).

In addition to visuo-spatial representation and verbal-propositional representation, it is clear that the system elaborated in our earlier work needs to be provided with some form of 'body representation'. That is, we take it that kinaesthetic awareness of one's own bodily position, as well as its (visually perceived) relation to the external world, is subserved by a dedicated system, with its own proprietary vocabulary and properties. This system also mediates between one's perception of the body movements of others and copying them on one's own body. It is significant that Christopher performed poorly in copying movement in the apraxia tasks. Moreover, to the extent that autism is systematically associated with some form of apraxia, it would seem that the perception of the body movements of ourselves and of others may involve the same self–other distinction needed for success in theory of mind tasks (albeit with no belief or affect component). Additional evidence that the kinaesthetic representation of body movement is distinct from the visuo-spatial comes from the fact that Christopher had no problems in tests where he had to guess what picture there was on the other side of a flash card or what another person was able to see (Smith & Tsimpli, 1995: 176f.).

Given the above components of the mind and the aim of providing an account of the phenomena in (1a – j) above, we need to postulate an explicit link, or links, between language and the central system(s) in order to accommodate the mapping (in both directions) between natural language and the language of thought. More particularly, our model relates semantic representations, at LF in Chomsky's earlier (1995, 2000) sense, to relevance-theoretic 'explicatures' (Sperber & Wilson, 1986/1995; Carston, 2002): what Cormack & Smith (2002: 356) call 'LoTF' – representations in the language of thought. For this we suggest a model as indicated in fig. 27, modified from Smith & Tsimpli (1995: 170) by the elimination of 'surface structure', and by the explicit tie-up with the conceptual contrast between FLB and FLN of Hauser *et al.* (2002). FLB (the faculty of language in the 'broad' sense) is divided between the language module proper – FLN (the faculty of language in the 'narrow' sense) and the conceptual lexicon, itself a sub-part of the central system. FLN generates representations at LF and PF. The latter are outside the language module *stricto sensu*; the former are converted via the morphology interface to give representations in post-LF, which are in turn converted by relevance-theoretic processes into propositional representations ('explicatures') in the LoT. All these processes are taken to be potentially bidirectional to allow for the use of the system in parsing and production.

As discussed briefly above, part of the central system under our conception is a set of quasi-modules. Of these, the one most relevant for the current discussion

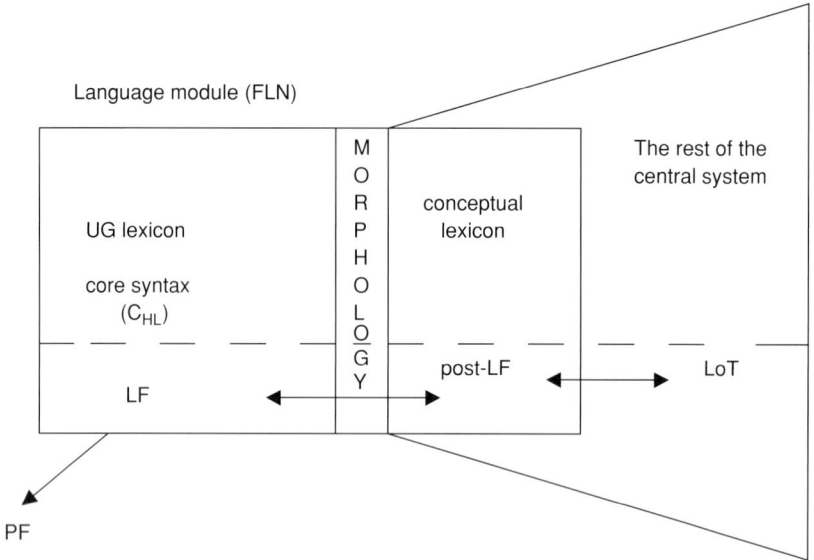

Figure 27 FLB (the faculty of language in the 'broad' sense)

is the theory of mind (ToM) (quasi-)module. The reason for its importance is the bidirectional interaction between the language faculty and the developing ToM – for detailed discussion see Tsimpli & Smith (1998). Its motivation in the case of Christopher is mainly to accommodate his differential behaviour on various false-belief tasks, where his performance constitutes a significant part of the evidence that he is mildly autistic. To include such additional structure in our model we need to elaborate the system as indicated in fig. 28, where a number of quasi-modules are specified (in particular, number, music, folk physics, moral judgement, social structure and so on). Note that we have excluded 'face recognition', which we included in that category in Smith & Tsimpli (1995), but which we now take to be one sub-part of the visual system. Only the interaction of ToM with the language faculty is explicitly indicated.

It is explicit in fig. 28 that ToM can manipulate LoT representations which have many of the properties of natural language representations. As we indicated previously, it must be the case that 'information from the central knowledge store including interpreted linguistic representations . . . must be accessible to [ToM]. That linguistic representations are shared by the Theory of Mind component and the language module does not necessarily entail the penetrability of the language system. Rather, Theory of Mind could either be parasitic on language or share with it linguistic structures of one particular type' (Tsimpli & Smith, 1998: 211–12). The structures characteristic of theory

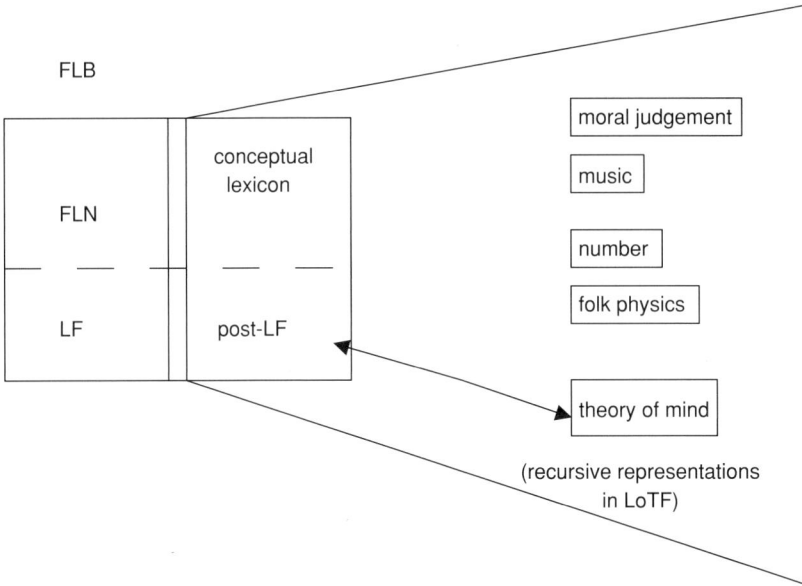

Figure 28 The quasi-modular structure of the central system

of mind are representations consisting of a very specific subset of linguistic structures: namely, sentences with at least one level of embedding, an epistemic modal operator ranging over the whole proposition and, in order to derive the self–other distinction, referential properties of the subjects included in the sentence. The major implication of such a position is that (*pace* Hauser *et al.*, 2002) recursion may not be limited to FLN but may also be a property of other faculties of mind. That is, more than one system exploits recursion but the primitives used are in each case different (see Smith, 2004; Smith & Law, 2007, for further discussion). A second major consideration, on which we remain for the moment agnostic, is the relation of ToM to pragmatics and 'metarepresentation' more generally. Our position is compatible with Wilson's (2003) claim that pragmatics is a sub-part of theory of mind – rather, what she calls a 'mind-reading' module – though we are prepared to grant the two systems autonomy. The issue will presumably be decided on the basis of possible dissociations: we suspect that it is possible to show some conventional socio-pragmatic abilities in the absence of other mind-reading skills (as, for example, in some autistic subjects) and perhaps vice versa, (as some Asperger Syndrome subjects can pass theory of mind false-belief tasks but their social skills are impoverished), suggesting that the two faculties are autonomous rather than being in a subset relation.

The model in fig. 28 happily accommodates two other domains with a potential interaction with the language faculty: the number sense and the music sense. Christopher's abilities in these areas are limited and, in the case of number, perhaps pathological. As reported in Smith & Tsimpli (1995: 5), on experimental testing, he displays a certain basic ability to carry out simple arithmetic calculations, but (often) fails to conserve number. Despite Chomsky's speculation (1991: 50) that the number sense is parasitic on the language faculty, the dissociations documented by Dehaene (1997) – e.g. acalculia in its various forms – suggests that they are autonomous, as is already implicit in the fact that the systems operate over different primitives (see also Gelman & Butterworth, 2005). As regards his musical ability, he has an avid interest in various forms of music, especially popular songs in a variety of languages, so he certainly does not suffer from amusia, even if his own singing is uninspired and somewhat tuneless.

At this point it is relevant to re-emphasise that physical location in a particular part of the brain is only one kind of evidence for the structure of the mind. The old view of areas of the brain being dedicated to processing unitary types of sensory input has largely been overtaken by recognition of the various integrational, multimodal (or supramodal) areas: for instance, the processing of sign language in auditory cortices. In general, multiple and integrated channels are exploited in all aspects of human activity, including communication.

Our main concern is the mental rather than the neural, though it is crucial that our model be compatible with whatever neural properties are known. In fig. 28 and elsewhere, we have substituted our own quasi-module for Fodor's language module, but we wish to retain his insight about the properties of other input systems and their relation to the central system. Accordingly, we maintain a model with Fodorian modular structure, while allowing for the possible fractionation as between conscious and unconscious processes mentioned above. For Fodor, as for us, the various input systems are all informationally encapsulated and cognitively impenetrable, so the only communication between the language system and these modules is via the central executive. As, on our account, (part of) the language faculty is a proper sub-part of the central system this gives rise to no problems of principle: relations between the various modules are always mediated centrally, most plausibly in a format close to or isomorphic with the natural language. One apparent problem that arises for this account, and one that is particularly relevant to any discussion of multimodal language processing, is typified by the McGurk effect (McGurk & MacDonald, 1976), where simultaneous auditory and visual input gives rise to a percept distinct from both. For instance, a subject hearing [p] but seeing a face articulating [k] will report hearing [t].[8] This suggests that there is interplay between the visual and auditory systems in a manner at variance with Fodor's claims. However, what the subject reports is presumably the result of passing the apparently contradictory input from the two modalities up to the central system for decision. If the integration takes place upstream of the input systems, or if both activities are in fact taking place in the language faculty (which is anyway parasitic on the visual and/or auditory systems), no problem arises. Indeed, the possibility of such interference suggests that Christopher (or anyone else) might experience problems when processing multiple inputs. It is a common observation in the autobiographical writing of subjects on the autistic spectrum that the need to process several inputs simultaneously gives rise to serious cognitive overload (see e.g. Williams, 1994: 22f; Willey, 1999: 22, 125ff.). This effect is accentuated in a situation where one of the modalities involved is required to process data distinct from that to which it is normally attuned as, for instance, when the visual system of a hearing person is called on to deal with lip-read input. All people, hearing and deaf, lip-read, with even normally hearing people relying appreciably on a visual input (see e.g. Dodd, 1987), and lip-reading also involves activation of the auditory cortex (Calvert *et al.*, 1997). One side-effect of the pervasiveness and efficacy of lip-reading is that congenitally blind children make characteristic phonological errors (Mills, 1987). So spoken language is perceived audio-visually but, for hearing people, what is visible in speech is relatively redundant and is less informative than the auditory signal. Accordingly, despite the fact that such dual input is always present, and that there appear to be specific areas of the brain in which the necessary integration takes place (MacSweeney *et al.*, 2004), problems arise when hearing people have to rely on vision in lip-reading, and deaf people are typically better lip-readers. Although we have no evidence on Christopher's ability to lip-read, inability to integrate information from various sources satisfactorily is characteristic of the weak central coherence suggested for him and other autistic subjects, so we would expect him to have some difficulty.

Whatever the implications of anomalous input (with a deliberately engineered mismatch between the auditory and the visual), it is clear that the language faculty must be closely linked to both the auditory and visual systems, the former for spoken language, the latter for signed language. Even in the case of 'spoken' language, reading necessitates the use of the visual mode, where disturbance can give rise to the specific pathology of dyslexia. There is no equivalent of dyslexia in the case of signing since there is no writing system for sign language, though aphasia is possible in either case, with comparable properties (see ch. 5 above). Moreover, it is known that children learn to fingerspell before they learn to read and at first do not recognise any relationship between written text and fingerspelling (Padden, 1991).[9]

In the case of both the auditory and the visual modalities it is important to remember that they serve non-linguistic as well as linguistic functions: we have not only the understanding of spoken language, but also the understanding of

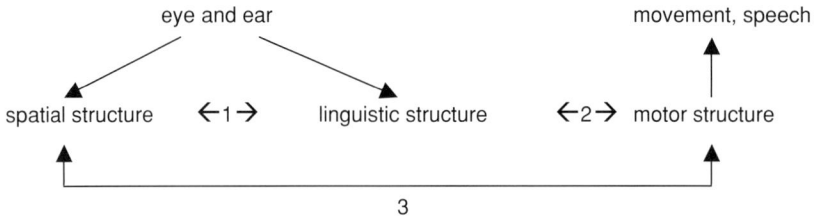

where:

Interface 1 maps spatial information to linguistic information and vice versa
Interface 2 maps linguistic information to motoric information and vice versa
Interface 3 maps spatial information into motoric information and vice versa

Figure 29 Components of the mind (from Van der Zee & Nikanne, 2000b)

music and noise (see Smith, 2002: ch. 6), the understanding of signed language and the interpretation of non-linguistic visual stimuli. Most relevantly, we also perceive and interpret gesture and the fusion of gesture with speech (see e.g. Goldin-Meadow & Wagner, 2005). That is, audition and vision license access to the same concepts in the central system as does the use of language: the sight or sound of the wind in the trees presumably triggers the same concept of tree as the word 'tree'. All these relationships must be explicitly allowed for in our model.

We turn next to language and spatial representation: a relation that our previous model ignored entirely. Although it is couched within a different theoretical framework, Jackendoff's (1997) 'representational modularity of mind', we are sympathetic – with certain reservations – to the basic assumptions made in Van der Zee & Nikanne's (2000b: 2) model of the 'components of the mind', shown schematically in fig. 29.

The model sketched in fig. 29 is elaborated in Nikanne (2000: 78) by the addition of 'body position senses', a 'motor faculty', a 'haptic faculty' and a 'social faculty', all supposedly centred on 'conceptual structure' (in the sense of Jackendoff, 1983). However, the link between spatial cognition and language is then mediated by conceptual structure, so it would seem to follow that, at least for Nikanne, spatial representations are not themselves conceptual representations. This seems unfortunate for signed languages. It is not contested that spatial concepts which are linguistic should differ from those that are non-linguistic: such a contrast is parallel to the distinction between linguistic sound and non-linguistic but informative noises such as coughs. But all of these are 'conceptual', unless one draws explicitly the distinction we have made above with regard to LF and LoTF, and defines representations at LF, whether signed or spoken, to be 'preconceptual' (as in Fodor, 2008). Whatever the correct interpretation,[10] our position is that we need both a linguistic and a conceptual interface for spatial representations. In users of signed languages spatial cognition interfaces with language directly, while in those using only spoken languages this interface might not be activated. That is, signers have control of both interfaces but those who can only speak may not have a linguistic interface with spatial concepts.

The 'spatial structure' in fig. 29 corresponds in essential respects to Anderson's visuo-spatial special processor, and the 'motor structure', insofar as it pertains to verbal action, corresponds to our PF interface. What is still lacking in our model is an explicit link between the articulatory–perceptual interface (simply hinted at by the label 'PF' in fig. 27) and the kinaesthetic system (normally deployed for proprioception) when this is exploited for speech or sign. We believe that our investigations of Christopher and the comparator group cast light on this relation, and enable us to simplify the model we are constructing. In particular, we suspect that the relation between proprioception and the articulatory–perceptual interface is mediated by another quasi-module 'kinaesthesis' that enables the central monitoring of all motor activities including those that subserve language. This suggests – as others have also claimed – that there needs also to be some integration of working memory and motor representations. Thus Emmorey & Wilson (2004), in a review comparing studies of working memory for sign language and spoken language, cite Boutla *et al.*'s (2004) observation that sensory traces persist longer in the auditory system, which shows superior coding of serial order, whereas sensory traces are less persistent in the visual system, which is superior at spatial coding. This provides strong support for the role of modality-specific rather than amodal representations in working memory, an observation which is relevant to Christopher's differential performance in signed and spoken languages. In fact, we suspect that sensory traces of written words are even more salient for Christopher than are auditory traces, which are different again from sensory traces of spatial relations.

With the addition of kinaesthesis to the set of quasi-modules these considerations lead to the suggestion that the structure of the mind be characterised in terms of correlated (Fodorian) input modules and quasi-modules, allowing us to dispense with separate (Andersonian) specific processors. That is, once we have the (central) structure provided by a set of quasi-modules, the functions of the specific processors can be taken over by them. The justification for this claim comes from the interpretation of Christopher's differential success in mastering the ways that BSL makes use of space, as discussed in chapter 3. We spell out the details of this below.

Some notion of proprioceptive 'body representation' is necessary for both the signed and the spoken modalities. Presumably, the modality that you are used to becomes so automated that you are only aware of it in anomalous conditions (e.g. delayed auditory feedback sabotages one's ability properly to monitor one's own output). Unfortunately there haven't been any studies of the effect on signers of delayed visual feedback, but Arena *et al.* (2007) have studied signers with reduced visual field. They show reduced size of signing space, suggesting that – as expected – this is calibrated using vision. As operating in a new domain is always problematic, a second anomalous condition arises when one is confronted with a new language. Getting used to a new language in the same modality as the previously dominant one is intuitively difficult, as witness the fact that all second language learners carry over linguistic properties from their first language, leading to both negative and positive transfer effects. Getting used to a new modality as well as a new language involves calling on resources, both modular and central, that are not normally used in this way.[11] Some diminution in the effort involved in mastering the visual modality when first learning a signed language may come from taking advantage of gesture. Most adult learners use centrally mediated strategies exploiting the iconicity of gesture to construct linguistic representations on the basis of the visual input.

Just as the language faculty is partly central and partly (Fodorian) modular, we have suggested that some of the other 'input' systems have central counterparts, as one would expect given that in several instances they interface with the language faculty themselves. That is, we have seen that there is a close relation between *audition* and spoken language, between *vision* and signed language, between *vision* and the reading of (spoken) language, and between *vision* and lip-reading. Similarly, there is a close relation between *kinaesthesis* and signed language, and between *kinaesthesis* and the reading of Braille or the haptic mode used in Tadoma (Smith, 2002: ch. 2). The deaf-blind form a particularly interesting study in their use of 'hands-on' sign language. Although there are as yet no experimental investigations, it is clear that those using hands-on signing have their limbs moved passively at the beginning of a sentence, but as processing takes place they begin to move their hands actively to anticipate the likely end to the sentence. This has implications for the functioning of the mind with relation to the various feedback loops it is necessary to postulate.

Thus all three of these sensory systems are directly implicated in the operation of the language faculty, and all three may undergo particular pathological disruptions to that faculty, resulting in aphasia, dysarthria, apraxia, anomalies of proprioception and so on. Accordingly, we have postulated quasi-modular correlates of these three input systems, simultaneously replacing Anderson's two specific processors. We remain agnostic about the need for multiplying quasi-modules beyond this: of the senses, olfaction and taste have no link via language to the central system, so we exclude them. The system must be rich enough to accommodate the differential accessibility to consciousness of different activities, and we suggest that the duplication of input systems and

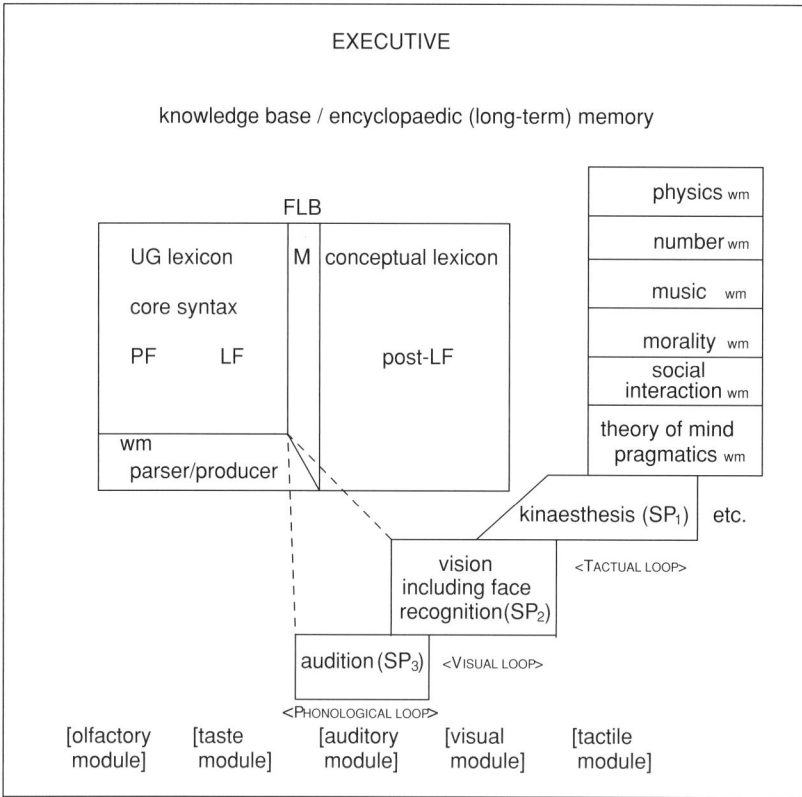

Figure 30 A model of (relevant parts of) the mind

dedicated quasi-modules for auditory, visual and kinaesthetic judgement allows precisely this. More specifically, the output from the visuo-spatial quasi-module has two potential paths: either interacting or not with a quasi-module devoted to kinaesthesis, hence giving rise via executive control to consciousness effects, or by-passing this quasi-module and hence directly affecting the operation of the motor system, (perhaps also mediated by the executive, hence with potential consciousness effects).

We are now in a position to extend the model we have been developing, this time incorporating Fodorian modules as well as an elaboration of the quasi-modular structure of the central system. Consider fig. 30.

Fodorian modules, corresponding to each of the senses – and only these – are enclosed in [square brackets]. The separation between them indicates informational encapsulation.

Quasi-modules are represented in boxes, with the lowest three incorporating (the function of) Anderson's 'specific processors'. The adjacency of the boxes indicates informational penetrability. We have no evidence for the relationships between e.g. '(folk) physics', 'number' and 'music', but there are close links between 'social interaction' (itself divided into 'social cognition' and 'social affect') and 'theory of mind'. For detailed discussion, see Smith *et al.*, 2003.

The parser/producer is a simplistic idealisation – the processes are not really simply reversible. Moreover, some constraints are specific to the parser (such as late closure) and others are characteristic of the producer, which is more closely linked to the conceptual lexicon. In Levelt's (1989) system for speaking you start from the concept and then you access the lemma containing syntactic and semantic information. In our system, designed to accommodate speaking and understanding, there is no distinction in the direction of the link between the conceptual lexicon and the parser or the producer. The link with working memory is underspecified but must include at least phonological working memory.

In the model:

'M' indicates 'morphology', the interface between the UG lexicon and the conceptual lexicon. We assume that the parser has access to this morphological interface.

Anderson's basic processing mechanism is reinterpreted as a constraint on the system as a whole.

The knowledge base/encyclopaedic memory is taken to pervade the entire system though without any implication that processes must be 'top-down'.

The executive controls – in unknown fashion – the operation of the whole.

'wm' indicates 'working memory' dedicated to the respective quasi-modules, including the language faculty.

The three 'loops' correspond to Baddeley's 'phonological loop' and its visual and kinaesthetic congeners. It is important to note that, despite the name, they are not entirely comparable. The 'visual loop' is different in nature from the auditory loop in that, with audition, we hear ourselves essentially as we hear others[12] – there is an intrinsic symmetry – whereas with vision we do not see others' actions as we see our own (especially in signing), though there may be a feedback mechanism which relies on mirror neurons. A kinaesthetic loop is unlike the other two in that it is not intrinsically interactional: that is, it provides no information to the perceiver. In the light of this asymmetry, it is of interest that recent work by Emmorey *et al.* (2009) shows that signers are better at monitoring their own production when seen from the other's perspective than their own.

6.7.2   *Exemplification*

Given the model in fig. 30, we can now return to the list of phenomena in (1) on page 163 and see how each is accounted for.

(1a) – the comprehension of language – spoken, written and signed – is accommodated as follows: the Fodorian input systems take an auditory or visual stimulus and transduce it into a format accessible to the language system. This input is analysed by the parser in conjunction with the grammar into a form which results first in LF (the internal semantic interface) and then in Post-LF. This linguistic representation is further converted by inferential processes à la Relevance theory into a format which gives representations in LoTF, which allow integration into the knowledge base or encyclopaedic memory. We take it that the main differences between spoken, written and signed inputs are that the first is auditorily transduced, while the second and third are visually transduced, and that signed input may also be affected by interaction between the language and kinaesthesis quasi-modules. Silent reading need not involve any kinaesthetic activity at all. We hypothesise that such interaction among quasi-modules is minimised – perhaps entirely[13] – in the comprehension of the first language, but may be pervasive in the comprehension of second language input. This will be most obvious in the case of those whose first language is spoken and who are learning sign as a second language; but there may equally be interaction between the auditory and visual (and kinaesthetic) quasi-modules in those whose first language is signed. The situation is, however, inherently asymmetric in that hearing people can be bilingual with two 'first' languages – signed and spoken – but are unlikely to have sign as an exclusively first language. A major difference between this account and our earlier one is that we no longer see any role for Anderson's specific processors, taking their functions now to be subsumed under those of the respective quasi-modules.

(1b) – spontaneous speaking/writing/signing – proceeds as follows. At the behest of the executive, the pragmatic component (whether this is a sub-module of the theory of mind quasi-module, an autonomous quasi-module in its own right or some amalgam of sub-parts of the central system) formulates some representation in the language of thought. This is then sent to the language faculty to be converted into a representation at LF, which is in turn paired via the grammar with a PF representation, which functions to provide instructions to the articulatory system. Again, there is differential involvement of the kinaesthetic quasi-module, depending on whether the default mode being used is speech or sign. We assume that writing, in virtue of being ontogenetically parasitic on a speakable or signable base, is initially less spontaneous than either of these natural output systems, and may involve a further translational step. In the model we are using this translates as a transformation of the PF (signed or spoken) into a written format. For the literate adult, for whom writing may be the default externalised form of language, writing presumably bypasses this translational step. Indeed, the PF, which we are assuming to be conceptually comparable for signed and spoken languages, may develop a further autonomous form for reading and writing.

(1c) – conversation – is accommodated by a combination of (a) and (b) together with the necessary participation of theory of mind. In our earlier work (see in particular Smith & Tsimpli, 1995: 169) we made crucial reference to the role of the 'executive' in accounting for the asymmetry between Christopher's general linguistic facility on the one hand, and his stilted and monosyllabic conversational ability on the other. While we still think that the executive is involved, as is further borne out by his performance on the Hayling sentence completion test (ibid: app. VI), our current model allows us to invoke the impairment in his theory of mind quasi-module as a contributory – and more explicit – cause. Moreover, to the extent that the executive is equipped with inhibitory control in the form of the supervisory attentional system, this will also accommodate Christopher's conversational oddities, either in the form of his responses to language tasks or in the form of his inability to control an inappropriate response. That is, the monosyllabic and staccato nature of his conversational contributions can be attributed, at least in part, to his failure to take proper account of his interlocutor's point of view, which requires the involvement of ToM in ordinary everyday interactions. The observations about interaction with the kinaesthesis quasi-module that have been adduced to account for asymmetries in his signed and spoken perception and production, carry over to conversation in a purely cumulative fashion

(1d) – translation – needs to be treated under various sub-headings: lexical, sentential; spoken/spoken; signed/spoken; spoken/signed. Lexical translation can be accommodated much as before as long as cognisance is also taken of Christopher's inefficient inhibitory control, which is responsible for his not suppressing inappropriate lexical items. With a written or signed input the vision module feeds a signal into the visual quasi-module with, in the case of signed input, concomitant activation of the kinaesthesis quasi-module. This is then transmitted to a multi-dimensional lexicon (see Smith & Tsimpli, 1995: 171) and a simple replacement operation substitutes one form for another. The relative difficulty of providing translations for signed as opposed to spoken input is then a joint function of the involvement of the extra quasi-module and the radically different nature of the signed representation as opposed to the orthographic representation for items in the various spoken languages as well as the respective subserving memory systems. Spoken input is handled in comparable fashion, except that only the auditory module is initially involved. However, the stored representation of the required response may automatically trigger competing formats (visual – either orthographic or signed, auditory, conceptual, etc.) with associated knock-on effects in terms of the involvement of other components of the mind. Sentential translation in typical subjects necessitates the involvement of the core syntax to a greater or lesser extent, depending on properties of the languages involved. Core syntax may be exploited only minimally except when syntactic processing is obstructed by important differences between the source and the target language. In the ordinary case, translation is rather 'shallow' in terms of syntactic look-up and in Christopher's case this involvement is minimised, depending on his familiarity with the languages concerned. That is, he often seems to treat translation simply as a process of successive lexical look-up, irrespective of the syntactic (or pragmatic) context (which is in fact what some translators do in the early stages of their professional training). In other cases, he clearly accesses at least the English part of his core syntax, but fails to accommodate cross-linguistic differences, fails to monitor the process appropriately, and hence fails to inhibit a syntactically incorrect or contextually inappropriate response. An important caveat to this simplistic account is necessitated by Christopher's expertise at producing the correct morphology in many of his languages. This shows that some aspects of the syntax, or at least the surface effects of morphological spell-out conditions, must have been activated to trigger (e.g.) the correct agreement, but even this frequently leaves it unclear whether the syntax involved is specific to the language putatively being translated or is an abstraction based on English.

(1e) – giving judgements of well-/ill-formedness – also largely involves components we have already looked at. It is important to highlight the difference between giving judgements on one's native language and on non-native languages. In making non-native acceptability judgements, Christopher seems to use his explicit metalinguistic knowledge only in forced-choice tasks. A typical example is provided by his reaction to word-order mistakes in German (for discussion, see Smith & Tsimpli, 1995: 158f.). His initial judgements are determined by the syntactic patterns dictated by his native language equivalent of the target sentence, and only with considerable difficulty can he inhibit this as the basis of his judgement. When it comes to English, his implicit knowledge of the language enables him to produce typical native speaker judgements, except in the case of structures, such as topicalisation, that involve Post-LF or discourse-related conditions. This asymmetry results from the fact that giving such judgements necessitates both the accessing of the core syntax (or its output as produced by the syntactic parser) and higher levels of processing. It is moot whether Christopher consciously accesses the result of the processing, as if he did, he should be able to backtrack and reanalyse locally ambiguous sentences, something he is typically unable to do. Whether our earlier argument for a conscious/unconscious duality in (quasi-)modular activity is relevant here or not, we take it that this pattern of responses can only result from the activity of the executive, which is responsible for the appropriate integration of such representations, monitoring the output of each of the other components. As Christopher's performance on such tasks is not usually amenable to conscious filtering or introspection, as witness his characteristic inability to modify his initial judgements, it appears that his executive is to some degree defective, especially insofar as inhibition is concerned.

(1f) – the roles of iconicity and gesture – involve interplay between the language faculty, the kinaesthesis quasi-module and the visual system. Neither gestures nor iconic elements more generally are represented within the language faculty: hence they are largely inaccessible to Christopher and irrelevant to children acquiring a first language. However, the identification of iconicity crucially presupposes the effect of the encyclopaedic knowledge base of the central system on the interpretation of linguistic stimuli, whether auditory or visual. It is the need for prolonged experience to develop the encyclopaedic information associated with individual lexical entries which underlies the different relevance of iconic clues to children and adults. This interaction between the knowledge base and the language faculty again suggests some inferential role for the executive.

(1g) – facial action. Earlier we distinguished between facial action and facial expression, where the former is part of the linguistic system proper and the latter is paralinguistic – used for conveying emotion and attitude. We further contrasted the use of facial action as used in BSL for drawing lexical as opposed to grammatical distinctions, and we observed that facial action comes in a variety of types: the use of the brows, the eyes, the mouth, where this last is in turn partitioned into 'mouthings' and 'mouth gestures'. In his spoken languages Christopher's expression is characteristically deadpan and, not surprisingly, his facial expression in using BSL was minimal. His use of linguistically important facial action was similarly minimal – we recorded only one appropriate example – and even his interpretation of its use by other signers was generally defective. However, as he gradually managed to engage in eye-contact with his interlocutors he did give evidence of some understanding of facial action in the signing of his tutor, manifesting as elsewhere a contrast between perception and production. We assume that his insensitivity to facial action, even when that encodes linguistic contrasts, is a direct function of his impaired theory of mind,[14] accentuated by the different modality of the new language to which he was exposed as an adult learner. We do not know if his mild autism would have inhibited his ability to process facial action had he been exposed to BSL as a child. Given his general linguistic proficiency Christopher's limited ability with intonation in spoken language is a little surprising: it is perhaps reminiscent of his problems with encoded cases of interpretive use (see above p. 36).

(1h) – doing IQ tests. Depending on the nature of the stimulus (verbal or non-verbal, visual or auditory) such tests would involve first the relevant input module or modules, then the corresponding quasi-modules, and finally the problem-solving mechanisms of the central system. Sadly, we have virtually nothing to say about these central mechanisms except that, in virtue of being a savant, Christopher's are by hypothesis somewhat degraded. It is moreover likely that his poor performance on such tests as the Rey-Osterrieth is at least in part a function of impoverishment in the visual loop as well as central deficits. This shared explanation would comport well with his difficulty with 180 degree rotation tasks.

(1i) – doing theory of mind tests (of false belief) and their differential results. We established earlier (1.4.4) that tasks which require no ascription of belief, such as taking a different physical perspective or doing the Zaitchik photographic tests, were systematically within Christopher's capabilities, but that tasks which necessitate the imputation of false belief to others were difficult or impossible. Further, his performance in this latter domain was interestingly inconsistent. For instance, he systematically failed the 'Sally-Anne' test but passed the 'Smarties' test, indicating that he is sometimes able to compensate for any defects in his theory of mind through linguistic and encyclopaedic knowledge. Our modification of Anderson's model in favour of the version in fig. 30 suggests that Christopher has a somewhat defective theory of mind quasi-module but good encyclopaedic access to relevant information. Crucially, what is relevant, and hence what is facilitated by his language-obsessed executive, is linguistic information. Moreover, our fractionation of working memory such that it is potentially different for each of the quasi-modules and the language faculty makes it possible to suggest that Christopher's language working memory is markedly superior to his theory of mind or (non-linguistic) visuospatial working memory. This leads naturally to the final domain of interest, Christopher's unusual memory.

(1j) – memory anomalies. If working memory is distributed in the way indicated in fig. 30 it allows for two kinds of dissociation: the sub-parts could be independently impaired or enhanced in a particular individual, and they could be differentially refined for signers and non-signers. We have already seen evidence of the enhancement and impairment in Christopher's skewed abilities; evidence for the second strand comes from the differential performance by signers and non-signers on working memory tasks, as described in Keehner & Gathercole (2007: 760) who claim that 'experience with sign language influences cognitive functions beyond the linguistic domain. A novel conclusion from the present study is that visuo-spatial working memory functions accrue adaptations even in hearing people who learn to sign in adulthood.'

6.8   Conclusions

6.8.1   *Neuropsychology and linguistic talent*

We suggested in the introduction that there is an asymmetry in our understanding of the relations between the neurological and the psychological. There has been huge progress in teasing apart the neurological (and genetic) determinants of various pathologies but, despite improved insight into the correlations between brain function and psychological processes, there has been minimal progress in getting to grips with talents. The most infamous parallel can be seen in the controversy over Einstein's brain: despite a plethora of speculative articles about its structure, nothing of scientific value has come from its study. We are optimistic enough to believe that the combination of current imaging studies and meticulous psycholinguistic documentation and experimentation can gradually ameliorate the situation as it pertains to signers both normal and abnormal, but sadly Christopher provides no relevant evidence.

6.8.2   *Modularity, modality and mind*

It is time to take stock. We began with the aim of confronting linguistic talent with apraxic autism in order to test a number of hypotheses and speculations. Some of these have been confirmed; others have remained obscure or have given rise to further questions.

At the most general level it is clear that Christopher treated BSL as a natural language with all the properties that this implies. Further, we have confirmation of the fundamental relevance of the competence–performance dichotomy: due to his apraxia, Christopher's BSL comprehension was considerably better than his BSL production. Similarly, his mild autism, with his reluctance to engage in eye-contact, made us predict his poor performance in using BSL for communication and his almost total lack of mastery of facial action.

We had also predicted his superior performance on the lexicon as opposed to the syntax; we had anticipated the negative effect of there being no written form for BSL, depriving him of his major source of linguistic data for his other 'second' languages; we confirmed not only that his general intellect is impoverished but also that his language processor suffers from deficiencies in capacity. By contrast, our assumption that there would be significant transfer effects from the syntax of English was disconfirmed by his success on BSL word-order, and we did not find evidence to support our prediction that his mastery of BSL verb morphology would be better than his mastery of BSL syntax, even though his misanalysis of the head-shake in negatives as being a morphological rather than a supra-segmental feature was suggestive.

We would like to conclude with speculations on modularity, modality, mind and memory. The hypothesis that the mind is modular is basically supported, provided that modularity is suitably defined to accommodate quasi-modules (for the central system) as well as Fodorian input systems. There is even evidence in the interaction of the linguistic and the visuo-spatial for a kinaesthesis quasi-module.

The hypothesis that natural language is basically modality-neutral is also supported. Modality effects are present but they are not a major determinant of Christopher's linguistic abilities except when it comes to the use of classifiers and the simultaneous exploitation of linguistic and topographic space. It is the representation of spatial relations in the signed input which causes him problems: that is, he did not use representational space or classifiers to stand for objects at all. His poor overall performance with classifiers contrasts sharply with the performance of the comparators on the one hand, and his own better performance on agreement, negation and the lexicon, on the other. That is, he has problems with features that draw on or interface with spatial cognition. This may make the hypothesis appear suspect. Christopher was incompetent in his use of sign space, with reference-assignment being difficult for him. But this was probably caused by factors that lie outside the grammatical system, most plausibly mastery of the syntax–discourse interface. Rather than constructing a sign space, Christopher relied on deictic reference, using real objects rather than classifiers. Because of his apraxia and his autism the modality cancelled out his talent: he typically performed within the limits defined by the comparator group but at the poor end of the spectrum; he would almost certainly have performed better in another spoken language. Nonetheless his success across a wide range suggests that the core aspects of the language faculty are neutral as between speech and sign.

As well as its implications for modularity and modality, Christopher's case has also provided evidence for the nature of memory, viz. Baddeley's model of working memory, with its modified structure incorporating an episodic buffer as well as the phonological loop and the visuospatial sketchpad.

Confronting Christopher with the task of learning a sign language has enabled us to refine our understanding of his mind and the human mind more generally. In particular, his weak central coherence and lack of executive control of inhibition cast light on the functioning of the mind in autism and in typical development. Our speculative fig. 30 makes specific predictions that can be tested on other populations. To some extent we have begun that enterprise with our comparison of Christopher and other abnormal signers.

To the extent that the dissociations shown by Christopher were reproduced in other subjects, the discussion of ch. 5 reveals not only commonalties across different pathological cases, but tentative corroboration of the categories and constructs we have been developing. Thus we find that the aphasics show the same sorts of dissociations between topographic and non-topographic processing as Christopher, confirming the hypothesis that they arise from impairments external to language. We find in Charles a double dissociation of sign and gesture in the mirror image of Christopher. We find in both Heather and the Down Syndrome twins a parallel dissociation of the linguistic and the visuo-spatial, especially with regard to the topographic use of space. In the twins we even find an asymmetry between lexical and syntactic proficiency, with a plateau effect in the latter entirely comparable with what we have seen in Christopher.

These comparisons are at best suggestive, but we finish in the same terms as in our previous book: 'Christopher has provided us with a wealth of evidence about the nature of mind and language. He has also provided us with insight into the nature of humanity, and in the process he has enriched our lives.'

Appendix 1 Stroop tests

We started with a basic Stroop test (http://faculty.washington.edu/chudler/words.html#seffect), which we ran twice – initially with the congruent stimuli first, as in (i), then a few minutes later with the incongruent stimuli first, as in (ii):

(i)   Stroop – congruent stimuli

RED	GREEN	BLUE	YELLOW	PINK
ORANGE	BLUE	GREEN	BLUE	WHITE
GREEN	YELLOW	ORANGE	BLUE	WHITE
BROWN	RED	BLUE	YELLOW	GREEN
PINK	YELLOW	GREEN	BLUE	RED

(ii)   Stroop – incongruent stimuli

RED	GREEN	BLUE	YELLOW	PINK
ORANGE	BLUE	GREEN	BLUE	WHITE
GREEN	YELLOW	ORANGE	BLUE	WHITE
BROWN	RED	BLUE	YELLOW	GREEN
PINK	YELLOW	GREEN	BLUE	RED

The results in (iii):

(iii)   Congruent first: incongruent 30 secs; congruent 14 secs.
        Incongruent first: incongruent 34 secs; congruent 15 secs.

put Christopher in the bottom third of the normed population. He made no mistakes with the congruent stimuli and his responses to the incongruent stimuli are given in (iv a) and (iv b):

(iv)a   RED   GREEN/yellow   white   RED   PINK
        blue   red   yellow   green   blue
        red   blue   green   red   (red)
        blue   yellow   (red)   green   orange
        PINK   YELLOW/blue   orange   red   green

Capitals indicate an incorrect response, an oblique stroke marks a spontaneous self-correction, and parentheses indicate a wrong choice of colour name ('red' for 'pink') but a choice not caused by the written stimulus. His response on the second exposure (in iv b) when the incongruent stimuli came first was slower and impressionistically more deliberate, even though he made more mistakes (the double oblique stroke indicates that he started the last row twice):

(iv)b   RED/green   yellow   white   (red)   PINK
        ORANGE   BLUE/red   yellow   green   blue
        red   YELLOW/blue   green   red   (red)
        blue   yellow   (red)   green   GREEN/(red)
        PINK   YELLOW//
        PINK   blue   orange   red   green

We also did an animal Stroop test, shown with incongruent stimuli in (v). With congruent stimuli he made one mistake, saying 'elephant' for 'bear', despite the word being written on it, and he took 17 seconds. With incongruent stimuli he made two mistakes: 'elephant' for 'bear' again, and 'fish' for 'snake' (immediately self-corrected to 'snake'), and he took 23 seconds. These figures put him in the middle third of the population – so there was no obviously abnormal inhibitory impairment.

(v)   Animal Stroop test (incongruent stimuli)

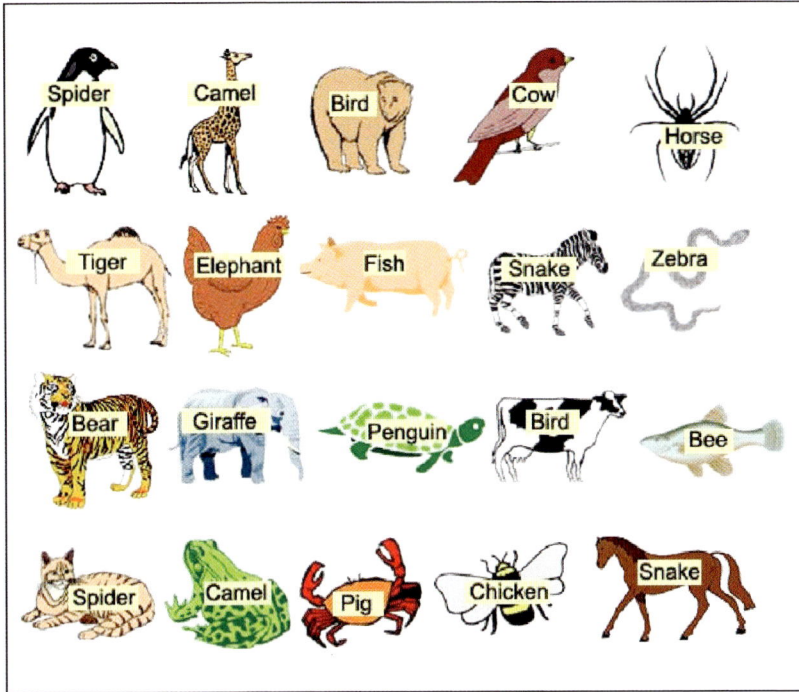

   To confirm these results we also devised Stroop variants using Greek and
English stimuli. There were four sets, two English and two Greek, each of 14
words – seven in colour, seven in black, as shown for Greek in (vi) and (vii)
The coloured examples were uniformly congruent (vi) or incongruent (vii).
We tested Christopher twice (half an hour apart), first with the incongruent
examples first, then with the congruent examples first; each time we did English
before Greek, and Christopher was instructed to "Name the colour of the word
you see." The results were:

English –	Incongruent first:	Incongruent 15 secs; Congruent 11 secs.
	Congruent first:	Incongruent 20 secs; Congruent 12 secs.
Greek –	Incongruent first:	Incongruent 15 secs; Congruent 13 secs.
	Congruent first:	Incongruent 16 sccs; Congruent 12 sccs.

(vi)   <u>Greek stimulus</u>   <u>English equivalent</u>

Κίτρινο	Yellow
Μπλε	Blue
Κίτρινο	Yellow
Μπλε	Blue
Κόκκινο	Red
Πράσινο	Green
Κόκκινο	Red
Κίτρινο	Yellow
Μπλε	Blue
Κόκκινο	Red
Μπλε	Blue
Κίτρινο	Yellow
Κόκκινο	Red
Πράσινο	Green

(vi)   <u>Greek stimulus</u>   <u>English equivalent</u>   <u>C's response</u>

Μπλε	Blue	'blue'
Πράσινο	Green	'green'
Κόκκινο	Red	'black'
Μπλε	Blue	'red ... blue'*
Κίτρινο	Yellow	'... yellow'
Πράσινο	Green	'black'
Πράσινο	Green	'blue'
Μπλε	Blue	'black'

Κόκκινο	Red	'yellow'
Κίτρινο	Yellow	'... yellow'
Κόκκινο	Red	'black'
Πράσινο	Green	'black'
Μπλε	Blue	'blue, yellow'
Μπλε	Blue	'black'

*At this point Christopher interjected a question about the Chinese for 'red' ... In the other examples [...] indicates a long pause.

On the first (incongruent) test, Christopher frequently translated the Greek word into English, rather than giving us the colour in which it was written, indicating that word meaning overrides colour naming. Accordingly in (vii) we have given not only the Greek stimulus and its English translation but also Christopher's reaction in 'inverted commas'. He made five mistakes in his responses out of a total of fourteen (36%). We construe this high incidence of mistakes as evidence for his having problems with inhibiting the incorrect response.

Appendix 2   List of example signs used in vocabulary tests in comprehension and production

Comprehension	Production
CAMERA	BLACK
KEY	YELLOW
CAR	GREEN
BOX	CHEF
WINDOW	WAITRESS
KNIFE	FIREMAN
BUS	DOG
SUITCASE	HORSE
MICROPHONE	RABBIT
WOMAN	KEY
PAINTER	CAR
SMOKE	BOX
DEER	ICE CREAM
ROPE	BALLOON
KITE	DOOR
CANDLE	UMBRELLA
CHILDREN	RAIN
FOUNTAIN	SUMMER
STAIRS	WINTER
APPLE	SNOW

Notes

PREFACE

1. There are also a number of video clips available at www.uga.edu/lsava/Smith/ Smith.html. These derive from a Dutch TV programme 'Het Talenwonder' (produced by Norderlicht in 1994). Christopher has also featured on television in the USA ('The Mystery of Genius', A and E Network, 2005) and in the UK on 'Horizon' (BBC 2, November, 2009; www.bbc.co.uk/programmes/b00nx7n4).

CHAPTER 1

1. As Christopher was immediately able to tell us, their deaths took place in 1989 and 1985 respectively.
2. It is relevant to note that, despite the usual observation about the limited verbal ability of autists, autistic *savants* characteristically have higher verbal abilities than their non-savant peers (Howlin *et al.*, 2009). This makes the rarity of cases like Christopher all the more remarkable.
3. This standard assumption is challenged by some recent work on 15-month-olds (Onishi & Baillargeon, 2005) which seems to show that they can entertain false belief but require years' more maturation before they are able to express this cognitive competence in language.
4. Even this is controversial, in that it has been claimed that the same problems arise with true belief. (For discussion, see Russell, 2005.)
5. We are grateful to Alan Wing and Marietta Remondou of the University of Birmingham for conducting these tests for us (on 4 June 1999).
6. We are grateful to Peter Lovatt of the University of Hertfordshire for help with these tests.
7. Nonetheless, as Alan Baddeley reminds us (p.c.), the original 4.5 span is unexpectedly low for someone with Christopher's linguistic ability.
8. That is, the use of encyclopaedic or 'long-term' memory to facilitate recall.
9. Christopher is good at solving anagrams; see Smith & Tsimpli (1995: 19).
10. We are grateful to Peter Möbius for help with this test.
11. We are grateful to Zoe Bablekou for discussion of this issue.
12. The improvement is not as clear-cut as one might wish, because of the ceiling effect; nonetheless even an unchanged performance would have been striking.
13. We are grateful to Annette Karmiloff-Smith, who helped us in conducting this and the next experiment in May 1996.

191

14. It may be necessary to fractionate further: mid-term memory (Where did you park the car this morning? What did you have for breakfast?) may be distinct from STM and LTM. Similarly, the tasks Christopher was performing with a retention interval of a few minutes to an hour exemplify neither classical STM nor LTM.

15. A third issue concerns whether memory is best viewed as 'information processing' or in terms of 'levels of processing' (see Brown & Craik, 2000: 94), where the former involves three stages of encoding, storage, and retrieval, but the latter does without the [short-term] memory store, attributing its putative properties to processes of encoding and retrieval: specifically whether the processing is deep (= semantic) or shallow (= sensory, phonetic).

16. 'Consolidation' 'refers to the idea that neural processes transpiring after the initial registration of information contribute to the permanent storage of memory . . . what has been learned is not instantly made permanent' (Nadel & Moscovich, 1997: 217). Consolidation takes place most efficiently during sleep (see Marshall & Born, 2007), but this is clearly not involved here.

17. These are sentences constructed from a highly limited set of nouns, verbs and adjectives, giving rise to semantically bland content which obviates the effect of conceptual difficulty on recall.

18. We have not yet carried out with him the experiments Baddeley uses to motivate a direct link.

19. As Fodor (2000: 63) put it: 'it's informational encapsulation . . . that's at the heart of modularity'. Importantly, for Fodor, modular structure cannot exhaust the mind's resources, because of the problem of abduction. Our postulation of an executive is tacit acceptance of this position.

20. Even this apparently innocuous remark is controversial. Many researchers are convinced that linguistic knowledge is no different in kind from non-linguistic knowledge (see e.g. Hudson, 2002), or is at least ontogenetically not distinct (see e.g. Elman *et al.*, 1996: 170). We do not have the space to rehearse the various arguments here, but are convinced that the case of Christopher constitutes relevant evidence for our position.

21. It is perhaps worth making explicit that Chomsky's use of the term *modular* varies according to context between an interpretation in which the language faculty is a module, and one in which e.g. Case theory is a module.

22. It should go without saying that the framework is itself a matter of controversy (for discussion, see e.g. Newmeyer, 2005; Biberauer, 2008).

23. Parametric variation is operative in the phonology as well as the syntax, but the restriction to functional categories pertains only to the syntax. For discussion of the identity criteria for parametric as opposed to non-parametric variation, see Smith & Law (2009).

24. Usually, the dissociation is between irregular morphology and regular morphology cum syntax.

25. The developmental pathways seem to be comparable in the two populations even though the underlying cause is radically different.

26. It is of interest that Nazeer (2006: 71) chooses the 'Smarties' test to argue against the idea that autism is correctly characterised by the absence, rather than late development, of a theory of mind.

27. This familiarity effect is now underpinned by evidence that 'mechanisms for maintaining novel information in working memory could differ from mechanisms for maintaining familiar information' (Hasselmo & Stern, 2006: 487).
28. It has been claimed (Plomin & Spinath, 2002) that there is an apparent tension between the pervasive ('molar') effect of *g* and (Fodorian) modularity, and they suggest further that *g* equates with 'working memory' (p. 173). It's not obvious that this is compatible with Christopher's asymmetric results as discussed in section 1.2. In a similar critique of modular accounts, Kaan & Swaab (2002: 355) claim that 'Syntactic processing ... recruits not one brain region but multiple areas that are not each uniquely involved in syntactic tasks. This is inconsistent with a strict modular view of syntactic processing.' This confuses neurological localisation with psychological modularity. The latter is compatible with localised or distributed architecture.
29. Though Frith (1989/2003: 167) allows the possibility that some autistic subjects might show strong central coherence.
30. It may be that Down Syndrome or retarded non-autistic individuals are affected by capacity problems whereas Asperger's subjects suffer from defective pragmatics. Christopher might have both problems.
31. In fact the presence of the negative in example (11) entails that it can only be construed naturally when used interpretively, so Christopher's problem with such examples may be attributable to this property.
32. Frith (1989/2003: 154) refers to 'the unusual ability to disregard context'.
33. This level of representation, 'LF prime', has fallen into desuetude, but some comparable level outside the language faculty is still presupposed.
34. The 'lemma' embraces the semantic and syntactic properties of words but excludes their morpho-phonological properties (see Caplan, 1992, e.g. p. 106 – following, among others, Levelt, 1989). We are not committed to this precise demarcation but we are sympathetic to the principle of such a distinction.
35. It should be pointed out however, that even 'normal' comprehenders seem unable to completely suppress the initial mistaken interpretation of garden-path structures, although they can backtrack and reanalyse (Ferreira *et al.*, 2001).
36. We say 'normal' acquisition of BSL as a second language, but there have been no research studies on this topic and only very limited research on other signed languages.

CHAPTER 2

1. This is not to deny that there is a considerable role for the right hemisphere in normal (speaking) subjects (see e.g. Chiarello, 2003).
2. That is, those which recreate a map of the real world.
3. As it differs from grammaticisation, we use the neologism 'linguisticisation' (MacSweeney *et al.*, 2008b) for the phenomenon of gesture becoming part of language. In linguisticisation, material from gesture becomes directly grammatical without going through a lexical stage. This process may also be seen in vocal gesture (rising intonation expressing uncertainty) becoming linguisticised into question prosody in spoken language.

4. For recent research on the role of the mouth in signed languages, see e.g. Sutton-Spence & Day (2001), and other papers in Boyes-Braem & Sutton-Spence (2001).
5. Signed sentences that appear in the text follow standard notation conventions. Signs are represented by upper-case English glosses. Unless otherwise specified, examples are from BSL. When more than one English word is needed to capture the sign's full meaning this is indicated through a hyphenated gloss. Repetition of signs is marked by '+'. 'IX' is a point to an area of sign space which acts as a syntactic index for referring to an argument in the sentence. Subscripted upper-case letters, R, L and C, indicate locations in sign space, namely right, left and centre; subscripted lower-case letters indicate coindexation. Above the glosses, non-manual markers such as eye closes (∅∅) and upper face and head movements are indicated by a horizontal line across the affected segment(s). A signed sentence which contains classifier constructions is glossed by first indicating the use of a classifier (CL), then the classifier and lastly the predicate. This gloss is transcribed as one complex construction by each piece of information being placed in a hyphenated string, e.g. TABLE CUP CL-C-ON-CL-B 'the cup is on the table' – where C marks a curved object, and B marks a flat object.
6. A sign's place of articulation can vary radically in particular contexts. A sign that is normally articulated on the forehead (e.g. DANGEROUS) may be articulated above the head if the signer is 'shouting' to gain attention when the addressee is some way in the distance, or it may be articulated on the stomach when the signer is 'whispering' to the addressee in an intimate or casual register (Crasborn, 2000).
7. That is, facial action, like intonation, may be grammaticalised or function as an affective device, though whether intonation is a feature of the grammar depends on the theory adopted (see Nespor and Sandler, 1999).
8. It is possible that a Parisian child reared within sight of the tower or a child reared on a farm might see the PARIS or MILK link more quickly and expand their encyclopaedic knowledge earlier. This still does not imply that such a child will learn the relevant sign earlier or with greater ease than another child.
9. This is in accordance with Sperber & Wilson's (1986/1995) account of concepts where a concept is a tripartite entity having lexical, logical and encyclopaedic sub-parts. The UG lexical entry corresponds to their 'lexical' part, the conceptual entry corresponds to their encyclopaedic part.
10. 'IX' indicates an indexical point to sign space.
11. MAN and its associated classifier are signed with the left hand; CAR is a 2-handed sign; the left hand then signs the G classifier again at the same time as the right hand signs the B classifier and moves it to contact the left hand.
12. The representation 'NOTHING' disguises the fact that the sign can be used either for an argument (as in 'he ate nothing') or as a simple negator, as in example (8).

CHAPTER 3

1. 'Signature' (Council for the Advancement of Communication with Deaf People), Level 1 (Basic) Certificate in BSL. The curriculum is available from Signature, Mersey House, Mandale Business Park, Belmont, Durham DH1 1TH, UK.

2. Note that Epun is an invented language; it has nothing in common with the Kwa language Nupe.
3. There are no other documents in Epun, and Christopher's mastery of the Arabic script in which Berber is usually written is inadequate to let him read primary material in this language.
4. This marks a level of attainment sufficient for starting a University degree in the literature of that language in the UK.
5. It is hard to describe the representation of any sign while abstracting away from syntactic space. The point is that the mapping between a sign in syntax space and actual physical space varies, with spatial classifiers instantiating the clearest case of close mapping.

CHAPTER 4

1. As explained in chapter 3.3 (pp. 80–1) not all members of the comparator group completed all the tests, but we report on all the available numbers. Most test results include between ten and twenty-five learners, most frequently about fifteen to twenty. Where appropriate we use group averages.
2. It is impossible to speak English and sign BSL simultaneously because of differences in word-order, but silent mouthing of words often accompanies signs.
3. 'A', 'B', etc. refer to various members of the comparator group.
4. An alternative reason for this mistake may be that the sign CAN looks very much like a 'size and shape specifier' for a nose. However, as Christopher made many more mistakes because of confusion of location than because of the over-use of size and shape specifiers, we are reasonably confident that it was a location error.
5. Text in lower case indicates that a gesture was used with a sign.

CHAPTER 5

1. This test examines understanding of three categories of verbs in single sentences: simple verbs, verbs that require person agreement and spatial verbs.

CHAPTER 6

1. We do not disagree with Hohenberger *et al.*'s observation (2002: 131) that the typological restriction to the 'fusional', characteristic of all sign languages, is modality-dependent.
2. This term refers to processes of word formation other than the simple stringing together of morphemes. Thus English *cat/cats* is concatenative, but *foot/feet* is non-concatenative. Much of the original motivation for the contrast came from analyses of the intercalation of vowels into a (typically triliteral) consonantal root that is characteristic of Semitic (see e.g. McCarthy, 1981).
3. We use the term 'phonetic-semantic' to refer to Chinese orthography, about 90 per cent of whose lexical entries are 'phonetic semantic compounds'. The traditional term 'ideographic' is at best true of a tiny minority of entries.
4. Signwriting <www.signwriting.org> has been developed for the writing of sign languages and is used in some countries for the education of deaf children; it is not, however, in use in Britain.

5. It may be that music should be excluded from consideration here. The essence of 'conceptual' as opposed to perceptual representations is that they can serve as the premises or conclusions for inferencing, and it is reasonably clear that musical representations do not have this function. As always we need a richer ontology.

6. Also known as the Ebbinghaus illusion.

7. What we are referring to here as 'unconscious' representation corresponds to Fodor's (2008: 169ff.) 'preconceptual representation'.

8. The face dominates the sound percept – where [p] is seen but [k] is heard, the subject reports a fusion [kp].

9. It would be interesting to know if there are cases of signers with an acquired lesion showing differential impairments in the processing of fingerspelling and reading. We know of no such cases.

10. We have other qualms about this system, as the enterprise is explicitly anti-Fodorian (and implicitly anti-Chomskian) in that e.g. 'the meaning of a linguistic utterance consists of all its associations to non-linguistic levels of representation' (Nikanne, 2000: 80). It seems to us that we need both a semantics/pragmatics distinction, and a NL/LoT contrast, if we are to do justice to the complexity of the mind.

11. To highlight this difference, Deborah Chen Pichler (personal communication) has contrasted L2 with M2 (modality2).

12. There are, of course, interesting differences, as in our perception of our own voice quality, which becomes salient when we hear our voice on tape.

13. Except in the case of parsing problems of the kind occasioned by garden-path phenomena, and other cases where the input part of the language system is 'sabotaged'. In such cases we assume that central system back-up is invoked.

14. Ultimately probably attributable to deficiencies in the mirror neuron system (see Iacoboni, 2008).

References

Adams, K. & **N. Conklin** (1973) 'Toward a theory of natural classification'. *Papers from the Ninth Regional Meeting, Chicago Linguistic Society*, pp. 1–10.

Aikhenvald, A. Y. (2000) *Classifiers: A Typology of Noun Categorization Devices*. Oxford: Oxford University Press.

(2003) 'Commentary: classifiers in spoken and in signed languages: how to know more'. In **K. Emmorey** (ed.) *Perspectives on Classifier Constructions in Sign Languages*. Mahwah, NJ: Erlbaum, pp. 87–90.

(in press) 'A morphosyntactic typology of classifiers and classifier constructions in sign languages'. MS, La Trobe University.

Allan, K. (1977) 'Classifiers'. *Language*, **53**: 285–311.

Anderson, D. & **J. Reilly** (2002) 'The MacArthur Communicative Development Inventory for American Sign Language'. *Journal of Deaf Studies and Deaf Education*, **7**: 83–106.

Anderson, E. S. (1978) 'Lexical universals of body-part terminology'. In **J. Greenberg**, **C. Ferguson** & **E. Moravcsik** (eds.) *Universals of Human Language*. Vol. 3: *Word Structure*. Stanford, CA: Stanford University Press, pp. 335–69.

Anderson, M. (1992) *Intelligence and Development: A Cognitive Theory*. Oxford: Blackwell.

Antzakas, K. (2006) *Features of Negation in Greek Sign Language* (in Greek). *Meletes gia tin Elliniki glossa* (forthcoming *Proceedings of the 23rd annual meeting of the Institute of Linguistics*, Department of Philology, School of Philosophy, Aristotelian University of Thessaloniki).

Arena, V., A. Finlay & **B. Woll** (2007) 'Seeing sign: the relation of visual feedback to sign language sentence structure'. Poster presented at the City University of New York Conference on Human Sentence Processing. La Jolla, CA.

Aronoff, M., I. Meir & **W. Sandler** (2005) 'The paradox of sign language morphology'. *Language*, **81**: 301–44.

Atkinson, J., R. Campbell, J. Marshall, A. Thacker & **B. Woll** (2004) 'Understanding "not": Neuropsychological dissociations between hand and head markers of negation in BSL'. *Neuropsychologia*, **42**: 214–29.

Atkinson, J., J. Marshall, B. Woll & **A. Thacker** (2005) 'Testing comprehension abilities in users of British Sign Language following CVA'. *Brain and Language*, **94**(2): 233–48.

Atkinson, J., B. Woll & **S. Gathercole** (2002) 'The impact of developmental visuospatial learning difficulties on British Sign Language'. *Neurocase*, **8**: 424–41.

Baddeley, A. (1997) *Human Memory: Theory and Practice*. Hove: Psychology Press.

(2000a) 'The episodic buffer: A new component of working memory?' *Trends in Cognitive Sciences*, **4**: 417–23.

(2000b) 'Short-term and working memory'. In **E. Tulving** & **F. Craik** (eds.) *The Oxford Handbook of Memory*. Oxford: Oxford University Press, pp. 77–92.

(2007) *Working Memory, Thought and Action*. Oxford: Oxford University Press.

Baker, S., R. Golinkoff & **L. A. Petitto** (2006) 'New insights into old puzzles from infants' categorical discrimination of soundless phonetic units'. *Language Learning and Development*, **2**: 147–62.

Baker, S., W. Idsardi, R. Golinkoff & **L. A. Petitto** (2005) 'The perception of handshapes in American Sign Language'. *Memory & Cognition*, **33**: 887–904.

Baker, S. & **C. Padden** (1978) 'Focusing on the nonmanual components of American Sign Language'. In **P. Siple** (ed.) *Understanding Language through Sign Language Research*. New York: Academic Press, pp. 27–57.

Baranek, G., L. D. Parham & **J. W. Bodfish** (2005) 'Sensory and motor features in autism: Assessment and intervention'. In **F. R. Volkmar, R. Paul, A. Klin** & **D. Cohen** (eds.) *Handbook of Autism and Pervasive Developmental Disorders*, 3rd edn. Vol. 2: *Assessment, Interventions, and Policy*. Hoboken, NJ: John Wiley & Sons, pp. 831–57

Baron-Cohen, S. (2002) 'The extreme male brain theory of autism'. *Trends in Cognitive Sciences*, **6**: 248–54.

(2008) 'Autism and talent: the role of systemizing'. Paper presented at the joint meeting of the Royal Society and British Academy on *Talent and Autism*, London, 29 September 2008.

Barry, C., C. M. Morrison & **A. W. Ellis** (1997) 'Naming the Snodgrass and Vanderwart pictures: Effects of age of acquisition, frequency and name agreement'. *Quarterly Journal of Experimental Psychology*, **50A**: 560–85.

Battison, R. (1978) *Lexical Borrowing in American Sign Language*. Silver Spring, MD: Linstok Press.

Bavelier, D., M. Dye & **P. Hauser** (2006a) 'Do deaf individuals see better?' *Trends in Cognitive Sciences*, **10**: 512–18.

Bavelier, D., E. Newport, M. Hall, T. Supalla & **M. Boutla** (2006b) 'Persistent difference in short-term memory span between sign and speech: Implications for cross-linguistic comparisons'. *Psychological Science*, **17**: 1090–2.

Bellugi, U. (1990) 'Spatial language and spatial cognition'. Keynote address presented at the Boston Child Language Conference.

Bellugi, U. & **S. Fischer** (1972) 'A comparison of sign language and spoken language'. *Cognition* **1**: 173–200.

Bellugi, U., L. O'Grady, D. Lillo-Martin, M. O'Grady, K. van Hoek & **D. Corina** (1990) 'Enhancement of spatial cognition in deaf children'. In **V. Volterra** & **C. Erting** (eds.) *From Gesture to Language in Hearing and Deaf Children*. New York: Springer Verlag, pp. 278–98.

Biberauer, T. (2008) 'Introduction'. In **T. Biberauer** (ed.) *The Limits of Syntactic Variation*. Amsterdam: John Benjamins, pp. 1–72.

Birdsong, D. (1992) 'Ultimate attainment in second language learning'. *Language*, **68**: 706–55.

Bisang, W. (1999) 'Classifiers in East and Southeast Asian languages: Counting and beyond'. In **J. Gvozdanovic** (ed.) *Numeral Types and Changes Worldwide*. Berlin: Mouton de Gruyter, pp. 113–85.

Bishop, D. V. M. (1983/2003) *The Test for Reception of Grammar, version 2 (TROG-2)*. London: Psychological Corporation.

(1997) *Uncommon Understanding: Development and Disorders of Language Comprehension in Children*. London: Psychology Press.

Blakemore, S. J., C. D. Frith & D. M. Wolpert (2001) 'The cerebellum is involved in predicting the sensory consequences of action'. *Neuroreport*, **12**(9): 1879–84.

Bloom, P. (2000) *How Children Learn the Meaning of Words*. Cambridge, MA: MIT Press.

Bloom, P. & T. German (2000) 'Two reasons to abandon the false belief task as a test of theory of mind'. *Cognition*, **77**, B25-B31.

Bonvillian, J. D., K. Nelson & J. Rhyne (1981) 'Sign language and autism'. *Journal of Autism Developmental Disorders*, **11**: 125–37.

Borer, H. (1984) *Parametric Syntax*. Dordrecht: Foris.

Borer, H. & B. Rohrbacher (2003) 'Minding the absent: Arguments for the full competence hypothesis'. *Language Acquisition*, **10**(2): 123–76.

Boutla, M., T. Supalla, E. Newport & D. Bavelier (2004) 'Short-term memory span: Insights from sign language'. *Nature Neuroscience*, **7**(9): 1–6.

Bowerman, M. & S. Levinson (eds.) (2001) *Language Acquisition and Conceptual Development*. Cambridge: Cambridge University Press.

Boyes-Braem, P. B., E. Pizzuto & V. Volterra (2002) 'The interpretation of signs by (hearing and deaf) members of different cultures'. In **R. Schulmeister & H. Reinitzer** (eds.) *Progress in Sign Language Research. Fortschritte in der Gebärdensprachforschung*. Hamburg: Signum-Verlag, pp. 187–219.

Boyes-Braem, P. & R. Sutton-Spence (eds.) (2001) *The Hands are the Head of the Mouth*. Hamburg: Signum Press.

Brennan, M. (1990) *Word formation in British Sign Language*. Ph.D dissertation, University of Stockholm.

(1992) 'The visual world of BSL: an introduction'. In **D. Brien** (ed.) *Dictionary of British Sign Language/English*. London: Faber & Faber, pp. 1–134.

Brennan, S. E., M. W. Friedman & C. J. Pollard (1987) 'A centering approach to pronouns'. In *Proceedings of the 25th Meeting of the Association for Computational Linguistics*. Stanford, CA, pp. 155–62.

Brentari, D. (1998) *A Prosodic Model of Sign Language Phonology*. Cambridge, MA: MIT Press.

(2002) 'Modality differences in sign language phonology and morphophonemics'. In **R. Meier, K. Cormier & D. Quinto** (eds.) *Modality and Structure in Signed and Spoken Languages*. New York: Cambridge University Press, pp. 35–64.

Brentari, D., H. Poizner & J. Kegl (1995) 'Aphasic and Parkinsonian signing: Differences in phonological disruption'. *Brain and Language*, **48**: 69–105.

Brown, S. & F. Craik (2000) 'Encoding and retrieval of information'. In **E. Tulving & F. Craik** (eds.) *The Oxford Handbook of Memory*. Oxford: Oxford University Press, pp. 93–107.

Burgess, P. & T. Shallice (1996) 'Response suppression, initiation and strategy use following frontal lobe lesions'. *Neuropsychologia*, **34**: 263–73.

Calvert, G., E. Bullmore, M. Brammer, R. Campbell, S. Williams, P. McGuire, P. Woodruff, S. Iversen & **A. David** (1997) 'Activation of auditory cortex during silent lipreading'. *Science*, **276**: 593–6.

Campbell, R., P. Martin & **T. White** (1992) 'Forced choice recognition of sign in novice learners of British Sign Language'. *Applied Linguistics*, **13**: 185–201.

Campbell, R., B. Woll, P. Benson & **S. Wallace** (1999) 'Categorical perception of face actions: their role in sign language and in communicative facial displays'. *Quarterly Journal of Experimental Psychology*, **52A**(1): 67–95.

Caplan, D. (1992) *Language: Structure, Processing and Disorders*. Cambridge MA: MIT Press.

Carey, D. (2001) 'Do action systems resist visual illusions?' *Trends in Cognitive Sciences*, **5**: 109–13.

Carminati, M. (2002) *The Processing of Italian Subject Pronouns*. Ph.D dissertation, University of Massachusetts, Amherst.

Carston, R. (1996) 'The architecture of the mind: Modularity and modularization'. In **D. Green** *et al.* (eds.) *Cognitive Science: An Introduction*. Oxford: Blackwell, pp. 53–83.

(2002) *Thoughts and Utterances: The Pragmatics of Explicit Communication*. Oxford: Blackwell.

Casey, S. & **K. Emmorey** (2009) 'Co-speech gesture in bimodal bilinguals'. *Language and Cognitive Processes*, **24**(2): 290–312.

Cheek, A., K. Cormier, A. Repp & **R. P. Meier** (2001) 'Prelinguistic gesture predicts mastery and error in the production of early signs'. *Language*, **77**(2): 292–323.

Chiarello, C. (2003) 'Parallel systems for processing language: Hemispheric complementarity in the normal brain'. In **M. Banich** & **M. Mack** (eds.) *Mind, Brain and Language*. Mahwah, NJ: Lawrence Erlbaum, pp. 229–47.

Chiat, S. (1986) 'Personal pronouns'. In **P. Fletcher** & **M. Garman** (eds.) *Language Acquisition*. Cambridge: Cambridge University Press, pp. 339–55.

Chomsky, N. (1975) *Reflections on Language*. New York: Pantheon.

(1980) *Rules and Representations*. Oxford: Blackwell.

(1981) *Lectures on Government and Binding: The Pisa Lectures*. Dordrecht: Foris Publications.

(1984) *Modular Approaches to the Study of Mind*. San Diego: San Diego State University Press.

(1991) 'Linguistics and adjacent fields: A personal view'. In **A. Kasher** (ed.) *The Chomskyan Turn*. Oxford: Blackwell, pp. 3–25.

(1995) *The Minimalist Program*. Cambridge, MA: MIT Press.

(2000) *New Horizons in the Study of Language and Mind*. Cambridge: Cambridge University Press.

(2002a) 'An interview on minimalism'. In **N. Chomsky** (2002b), pp. 151–198.

(2002b) *On Nature and Language*. Cambridge: Cambridge University Press.

(2009a) 'Opening remarks'. In **M. Piattelli-Palmarini, J. Uriagereka** & **P. Salaburu** (eds.) *Of Minds and Language: A Dialogue with Noam Chomsky in the Basque Country*. Oxford: Oxford University Press, pp. 13–43.

(2009b) 'Conclusion'. In **M. Piattelli-Palmarini, J. Uriagereka** & **P. Salaburu** (eds.) *Of Minds and Language: A Dialogue with Noam Chomsky in the Basque Country*. Oxford: Oxford University Press, pp. 379–409.

Clahsen, H. (1999) 'Lexical entries and rules of language: A multidisciplinary study of German inflection'. *Behavioral and Brain Sciences*, **22**: 991–1060.

Clahsen, H. & **M. Almazan** (1998) 'Syntax and morphology in children with Williams' Syndrome'. *Cognition*, **68**: 167–98.

Coltheart, M. (1999) 'Modularity and cognition'. *Trends in Cognitive Sciences*, **3**: 115–20.

Corina, D. (1998) 'Aphasia in users of signed language'. In **P. Coppens, Y. Lebrun** & **A. Basso** (eds.) *Aphasia in Atypical Populations*. London: Lawrence Erlbaum, pp. 261–310.

(1999) 'Neural disordersof language and movement: Evidence from American Sign Language'. In **L. Messing** & **R. Campbell** (eds.) *Gesture, Speech and Sign*. Oxford: Oxford University Press, pp. 27–42.

Corina, D. & **W. Sandler** (1993) 'On the nature of phonological structure in sign language'. *Phonology*, **10**: 165–207.

Cormack, A. & **N. V. Smith** (2002) 'Compositionality, copy theory and control'. *UCL Working Papers in Linguistics*, **14**: 355–73.

Crasborn, O. (2000) '"Loud" and "soft" signing in the Sign Language of the Netherlands: evidence against hand-shape as a phonological entity'. Paper presented at the 7th International Conference on Theoretical Issues in Sign Language Research. Amsterdam, The Netherlands.

Crystal, D. (1975) *The English Tone of Voice: Essays in Intonation, Prosody and Paralanguage*. London: Edward Arnold.

Culicover, P. (2004) 'Review article of R. Huddleston & G. K. Pullum (2002) *The Cambridge Grammar of the English Language*, Cambridge: Cambridge University Press'. Language, **80**: 127–41.

Daley, K. (1998) *Vietnamese Classifiers in Narrative Texts*. Dallas: Summer Institute of Linguistics and University of Texas at Arlington Publication in Linguistics **125**.

Damasio, A. (1994) *Descartes' Error: Emotion, Reason and the Human Brain*. New York: Putnam.

Damasio, H., T. Grabowski, D. Tranel, L. Ponto, R. Hichwa & **A. Damasio** (2001) 'Neural correlates of naming actions and of naming spatial relations'. *Neuroimage*, **13**: 1053–64.

Daneman, M. & **P. Carpenter** (1980) 'Individual differences in working memory and reading'. *Journal of Verbal Learning and Verbal Behaviour*, **19**: 450–66.

de Groot, A. (1993) 'Word type effect in bilingual processing tasks: Support for a mixed representational system'. In **R. Schreuder** & **B. Weltens** (eds.) *The Bilingual Lexicon*. Amsterdam: John Benjamins Publishing Company, pp. 27–52.

Dehaene, S. (1997) *The Number Sense*. Oxford: Oxford University Press.

Demey, E. & **E. van der Kooij** (2008) 'Phonological patterns in a dependency model: Allophonic relations grounded in phonetic and iconic motivation'. *Lingua*, **118**: 1109–38.

Deuchar, M. (1983) 'Is British Sign Language an SVO language?' In **J. Kyle** & **B. Woll** (eds.): *Language in Sign: An International Perspective on Sign Language*. (Proceedings of the 2nd International Symposium of Sign Language Research) London: Croom Helm, pp. 69–76.

de Villiers, P., J. de Villiers, B. Schick & **R. Hoffmeister** (2000) 'Theory of mind development in signing and non-signing Deaf children: The impact of sign language on social-cognition'. Paper presented at the 7th International Conference on Theoretical Issues in Sign Language Research, Amsterdam, The Netherlands.

Dobbelsteen, J. J. van den (2003) 'The ability to align vision and kinaesthesia'. http://www.eur.nl/fgg/medbib/EUR-diss/Dobbelsteen_J_vd/01.pdf

Dodd, B. (1987) 'The acquisition of lip-reading skills by normally hearing children'. In **B. Dodd** & **R. Campbell** (eds.) *Hearing by Eye: The Psychology of Lip-reading.* London: Lawrence Erlbaum, pp. 163–75.

Duffy, J. R. (1995) *Motor Speech Disorders: Substrates, Differential Diagnosis, and Management.* St Louis: Mosby.

Ebbinghaus, H. (1913) *Memory: A Contribution to Experimental Psychology.* New York: Publications, Inc.

Ekman, P. (2007) *Emotions Revealed: Recognizing Faces and Feelings to improve Communication and Emotional Life,* 2nd edn. New York: Henry Holt & Co.

Ellis, N. C. & **A. Beaton** (1995) 'Psycholinguistic determinants of foreign language vocabulary learning'. In **B. Harley** (ed.) *Lexical Issues in Second Language Learning.* Amsterdam: John Benjamins, pp. 107–65.

Elman, J., E. Bates, M. Johnson, A. Karmiloff-Smith, D. Parisi & **K. Plunkett** (1996) *Rethinking Innateness: A Connectionist Perspective on Development.* Cambridge, MA: MIT Press.

Emmorey, K. (1996) 'The confluence of space and language in signed languages'. In **P. Bloom, M. Peterson, L. Nadel** & **M. Garrett** (eds.) *Language and Space.* Cambridge, MA: MIT Press, pp. 171–209.

(1999) 'Do signers gesture?' In **L. Messing** & **R. Campbell** (eds.) *Gesture, Speech and Sign.* New York: Oxford University Press, pp. 133–59.

(2002) *Language, Cognition, and the Brain: Insights from Sign Language Research.* Mahwah, NJ: Lawrence Erlbaum Associates.

(ed.) (2003) *Perspectives on Classifier Constructions in Sign Languages.* Mahwah, NJ: Erlbaum.

Emmorey, K., U. Bellugi, A. Friederici & **P. Horn** (1995) 'Effects of age of acquisition on grammatical sensitivity: Evidence from on-line and off-line tasks'. *Applied Psycholinguistics,* **16**: 1–23.

Emmorey, K., R. Bosworth & **T. Kraljic** (2009) 'Visual feedback and self-monitoring of sign language'. *Journal of Memory and Language,* **61**: 398–411.

Emmorey, K. & **D. Corina** (1990) 'Lexical recognition in sign language: Effects of phonetic structure and morphology' *Perceptual & Motor Skills* **71**: 1227–52.

Emmorey, K., H. Damasio, S. McCullough, T. Grabowski, L. Ponto, R. Hichwa & **U. Bellugi** (2002) 'Neural systems underlying spatial language in American Sign Language'. *Neuroimage,* **17**: 812–24.

Emmorey, K. & **B. Falgier** (1999) 'Talking about space with space: Describing environments in ASL'. In **E. Winston** (ed.) *Story Telling and Conversation: Discourse in Deaf Communities.* Washington DC: Gallaudet University Press, pp. 3–26.

Emmorey, K., E. Klima & **G. Hickok** (1998) 'Mental rotation within linguistic and non-linguistic domains in users of American Sign Language'. *Cognition,* **68**(3): 221–46.

Emmorey, K., S. Kosslyn & **U. Bellugi** (1993) 'Visual imagery and visual-spatial language: Enhanced imagery abilities in deaf and hearing ASL signers'. *Cognition,* **46**: 139–81.

Emmorey, K. & **M. Wilson** (2004) 'The puzzle of working memory for sign language'. *Trends in Cognitive Sciences*, **8**: 521–3.

Fabbro, F. (2000) 'Introduction to language and cerebellum'. *Journal of Neurolinguistics*, **13**: 83–94.

Fabbro, F., **R. Moretti** & **A. Bava** (2000) 'Language impairments in patients with cerebellar lesions'. *Journal of Neurolinguistics*, **13**: 173–88.

Ferreira, F., **K. Christianson** & **A. Hollingworth** (2001) 'Misinterpretations of garden-path sentences: Implications for models of sentence processing and reanalysis'. *Journal of Psycholinguistic Research*, **30**(1): 3–20.

Ferreira, F. & **C. Clifton** (1986) 'The independence of syntactic processing'. *Journal of Memory and Language*, **25**: 348–68.

Fodor, J. (1975) *The Language of Thought*. New York: Crowell.

(1983) *The Modularity of Mind*. Cambridge, MA: MIT Press.

(1992) 'A theory of the child's theory of mind'. *Cognition*, **44**: 283–96.

(2000) *The Mind Doesn't Work That Way: The Scope and Limits of Computational Psychology*. Cambridge, MA: MIT Press.

(2008) *LOT 2: The Language of Thought Revisited*. Oxford: Clarendon Press.

Frith, U. (1989/2003) *Autism: Explaining the Enigma*. Oxford: Blackwell.

Gafos, A. (1998) 'Eliminating long-distance consonantal spreading'. *Natural Language and Linguistic Theory*, **16**: 223–78.

Gelman, R. & **B. Butterworth** (2005) 'Number and language: how are they related?' *Trends in Cognitive Sciences*, **9**: 6–10.

Goldin-Meadow, S. & **S. Wagner** (2005) 'How our hands help us learn'. *Trends in Cognitive Sciences*, **9**: 234–41.

Goodglass, H. & **E. Kaplan** (1972) *The Assessment of Aphasias and Related Disorders*. Philadelphia, PA: Lea and Febiger. [Revised edn, 1983.]

Gopnik, M. (1997) 'Language deficits and genetic factors'. *Trends in Cognitive Sciences*, **1**: 5–9.

Green, D. W. (1998) 'Mental control of the bilingual lexico-semantic system'. *Bilingualism: Language and Cognition*, **1**: 67–81.

Grégoire, A. (1937) *L'Apprentissage du Langage: Les deux Premières Années*. Paris: Félix Alcan.

Grosjean, F. (1981) 'Sign and word recognition: A first comparison'. *Sign Language Studies*, **32**: 195–220.

Grosjean, F. & **H. Lane** (1981) 'Temporal variables in the perception and production of spoken and sign languages'. In **P. Eimas** & **J. Miller** (eds.) *Perspectives on the Study of Speech*. Hillsdale, NJ: Lawrence Erlbaum, pp. 207–37.

Grosz, B. J., **A. K. Joshi** & **S. Weinstein** (1995) 'Centering: A framework for modeling the local coherence of discourse'. *Computational Linguistics*, **21**(2): 203–25.

Happé, F. & **P. Vital** (2009) 'What aspects of autism predispose to talent?' *Philosophical Transactions of the Royal Society of London, Series B*, **364**: 1369–75.

Hasselmo, M. & **C. Stern** (2006) 'Mechanisms underlying working memory for novel information'. *Trends in Cognitive Sciences*, **10**: 487–93.

Hauser, M., **N. Chomsky** & **W. Tecumseh Fitch** (2002) 'The faculty of language: What is it, who has it, and how did it evolve?' *Science*, **298**: 1569–79.

Hawkins, R. (2001) *Second Language Syntax: A Generative Introduction*. Oxford: Blackwell.

Hawkins, R. & **H. Hattori** (2006) 'Interpretation of English multiple Wh-questions by Japanese speakers: a missing uninterpretable feature account'. *Second Language Research*, **22**(3): 269–301.

Hickok, G., U. Bellugi & **E. Klima** (2002) 'Sign language in the brain'. *Scientific American*, **12**: 46–53.

Hickok, G., H. Pickell, E. Klima & **U. Bellugi** (2009) 'Neural dissociation in the production of lexical versus classifier signs in ASL: Distinct patterns of hemispheric asymmetry'. *Neuropsychologia*, **47**: 382–7.

Hickok, G., M. Wilson, K. Clark, E. Klima, M. Kritchevsky & **U. Bellugi** (1999) 'Discourse deficits following right hemisphere damage in deaf signers'. *Brain and Language*, **66**: 233–48.

Hohenberger, A., D. Happ & **H. Leuninger** (2002) 'Modality-dependent aspects of sign language production: Evidence from slips of the hands and their repairs in German Sign Language'. In **R. Meier, K. Cormier** & **D. Quinto** (eds.) *Modality and Structure in Signed and Spoken Languages*. New York: Cambridge University Press, pp. 112–42.

Holowka, S. & **L. A. Petitto** (2002) 'Left hemisphere cerebral specialization for babies while babbling'. *Science*, **297**: 1515.

Howlin, P., S. Goode, J. Hutton & **M. Rutter** (2009) 'Savant skills in autism: Psychometric approaches and parental reports'. *Philosophical Transactions of the Royal Society of London, Series B*, **364**: 1359–67.

Hudson, R. A. (2002) 'Word grammar'. In **K. Sugayama** (ed.) *Studies in Word Grammar*. Kobe: Research Institute of Foreign Studies, Kobe City University of Foreign Studies, pp. 7–32.

Hulst, H. van der (1996) 'On the other hand'. *Lingua*, **98**: 121–43.

Iacoboni, M. (2008) *Mirroring People*. New York: Farrar, Strauss & Giroux.

Ingram, J. (2007) *Neurolinguistics: An Introduction to Spoken Language Processing and its Disorders*. Cambridge: Cambridge University Press.

Jacquemot, C. & **S. Scott** (2006) 'What is the relationship between phonological short-term memory and speech processing?' *Trends in Cognitive Sciences*, **10**: 480–6.

Jackendoff, R. (1983) *Semantics and Cognition*. Cambridge, MA: MIT Press.

(1997) *The Architecture of the Language Faculty*. Cambridge, MA: MIT Press.

Jakobson, R. (1941) *Kindersprache, Aphasie und Allgemeine Lautgesetze*. The Hague: Mouton.

(1957) *Shifters, Verbal Categories, and the Russian Verb*. Harvard University, Department of Slavic Languages and Literatures.

Jarrold, C., A. Baddeley & **A. Hewes** (1999) 'Genetically dissociated components of working memory: Evidence from Down's and Williams syndrome'. *Neuropsychologia*, **37**: 637–51.

Joanisse, M. & **M. Seidenberg** (1998) 'Specific language impairment: a deficit in grammar or processing?' *Trends in Cognitive Sciences*, **2**: 240–7.

Jueptner, M., I. H. Jenkins, D. J. Brooks, R. Frackowiak & **R. Passingham** (1996) 'The sensory guidance of movement: a comparison of the cerebellum and basal ganglia'. *Experimental Brain Research*, **112**: 462–74.

Jusczyk, P. (1997) *The Discovery of Spoken Language*. Cambridge, MA: MIT Press.

Kaan, E. & **T. Swaab** (2002) 'The brain circuitry of syntactic comprehension'. *Trends in Cognitive Sciences*, **6**: 350–6.

Kanwisher, N. & M. Moscovitch (2000) 'The cognitive neuroscience of face process-ing: Introduction'. In **N. Kanwisher & M. Moscovitch** (eds.) *Cognitive Neuropsy-chology of Face Processing*. Philadelphia, PA: Psychology Press, pp. 1–11.

Kargopoulos, P., Z. Bablekou, E. Gonida & G. Kiosseoglou (2003) 'Effects of face and name presentation on memory for associated verbal descriptors'. *American Journal of Psychology*, **116**(3): 415–30.

Karmiloff-Smith, A. (1979) *A Functional Approach to Child Language: A Study of Determiners and Reference*. Cambridge: Cambridge University Press.

Keehner, M. & S. Gathercole (2007) 'Cognitive adaptations arising from nonna-tive experience of sign language in hearing adults'. *Memory & Cognition*, **35**: 752–61.

Kendon, A. (1980) 'The sign language of the women of Yuendumu: A preliminary report on the structure of Warlpiri sign language'. *Sign Language Studies*, **27**: 101–12.

Kimura, D. (1982) 'Left hemisphere control of oral and brachial movements and their relation to communication'. *Philosophical Transactions of the Royal Society of London, Series B*, **298**: 135–49.

Kirk, B., J. Kyle, J. Ackerman & B. Woll (1990) 'Measuring British Sign Language development in deaf school children'. In **J. Kyle** (ed.) *Deafness and Sign Language into the 1990s*. Bristol: Deaf Studies Trust, pp. 62–71.

Kjelgaard, M. & H. Tager-Flusberg (2001) 'An investigation of language impairment in autism: Implications for genetic subgroups'. *Language and Cognitive Processes*, **16**: 287–308.

Klima, E. & U. Bellugi (1979) *The Signs of Language*. Cambridge, MA: Harvard University Press.

Kroll, J. & E. Stewart (1994) 'Category interference in translation and picture naming: Evidence for asymmetric connections between bilingual memory representations'. *Journal of Memory and Language*, **33**: 149–74.

Lalonde, R. & T. Botez-Marquard (2000) 'Neuropsychological deficits of patients with chronic or acute cerebellar lesions'. *Journal of Neurolinguistics*, **13**: 117–28.

Lardiere, D. (2000) 'Mapping features to forms in second language acquisition'. In **J. Archibald** (ed.) *Second Language Acquisition and Linguistic Theory*. Oxford: Blackwell, pp. 102–29.

(2006) *Ultimate Attainment in Second Language Acquisition: A Case-study*. Mahwah, NJ: Lawrence Erlbaum Asssociates.

Lely, H. K. J. van der (1997) 'Language and cognitive development in a grammatical SLI boy: modularity and innateness'. *Journal of Neurolinguistics*, **10**: 75–107.

Lely, H. K. J. van der & L. Stollwerck (1997) 'Binding theory and grammatical specific language impairment in children'. *Cognition*, **62**: 245–90.

Leonard, L. (1998) *Children with Specific Language Impairment*. Cambridge, MA: MIT Press.

Levelt, W. (1989) *Speaking: From Intention to Articulation*. Cambridge, MA: MIT Press.

Levy, Y. & G. Kavé (1999) 'Language breakdown and linguistic theory: A tutorial overview'. *Lingua*, **107**: 95–143.

Lewin, D. (2006) 'British Sign Language, The Deaf Community and Mouthings'. Unpublished MA dissertation, University College London.

Liddell, S. (2003) *Grammar, Gesture and Meaning in American Sign Language*. Cambridge: Cambridge University Press.

Liddell, S. & **R. Johnson** (1989) 'American Sign Language: the phonological base'. *Sign Language Studies*, **64**: 195–277.

Lieberth, A. & **M. Gamble** (1991) 'The role of iconicity in sign language learning by hearing adults'. *Journal of Communication Disorders*, **24**: 89–99.

Lillo-Martin, D. (2002) 'Where are all the modality effects?' In **R. P. Meier, K. Cormier** & **D. Quinto-Pozos** (eds.) *Modality and Structure in Signed and Spoken Language*. Cambridge: Cambridge University Press, pp. 241–62.

MacSweeney, M., R. Campbell, B. Woll, V. Giampietro, A. David, P. McGuire, G. Calvert & **M. Brammer** (2004) 'Dissociating linguistic and nonlinguistic gestural communication in the brain'. *Neuroimage*, **22**: 1605–18.

MacSweeney, M., C. Capek, R. Campbell & **B. Woll** (2008a) 'The signing brain: The neurobiology of sign language'. *Trends in Cognitive Sciences*, **12**(11): 432–40.

MacSweeney, M., D. Waters, M. Brammer, B. Woll & **U. Goswami** (2008b) 'Phonological processing in deaf signers and the impact of age of first language acquisition'. *Neuroimage*, **40**: 1369–79.

MacSweeney, M., B. Woll, R. Campbell, G. Calvert, P. McGuire, A. David, A. Simmons & **M. Brammer** (2002) 'Neural correlates of British Sign Language processing: specific regions for topographic language?' *Journal of Cognitive Neuroscience*, **14**(7): 1064–75.

Maguire, E. (2008) 'Neural correlates of exceptional memory'. Paper presented at the joint meeting of the Royal Society and British Academy on *Talent and Autism*, London, 29 September 2008.

Marien, P., S. Engelborghs, B. A. Pickut & **P. P. DeDeyn** (2000) 'Aphasia following cerebellar damage: fact or fantasy?' *Journal of Neurolinguistics*, **13**: 145–71.

Marshall, J., J. Atkinson, E. Smulovich, A. Thacker & **B. Woll** (2004) 'Aphasia in a user of British Sign Language: Dissociation between sign and gesture'. *Cognitive Neuropsychology*, **21**: 537–54.

Marshall, L. & **J. Born** (2007) 'The contribution of sleep to hippocampus-dependent memory consolidation'. *Trends in Cognitive Sciences*, **11**: 442–50.

Masoura, E. V. & **S. Gathercole** (1999) 'Phonological short-term memory and foreign vocabulary learning'. *International Journal of Psychology*, **34**: 383–8.

Mayes, A. (2000) 'Selective memory disorders'. In **E. Tulving** & **F. Craik** (eds.) *The Oxford Handbook of Memory*. Oxford: Oxford University Press, pp. 427–40.

McBurney, S. L. (2002) 'Pronominal reference in signed and spoken language: Are grammatical categories modality-dependent?' In **R. Meier, K. Cormier** & **D. Quinto** (eds.) *Modality and Structure in Signed and Spoken Languages*. New York: Cambridge University Press, pp. 329–69.

McCarthy, J. (1981) 'A prosodic theory of nonconcatenative morphology'. *Linguistic Inquiry*, **12**: 373–418.

McCarthy, R. & **E. Warrington** (1990) *Cognitive Neuropsychology*. San Diego: Academic Press.

McGurk, H. & **J. MacDonald** (1976) 'Hearing lips and seeing voices'. *Nature*, **264**(5588): 746–8.

Meier, R. P. (1982) *Icons, Analogues and Morphemes: The Acquisition of Verb Agreement in American Sign Language*. PhD dissertation, University of California, San Diego.

(1987) 'Elicited imitation of verb agreement in American Sign Language: Iconically or morphologically determined?' *Journal of Memory and Language*, **26**: 362–76.

(1990) 'Person deixis in ASL'. In **S. Fischer** & **P. Siple** (eds.) *Theoretical Issues in Sign Language Research*. Volume 1: *Linguistics*. Chicago: University of Chicago Press, pp. 175–90.

(2000) 'Shared motoric factors in the acquisition of sign and speech'. In **K. Emmorey** & **H. Lane** (eds.) *The Signs of Language Revisited: An Anthology to Honor Ursula Bellugi and Edward Klima*. Mahwah, NJ: Erlbaum, pp. 333–56.

Meier, R. P., K. Cormier & **D. Quinto** (eds.) (2002) *Modality and Structure in Signed and Spoken Languages*. New York: Cambridge University Press.

Menn, L. & **C. Stoel-Gammon** (1995) 'Phonological development'. In **P. Fletcher** & **B. MacWhinney** (eds.) *The Handbook of Child Language*. Oxford: Blackwell, pp. 335–59.

Mills, A. (1987) 'The development of phonology in the blind child'. In **B. Dodd** & **R. Campbell** (eds.) *Hearing by Eye: The Psychology of Lip-reading*. London: Lawrence Erlbaum, pp. 145–61.

Mitchell, D. C. (1987) 'Lexical guidance in human parsing: Locus and processing characteristics'. In **M. Coltheart** (ed.) *Attention and Performance XII: The Psychology of Reading*. Hove, UK: Erlbaum, pp. 601–18.

Morgan, G. (1999) 'Event packaging in British Sign Language discourse'. In **E. Winston** (ed.) *Story Telling and Conversation: Discourse in Deaf Communities*. Washington, DC: Gallaudet University Press, pp. 27–58.

(2006) 'Children are just "lingual": The development of phonology in British Sign Language (BSL)'. *Lingua*, **116**: 1507–23.

Morgan, G., I. Barrière & **B. Woll** (2006) 'The influence of typology and modality in the acquisition of verb agreement in British Sign Language'. *First Language*, **26**: 19–43.

Morgan, G., R. Herman, I. Barrière & **B. Woll** (2008) 'The onset and mastery of spatial language in children acquiring British Sign Language'. *Cognitive Development*, **23**: 1–9.

Morgan, G., N. V. Smith, I.-M. Tsimpli and **B. Woll** (2002a) 'Language against the odds: The learning of British Sign Language by a polyglot savant'. *Journal of Linguistics*, **38**: 1–41.

(2002b) 'The effects of modality on British Sign Language development in an exceptional learner'. In **R. Meier, K. Cormier** & **D. Quinto** (eds.) *Modality and Structure in Signed and Spoken Languages*. New York: Cambridge University Press, pp. 422–41.

(2007) 'Classifier learning and modality in a polyglot *savant*'. *Lingua*, **117**: 1339–53.

Morgan, G. & **B. Woll** (eds.) (2002) *Directions in Sign Language Acquisition*. Amsterdam: John Benjamins.

(2003) 'The development of reference switching encoded through body classifiers in BSL'. In **K. Emmorey** (ed.) *Perspectives on Classifier Constructions in Sign Languages*. Mahwah, NJ: Lawrence Erlbaum, pp. 297–310.

(2007) 'Understanding sign language classifiers through a polycomponential approach'. *Lingua*, **117**: 1159–68.

Nadel, L. & **M. Moscovich** (1997) 'Memory consolidation, retrograde amnesia and the hippocampal complex'. *Current Opinion in Neurobiology*, **7**: 217–27.

Navon, D. (1977) 'Forest before trees: The precedence of global features in visual perception'. *Cognitive Psychology*, **9**: 353–83.

Nazeer, K. (2006) *Send in the Idiots: Or How We Grew to Understand the World*. London: Bloomsbury.

Neeleman, A. & **K. Szendrői** (2005) 'Pro drop and pronouns'. In **J. Alderete, C. Han** & **A. Kochetov** (eds.) *Proceedings of the 24th West Coast Conference on Formal Linguistics*. Medford, MD: Cascadilla Press, pp. 299–307.

Neidle, C., J. Kegl, D. MacLaughlin, B. Bahan & **R. Lee** (2000) *The Syntax of American Sign Language: Functional Categories and Hierarchical Structure*. Cambridge, MA: MIT Press.

Nespor, M. & **W. Sandler** (1999) 'Prosodic phonology in Israeli Sign Language'. *Language and Speech*, **42**: 143–76.

Neville, H. (1991) 'Neurobiology of cognitive and language processing: Effects of early experience'. In **K. Gibson** & **A. Petersen** (eds.) *Brain Maturation and Cognitive Development:Comparative and Cross-cultural Perspectives*. New York: Aldine de Gruyter Press, pp. 355–80.

Newmeyer, F. (2005) *Possible and Probable Languages: A Generative Perspective on Linguistic Typology*. Oxford: Oxford University Press.

Nichols, S., S Stich, A. Leslie & **D. Klein** (1996) 'Varieties of off-line simulation'. In **P. Carruthers** & **P. K. Smith** (eds.) *Theories of Theories of Mind*. Cambridge: Cambridge University Press, pp. 39–74.

Nikanne, U. (2000) 'Some restrictions in linguistic expressions of spatial movement'. In **E. Van der Zee** & **U. Nikanne** (eds.) (2000a), pp. 77–93.

Norman, D. A. and **T. Shallice** (1980/1986) 'Attention to action: Willed and automatic control of behaviour'. Centre for Human Information Processing (Technical Report #99). Reprinted in revised form in **R. J. Davidson, G. E. Schwartz** & **D. Shapiro** (eds.) (1986) *Consciousness and Self-Regulation*, Vol. 4. New York: Plenum.

O'Connor, N. & **B. Hermelin** (1991) 'A specific linguistic ability'. *American Journal on Mental Retardation*, **95**: 673–80.

O'Connor, N., N. V. Smith, C. Frith & **I.-M. Tsimpli** (1994) 'Neuropsychology and linguistic talent'. *Journal of Neurolinguistics*, **8**: 95–107.

Ohyama, T., W. Nores, M. Murphy & **M. Mauk** (2003) 'What the cerebellum computes'. *Trends in Neurosciences*, **26**(4): 222–7.

Onishi, K. & **R. Baillargeon** (2005) 'Do 15-month-old infants understand false beliefs?' *Science*, **308**: 255–8.

Orlansky, M. S. & **J. D. Bonvillian** (1984) 'The role of iconicity in early sign language acquisition'. *Journal of Speech and Hearing Disorders*, **49**: 287–92.

Padden, C. (1988) *Interaction of Morphology and Syntax in American Sign Language*. New York: Garland.

(1991) 'The acquisition of fingerspelling by deaf children'. In **P. Siple** & **S. Fischer** (eds.) *Theoretical Issues in Sign Language Research*. Vol. 2: *Psychology*. Chicago, University of Chicago Press, pp. 191–210.

Papagno, C., T. Valentine & **A. Baddeley** (1991) 'Phonological short-term memory and foreign-language learning'. *Journal of Memory and Language*, **30**: 331–47.

Paradis, M., M.-C. Goldblum & **R. Abidi** (1982) 'Alternate antagonism with paradoxical translation behaviour in two bilingual aphasic patients'. *Brain and Language*, **15**: 55–69.

Perlmutter, D. (1992) 'Sonority and syllable structure in American Sign Language'. *Linguistic Inquiry*, **23**: 407–42.

Perret, E. (1974) 'The left frontal lobe of man and the suppression of habitual responses in verbal categorical behaviour'. *Neuropsychologia*, **12**: 323–30.

Petitto, L. A. (1987) 'On the autonomy of language and gesture: Evidence from the acquisition of personal pronouns in American Sign Language'. *Cognition*, **27**: 1–52.

(2005) 'How the brain begets language'. In **J. McGilvray** (ed.) *The Cambridge Companion to Chomsky*. Cambridge: Cambridge University Press, pp. 84–101.

Petitto, L. A., R. Zatorre, K. Gauna, E. Nikelski, D. Dostie & **A. Evans** (2000) 'Speech-like cerebral activity in profoundly deaf people while processing signed languages: Implications for the neural basis of all human language'. *Proceedings of the National Academy of Sciences*, **97**: 13961–6.

Phillips, C. (1996) *Order and Structure*. Ph.D dissertation, MIT.

Pizzuto, E. & **V. Volterra** (2000) 'Iconicity and transparency in sign languages: A cross-linguistic cross-cultural view'. In **K. Emmorey** & **H. Lane** (eds.) *The Signs of Language Revisited : An Anthology to Honor Ursula Bellugi and Edward Klima*. Mahwah, NJ: Erlbaum, pp. 261–86.

Platzack, C. (2000) 'Multiple interfaces'. In **E. Van der Zee & U. Nikanne** (eds.) (2000a), pp. 21–53.

Plomin, R. & **F. Spinath** (2002) 'Genetics and general cognitive ability (*g*)'. *Trends in Cognitive Sciences*, **6**: 169–76.

Poizner, H., E. Klima & **U. Bellugi** (1987) *What the Hands Reveal about the Brain*. Cambridge, MA: MIT Press.

Pyers, J. & **K. Emmorey** (2008) 'The face of bimodal bilingualism: ASL grammatical facial expressions are produced when bilinguals speak to English monolinguals'. *Psychological Science*, **19**: 531–5.

Ranganath, C. & **S. Blumenfeld** (2005) 'Doubts about double dissociations between short- and long-term memory'. *Trends in Cognitive Sciences*, **9**: 374–80.

Rathmann, C. & **G. Mathur** (2002) 'Is verb agreement the same cross-modally?' In **R. P. Meier, K. Cormier** & **D. Quinto** (eds.) *Modality and Structure in Signed and Spoken Languages*. New York: Cambridge University Press, pp. 370–404.

Reilly, J. & **U. Bellugi** (1996) 'Competition on the face: Affect and language in ASL motherese'. *Journal of Child Language*, **23**: 219–36.

Reilly, J., M. McIntire & **U. Bellugi** (1991) 'BABYFACE: A new perspective on universals in language acquisition'. In **P. Siple** (ed.) *Theoretical Issues in Sign-Language Research: Psycholinguistics*. Chicago: University of Chicago Press, pp. 9–24.

Roberts, I. (1997) *Comparative Syntax*. London: Arnold.

Rudner, M. & J. Rönnberg (2006) 'Towards a functional ontology for working memory for sign and speech'. *Cognitive Processes*, **7** (Suppl. 1): S183–S186.

Russell, J. (2005) 'Justifying all the fuss about false belief'. *Trends in Cognitive Sciences*, **9**: 307–8.

Sacks, O. (1985) *The Man Who Mistook His Wife for a Hat*. New York: HarperCollins.

Saeed, J., R. Sutton-Spence & L. Leeson (2000) 'Constituent structure in declarative sentences in Irish Sign Language and British Sign Language – a preliminary examination'. Poster presented at the 7th International Conference on Theoretical Issues in Sign Language Research, Amsterdam, The Netherlands.

Sandler, W. (2009) 'Symbiotic symbolization by hand and mouth in sign language'. *Semiotica*, **174**: 241–75.

Sandler, W. & D. Lillo-Martin (2006) *Sign Language and Linguistic Universals*. Cambridge: Cambridge University Press.

Schembri, A. (2002) 'The representation of motion events in signed language and gesture: a preliminary report'. In **R. Schulmeister & H. Reinitzer** (eds.) *Progress in Sign Language Research: In Honor of Siegmund Prillwitz*. Hamburg: Signum, pp. 99–126.

(2003) 'Rethinking "classifiers" in signed languages'. In **K. Emmorey** (ed.) *Perspectives on Classifier Constructions in Sign Languages*. Mahwah, NJ: Lawrence Erlbaum Associates, pp. 3–34.

Schick, B. (1990) 'Classifier predicates in American Sign Language'. *International Journal of Sign Linguistics*, **1**: 15–40.

Shallice, T. & P. Burgess (1996) 'The domain of supervisory processes and temporal organization of behaviour'. *Philosophical Transactions of the Royal Society London B*, **351**: 1405–12.

Sieratzki, J. S. & B. Woll (2002) 'Toddling into language: precocious language development in motor-impaired children with spinal muscular atrophy'. *Lingua*, **112**: 423–33.

Smith, N. V. (1998a) 'Dissociations'. *Glot International*, **3**(9/10): 10.

(1998b) 'Jackdaws, sex and language acquisition'. *Glot International*, **3**(7): 7.

(2002) *Language, Bananas and Bonobos*. Oxford: Blackwell.

(2003) 'Dissociation and modularity: Reflections on language and mind'. In **M. Banich & M. Mack** (eds.) *Mind, Brain and Language*. Mahwah, NJ: Lawrence Erlbaum, pp. 87–111.

(2004) *Chomsky: Ideas and Ideals*. Cambridge: Cambridge University Press.

Smith, N. V., B. Hermelin & I.-M. Tsimpli (2003) 'Dissociation of social affect and theory of mind in a case of Asperger syndrome'. *UCL Working Papers in Linguistics*, **15**: 357–77.

Smith, N. V. & A. Law (2007) 'Twangling instruments: Is parametric variation definitional of human language?' *UCL Working Papers in Linguistics*, **19**: 1–28.

(2009) 'On parametric (and non-parametric) variation'. *Biolinguistics*, **3**: 332–43.

(in press) 'Parametric variation: Its relevance to language and birdsong'. In **J. Bolhuis & M. Everaert** (eds.) *Birdsong, Speech and Language: Converging Mechanisms*. Cambridge, MA: MIT Press.

Smith, N. V. & Tsimpli, I.-M. (1993) 'A specialist intelligence: the case of a polyglot savant'. *UCL Working Papers in Linguistics*, **5**: 413–50.

(1995) *The Mind of a Savant: Language Learning and Modularity*. Oxford: Blackwell.

Smith, N. V., I.-M. Tsimpli & **J. Ouhalla** (1993) 'Learning the impossible: The acquisition of possible and impossible languages by a polyglot savant'. *Lingua*, **91**: 279–347.

Sperber, D. & **D. Wilson** (1986/1995) *Relevance: Communication and Cognition*. Oxford: Blackwell.

Sperber, D. & **D. Wilson** (2002) 'Pragmatics, modularity and mind-reading'. *Mind & Language*, **17**: 3–23.

Stalnaker, R. (1972) 'Pragmatics'. In **D. Davidson** & **G. Harman** (eds.) *Semantics of Natural Language*. Dordrecht: Reidel, pp. 380–97.

Stokoe, W. (1960) *Sign Language Structure: An Outline of the Visual Communication of the American Deaf* (Studies in Linguistics Occasional Papers 8). Buffalo, NY: University of Buffalo, Department of Anthropology and Linguistics.

Stokoe, W., D. Casterline & **C. Croneberg** (1965) *A Dictionary of American Sign Language on Linguistic Principles*. Washington, DC: Gallaudet College Press.

Supalla, T. (1986) 'The classifier system in American Sign Language'. In **C. Craig** (ed.) *Noun Classification and Categorization*. Amsterdam: John Benjamins, pp. 181–214.

Sutton-Spence, R. & **L. Day** (2001) 'Mouthings and mouth gestures in British Sign Language'. In **P. Boyes-Braem** & **R. Sutton-Spence** (eds.) *The Hands Are the Head of the Mouth*. Hamburg: Signum Press, pp. 69–85.

Sutton-Spence, R. L. & **B. Woll** (1999) *An Introduction to the Linguistics of BSL*. Cambridge: Cambridge University Press.

Tallal, P. (1990) 'Fine-grained discrimination deficits in language learning impaired children are specific neither to the auditory modality nor to speech perception'. *Journal of Speech and Hearing Research*, **33**: 616–17.

Talmy, L. (2003) 'The representation of spatial structure in spoken and signed language'. In **K. Emmorey** (ed.) *Perspectives on Classifier Constructions in Sign Languages*. Mahwah, NJ: Lawrence Erlbaum, pp. 169–95.

Tammet, D. (2006) *Born on a Blue Day: A Memoir of Asperger's and an Extraordinary Mind*. London: Hodder & Stoughton.

Taub, S. F. (2001) *Language from the Body: Iconicity and Metaphor in American Sign Language*. Cambridge: Cambridge University Press.

Thompson, R., K. Emmorey & **T. Gollan** (2005) 'Tip-of-the-fingers experiences by ASL signers: Insights into the organization of a sign-based lexicon'. *Psychological Science*, **16**(11): 856–60.

Thompson, R., K. Emmorey & **R. Kluender** (2006) 'The relationship between eye gaze and agreement in American Sign Language: An eye-tracking study'. *Natural Language and Linguistic Theory*, **24**: 571–604.

Tolar, T. D., A. R. Lederberg, S. Gokhale & **M. Tomasello** (2007) 'The development of the ability to recognize the meaning of iconic signs'. *The Journal of Deaf Studies and Deaf Education*, **13**(2): 225–40.

Tomasello, M. (2000) 'Do young children have adult syntactic competence?' *Cognition*, **74**: 209–53.

Trask, L. (1996) *A Dictionary of Phonetics and Phonology*. London: Routledge.

Tsimpli, I.-M. (1996) *The Prefunctional Stage of Language Acquisition*. New York: Garland.

Tsimpli, I.-M. & M. Dimitrakopoulou (2007) 'The interpretability hypothesis: Evidence from Wh-interrogatives in second language acquisition'. *Second Language Research*, **23**(2): 215–42.

Tsimpli, I.-M. & A. Roussou (1991) 'Parameter-Resetting in L2?' *UCL Working Papers in Linguistics* **3**: 149–69.

Tsimpli, I.-M. & N. V. Smith (1991) 'Second-language learning: Evidence from a polyglot *savant*'. *UCL Working Papers in Linguistics* **3**: 171–83.

(1993) 'LF and post-LF in a polyglot savant's grammars'. *Newcastle and Durham Working Papers in Linguistics*, **1**: 276–91.

(1998) 'Modules and quasi-modules: Language and theory of mind in a polyglot savant'. *Learning and Individual Differences*, **10**: 193–215.

Tsimpli, I.-M. & S. Stavrakaki (1999) 'The effects of a morphosyntactic deficit in the determiner system: the case of a Greek SLI child'. *Lingua*, **108**: 31–85.

Tulving, E. (2000) 'Concepts of memory'. In E. Tulving & F. Craik (eds.) *The Oxford Handbook of Memory*. Oxford: Oxford University Press, pp. 33–43.

Tyrone, M. E., J. R. Atkinson, J. Marshall & B. Woll (in press) 'The effects of cerebellar ataxia on sign language production: a case study'.

Ussishkin, A. (2005) 'A fixed prosodic theory of nonconcatenative templatic morphology'. *Natural Language and Linguistic Theory*, **23**: 169–218.

Van der Zee, E. & U. Nikanne (eds.) (2000a) *Cognitive Interfaces: Constraints on Linking Cognitive Information*. Oxford: Oxford University Press.

Van der Zee, E. & U. Nikanne (2000b) 'Introducing cognitive interfaces and constraints on linking cognitive information'. In E. Van der Zee & U. Nikanne (eds.) (2000a), pp.1–17.

Vermeerbergen, M., L. Leeson & O. Crasborn (eds.) (2007) *Simultaneity in Signed Languages: Form and Function*. Amsterdam: John Benjamins.

Vigliocco, G., D. P. Vinson, T. Woolfe, M. W. Dye & B. Woll (2005) 'Words, signs and imagery: When the language makes the difference'. *Proceedings of the Royal Society B*, **272**: 1859–63.

Vinson, D., K. Cormier, T. Denmark, A. Schembri & G. Vigliocco (2009) 'The British Sign Language (BSL) norms for age of acquisition, familiarity, and iconicity'. *Behavior Research Methods*, **40**(4): 1079–87.

Vinson, D., G. Vigliocco, T. Woolfe, M. Dye & B. Woll (2005) 'Language and imagery: effects of language modality'. *Proceedings of the Royal Society B*, **72** (1574): 1859–63.

Warrington, E. K. (1984) *Recognition Memory Test*. Slough, UK: National Foundation for Education Research and Nelson Publishing Co.

Willey, L. H. (1999) *Pretending to be normal: Living with Asperger's Syndrome*. London: Jessica Kingsley Publishers.

White, L. (2003) *Second Language Acquisition and Universal Grammar*. Cambridge: Cambridge University Press.

Williams, D. (1994) *Somebody Somewhere*. London: Doubleday.

Williams, J. N. & P. Möbius (1997) 'Syntactic processing strategies in a second language'. *University of Cambridge Working Papers in English and Applied Linguistics* **4**: 173–208.

Wilson, B., J. Cockburn & **A. Baddeley** (1985) *The Rivermead Behavioural Meaning Test*. Reading, UK: Thames Valley Test Company.

Wilson, D. S. M. (2003) 'New directions for research for pragmatics and modularity'. *UCL Working Papers in Linguistics* **15**: 105–27.

Wilson, D. & **D. Sperber** (2002) 'Relevance theory'. *University College London Working Papers in Linguistics* **14**: 249–87.

Wilson, M. & **K. Emmorey** (1998) 'A "word length effect" for sign language: Further evidence for the role of language in structuring working memory'. *Memory and Cognition*, **26**: 3: 584–90.

(2006) 'Comparing sign language and speech reveals a universal limit on short-term memory capacity'. *Psychological Science*, **17**: 682–3.

Woll, B. (1998) 'The development of signed and spoken language'. In **S. Gregory, P. Knight, W. McCracken, S. Powers** & **L. Watson** (eds.) *Issues in Deaf Education*. London: Fulton, pp. 58–68.

(2001) 'The sign that dares to speak its name: Echo phonology in British Sign Language (BSL)'. In **P. Boyes-Braem** & **R. Sutton-Spence** (eds.) *The Hands are the Head of the Mouth*. Hamburg: Signum Press, pp. 87–98.

Woll, B. & **J. Sieratzki** (1998) 'Echo phonology: Signs of a link between gesture and speech'. *Behavioral and Brain Sciences*, **21**: 531–2.

Zaitchik, D. (1990) 'When representation conflicts with reality: The preschooler's problem with false beliefs and "false" photographs'. *Cognition*, **35**: 41–68.

Zeshan, U. (2004a) 'Hand, head, and face: Negative constructions in sign languages'. *Linguistic Typology*, **8**: 1–58.

(2004b) 'Interrogative constructions in signed languages: Cross-linguistic perspectives'. *Language*, **80**: 7–39.

Index